1970

GOGOL AS A SHORT-STORY WRITER

SLAVISTIC PRINTINGS AND REPRINTINGS

edited by

C. H. VAN SCHOONEVELD

Stanford University

LVII

1965

MOUTON & CO.

LONDON · THE HAGUE · PARIS

GOGOL AS A SHORT-STORY WRITER

A STUDY OF HIS TECHNIQUE OF COMPOSITION

by

F. C. DRIESSEN †

Translated from the Dutch by

IAN F. FINLAY

1965

MOUTON & CO.

PARIS · THE HAGUE · LONDON

Originally published in 1955
by "Hollandia", Baarn, Holland,
under the title

Gogol' als Novellist

PRINTED IN THE NETHERLANDS BY MOUTON & CO., PRINTERS, THE HAGUE

PREFACE

When Professor Driessen died on 31st January 1963 at the age of fifty-six, he had occupied the chair of Slavonic literatures at the University of Amsterdam for two and a half years only. His great interest in Slavonic studies, however, dated from his years as an undergraduate. He studied Dutch literature at Leyden, but chose Russian language and literature as a subsidiary subject, being one of van Wijk's first students. During the academic year 1932-1933 he studied in Prague.

Slavonic studies offered so few prospects in the Netherlands at that time that his career inevitably began as a teacher of Dutch at a secondary school. He was, from 1948 to 1960, headmaster of the Baarns Lyceum, one of the largest secondary schools in the Netherlands.

In addition to all his many activities, he nevertheless still found time to devote himself to investigations of the theory of the short story in general and the Russian short story in particular.

When, in 1960, a new chair was established at the University of Amsterdam for Slavonic literatures, Dr. Driessen was the obvious person to occupy it.

His work – written in Dutch – has not become very well known outside the Netherlands. This is, in our opinion, regrettable. In his book *Gogol as a short-story writer,* we find the results of his penetrating study of the short story. His work is interesting because of the method followed in the analysis of Gogol's short stories. He has thrown light on many previously unnoticed features in the composition of these works. In his formal analysis he discovered elements which cannot be explained from the structure and for which he found a psycho-analytical explanation. This warranted application of a non-literary method of approach offers a solution of various conflicting and doubtful interpretations of certain of Gogol's short stories.

We therefore consider it of scientific importance that the work should also become available outside the Netherlands in the form of the present translation. It can now take its rightful place amongst the literature devoted to Gogol.

University of Amsterdam

C. L. EBELING
J. VAN DER ENG

ACKNOWLEDGEMENT

In order to avoid the dangers inherent in "double translations", i.e. from Russian into Dutch into English, Dr. Driessen's Dutch translations of passages from Gogol's short stories were substituted in the present work by those of Constance Garnett for "Evenings in a Village near Dikanka" and "Mirgorod" and by that of David Magarshack for "The Overcoat". Thanks are offered to the respective publishers of these translations, namely Chatto & Windus, London and Doubleday & Company, Inc., New York, for permission to use them.

CONTENTS

LIST OF WORKS BY GOGOL, DISCUSSED OR QUOTED

Arabesques
Christmas Eve
Dead Souls
Diary of a Madman (The)
Evenings in a Village near Dikanka
Fair at Sorochintsy (The)
Government Inspector (The)
Hans Küchelgarten
Lost Letter (The)
Marriage
May Night (A)
Mirgorod
Nevsky Avenue
Nights at a Roman Villa
Nose (The)
Old-world Land-owners.
Overcoat (The)
Place Bewitched (A)
Portrait (The)
Rome
St. John's Eve
Selected Passages from the Correspondence with my Friends
Shponka (Ivan Fyodorovich) and his Aunt
The Tale of how Ivan Ivanovich Quarrelled with Ivan Nikiforovich
                                        (The Two Ivans)
Taras Bulba
Terrible Revenge (A)
Viy
Woman

ABBREVIATIONS USED, AND NOTE ON TRANSLITERATION

Kh. S.   *Kharkovsky Universitetsky Sbornik v pamyat V. A. Zhukovskogo i N. V. Gogolya* (Kharkov, 1903).

Mat.   V. I. Shenrok, *Materialy dlya biografiyi Gogolya,* 4 vols. (M., 1892–1897).

M. I.   *Materialy i Issledovaniya pod red. V. Gippiusa,* 2 vols. (M.-L., 1936).

P.   *Pisma N. V. Gogolya. Red. V. I. Shenrok,* 4 vols. (SPb., no date) (1902).

P. G. D.   *Pamyati Gogolya. Nauchno-literaturny sbornik, izd. Istoricheskym Obshchestvom Nestora Letopistsa, pod red. N. P. Dashkevicha* (Kiev, 1902).

P. G. V.   *Pamyati N. V. Gogolya. Sbornik rechey i statey, izd. Imp. Univ. Sv. Vladimira* (Kiev, 1911).

Rechi.   *N. V. Gogol, Rechi posvyashchenny ego pamyati* (SPb., 1902).

S. N.   *Sbornik izdanny Imp. Novorossiyskym Universitetom po sluchayu stoletiya so dnya rozhdeniya N. V. Gogolya* (Odessa, 1909).

Soch.   *Sochineniya N. V. Gogolya,* 10th edit., 7 vols. Vols. I-V edited by N. Tikhonravov, vols. VI and VII by V. Shenrok (M., 1889–1896).

Soch. A. N.   *N. V. Gogol. Polnoye sobraniye sochineny.* 14 vols. Edition of "Akademiya Nauk S.S.S.R." (M., 1937–1952).

The Russian personal names and words have in the text, the relevant notes, the index of persons (p. 242) and the list of Gogol's works (p. 11) been transliterated according to the system most current in England. For the sake of uniformity the Russian letter   has in all cases been transliterated by "ch", this necessitating the change of Garnett's "tch" to "ch".

In the bibliography (p. 233–241) on the other hand, the scientific system of transliteration used by Dr. Driessen has been preserved.

INTRODUCTION

The following study is concerned with certain of Gogol's short stories and relates particularly to their composition. The approach was not however the same for all the stories. Some allowed a comparison with a literary model, for certain of them there were one or more earlier versions which could be considered, while for others neither case obtained, and the short story was analysed as a separate entity. Whatever the manner of investigating the composition of the short stories, this was always done with a view to penetrating Gogol's intentions to a greater extent. This sometimes led to views about their content which differ from those customarily held.

When discussing Gogol's technique, I have used almost exclusively terms which are in general use, without defining them strictly. It was initially my intention to define them, and a general discussion of the nature of the "short story" would then have formed the introduction to a closer study of what I have here, for convenience, called "Gogol's short stories". On reflection, I decided, however, to omit this chapter. I feel that the problem posed by the short story as a form is, since Pabst's studies,[1] further from its solution than it ever was. It is also possible that it will, as Pabst suggests, turn out to have been a hypothetical problem. In any case, it is, in my opinion, becoming more and more difficult to speak about "the" short story or even about the short story of a given period in terms of a well-defined concept. This is why I did not attempt to decide whether "The Overcoat" for example represents a typically romantic or a classical form or, which seems most plausible, a cross between both. Gogol himself still found the

---

[1] Walter Pabst, "Die Theorie der Novelle in Deutschland (1920–1940)", in *Romanistisches Jahrbuch*, 1949, pp. 81–124. Idem, *Novellentheorie und Novellendichtung. Zur Geschichte ihrer Antinomie in den romanischen Literaturen* (Hamburg, 1953).

term "tales" too good for most of his short stories. All this work was, according to him, as yet "immature und unfinished".[2] It seemed to me more important to prove the groundless nature of Gogol's depression in this latter respect than to quarrel about a name. In other words, it is, I think, of greater use for our picture of Gogol as an artist to indicate the structure of his works and to show how closely this is related to their tenor than to establish that this structure can be classified in a given system of categories which still gives the impression of being more or less artificial.

Certain names of forms and of formal characteristics (e.g. "open short story", "Wendepunkt"[3]) are so widely used, even outside the relevant specialised literature, that I considered I could use them without explanation. Nothing further should be seen in them than useful aids in a description. Any misunderstanding which could theoretically be possible is excluded because of the context in which such terms are used.

It will perhaps appear strange that the place which these short stories occupy in Russian literature has been discussed indirectly only. Should this not have formed the background to the whole study? I however deliberately neglected to sketch the position of Gogol's work in his own time. My reason was that I was confronted with the choice either of borrowing from others or undertaking an independent investigation. The first choice, easy as it may have been, had to be avoided because, in so doing, I should immediately have linked myself with a given tradition of interpretation. The second choice was not really possible in the Netherlands. One would, after all, have had to have at one's disposal a number of Russian journals dating from the beginning of the nineteenth century and preferably also Russian translations of Western European writers from the same period. These are, however, not to be found in the Netherlands.

I have, therefore, examined certain short stories in isolation and have tried to derive conclusions concerning their interpretation mainly from their construction. In other words, after first having immersed myself in Gogol's works and the relevant literature, I tried to become "naïve" once again and to read the short stories "for the first time", free from any tradition as regards explanation. Thereafter, I naturally

---

[2]   *Soch. A. N.*, XI, 77.
[3]   Turning-point.

compared my results with the most important existing interpretations.

This method did not, however, appear to prove consistent for long. It is in fact abandoned as soon as we take into consideration an earlier version of a story. It is as if one were suddenly to move to a diachronous view of language when taking a synchronous view thereof. I had in the end to depart radically from the method used when certain sections of my material appeared to offer obstinate resistance to a purely formal investigation.

This latter fact forced me after all to make Gogol the man the subject of my investigation, this being something I should willingly have avoided. The majority of the stories seemed, in fact, to express one or other form of anxiety, and certain of them remained unintelligible if there were no attempt to find an object of anxiety in their author. For that reason, a chapter on "Gogol and anxiety" had to introduce the study. In this chapter the least possible use has been made of the stories as evidence, although it proved impossible to keep Gogol's works as a whole out of this explanatory description of the development of his anxiety.

The opposite is done in the remaining chapters. In most cases, information from the first chapter is left out of consideration there and, if it is used, this is only after aesthetic treatment.

Only in he final chapter ("Conclusion") are the results of the first combined with those of the following chapters, and is there an attempt at a sort of synthesis.

A choice had to be made from the material offered by Gogol's short stories. My choice has been arbitrary in so far as I have treated only one of the "St. Petersburg stories". It is, however, the most important one and my conclusions would have altered but little by a consideration of the others. Each of Gogol's short stories is worth a careful study, including the Ukrainian ones which I have not discussed. The fragments of stories which remained unfinished should certainly also have to be considered in an investigation concerned more with origins.

The present study is then an incomplete, deliberately one-sided one. It nevertheless forms, I think, a not entirely conventional approach to a subject which has innumerable aspects.

CHAPTER I

GOGOL AND ANXIETY

The following chapters will show that anxiety is a subject repeatedly treated by Gogol. We may, in fact, put it more strongly: anxiety is what concerned him more than anything else in his short stories. This fact automatically gives rise to a number of questions. Did Gogol himself suffer from one or more forms of anxiety? Did he project these into his work? Was this projection wholly or in part conscious? Does an answer to these questions help us in understanding his works? Is it justified, from the point of view of scientific method, to raise psychological questions in a study which is concerned primarily with the construction of Gogol's works? In other words, can it be shown that possible feelings or complexes of anxiety influenced that construction?

Bearing in mind that what follows contains the account of a step which was taken only after long hesitation and with great reluctance, we may give first the answer to the last question. It was in fact as a result of a number of problems regarding *form* that I found myself obliged to indulge in psychological matters concerning which I should rather have remained silent. When one, as in the present case, is quite aware of being about to enter a scientific field in which one is a layman, a field moreover in which there are innumerable riddles for the expert and in which generally accepted conclusions are rare, then one does this only when forced to by extreme necessity. It is obvious that anyone who writes a biography or who interprets a story more or less plays the part of a psychologist. Matters are however somewhat different in the present case. Moments do in fact occur in Gogol's work where the normal empathy ("Einfühlung") of the admiring reader – and what more can the philologist desire than to be a good reader? – deserts him. It is my view that psychology and, in particular, depth psychology can be of assistance here. It is even possible that it also provides a view on certain of Gogol's works which cannot be considered here.

Reservation is definitely desirable. Freudian studies of literature are often justifiably in bad odour. Yet, providing one is conscious of the limited validity of the results, something real can in fact be achieved by the psycho-analytical method. What? I think that Professor Trilling formulated this excellently in a small essay devoted to Freud and literature. In Trilling's opinion the critic or biographer certainly runs great risks if he sets to work psycho-analytically. He can however be warned against these dangers by the failures of others, particularly against that of forcing things into a system. "I think it is true to say", Trilling continues, "that now the motive of his interpretation is not that of exposing the secret shame of the writer and limiting the meaning of his work, but, on the contrary, that of finding grounds for sympathy with the writer and for increasing the possible significances of his work." [1]

These motives, namely an effort towards greater sympathy with the author and an attempt to give his work a wider meaning, led me to follow a psycho-analytical train of thought here and there. As mentioned above, I even felt myself forced to do this, because a method of investigation which initially seemed to me adequate turned out in the end to fail. No single method is of course the only true one. It is obvious that every work of art can be approached philologically, historically, sociologically, etc. An investigation of the literary form as well appeared to me promising in Gogol's case. It is still my conviction, however much "formalism" may be out of fashion in Russia, that a work of art can be seen as a system of technical "artifices",[2] which are used consciously or unconsciously. An attempt to regard such a technical whole, such a composition as "expression" or as "significant" leads of itself to the content of the work. This is why the study of a composition must always remain directed at the "sense" of the means used. It then, of course, often turns out that a review of the form leads to a better understanding of the sense. Yet, what are we to do if the work gives at certain points the impression of not being "formed"? This situation occurs repeatedly with Gogol. I would mention merely the numerous lyrical passages at points where one does not expect them at all. These sometimes have every appearance of not fitting either into the logical

[1] Lionel Trilling, "Freud and Literature", *The Liberal Imagination* (New York, 1954), p. 48.
[2] "Artifice" is not a complete translation of the Russian *priyom*. Insofar as it does not appear from what follows, it may be said that the theoretical "formalists", who went so far that they wanted to consider the work of art as *nothing but* a system of *priyomy*, were in my opinion defending an untenable point of view.

context of the content or into the aesthetic context of the form. Yet, there are also quite different cases, one of which will appear when discussing "Viy".

It can be assumed that such passages which "jump out of context" are expressions of Gogol's deepest thoughts or even of feelings which, however strong, were hidden from his consciousness. If this is considered to be the case, then the question arises as to what element in Gogol's inner self they express. One of the answers which will have to be given most often must be that this feeling is anxiety. The fact that this is not an arbitrary assertion can appear only from the whole of the present study. Yet, if this assertion is true, then it must also be expected that it would be a good idea to devote our attention to Gogol's own anxiety. It is then highly likely that the occasion which the "unformed" parts of his work gave us for directing our study to that anxiety will cause us to view his whole output once again in this new light. In other words, if we make a tentative and imperfect attempt to discover more about the anxieties which obsessed Gogol, then there is possibly a chance that we shall also gain a deeper insight into the nature and form of his incarnations of anxiety.[3]

It is high time that a skilled psychologist who knows Gogol's life and work thoroughly should undertake this very extensive investigation. At this stage, the present author can merely attempt this on the lines indicated above with the modest means at his disposal.

I should like earnestly to issue a warning about one misunderstanding. If a certain amount of depth psychology is cautiously used here and a search is made for an unconscious force which drove or hindered Gogol in his creative work, this in no way indicates that Gogol's work is really "nothing but" the processing of an unusual tendency in his libido, or the "result" of an infantile fixation. On the contrary, it is important only because and insofar as it is something else. It can, however, not be unimportant to know with what demon a person has wrestled if one wants to understand fully the demoniac element in his creations. I cannot conceive that it should ever be possible to "reduce" a work of art to anything. Our ultimate purpose is to understand an author, not a neurotic. If that author however forces us through his work itself to the question of a hidden driving-force, then we cannot see why that question should have to be answered if the answer can be: those historical circumstances, that social problem, that inner

[3] See Charles Odier, *L'angoisse et la pensée magique* (Neuchâtel-Paris, 1948), p. 45.

religious struggle, and not if we must say: that unconscious conflict. We must, in my opinion, use the unfortunately small number of facts available to review Gogol's neurotic anxiety as best we can. We do it in the knowledge of possibly making a mistake and, at the same time, in the realisation that all our efforts will be of no avail unless they lead us to that deeper and sympathetic experiencing referred to above.

These are then provisional answers to some of the principal questions posed at the beginning of this chapter. The proof has still to be given, and the following chapters will offer an opportunity for this. The rest of our argument will however appear to beg the question unless we first show that Gogol did suffer from anxiety and in fact from an anxiety which should be considered as neurotic. This latter point is the main one, for anxiety in one form or another is experienced by every person.

It would now be particularly easy if there were one definition of anxiety, if one description of the phenomenon of neurosis were accepted as being generally valid, and we could then investigate the extent to which Gogol's symptoms can be identified. There is, however, no question of this.

There is no agreement among psychologists and psychiatrists concerning matters such as neurosis and anxiety, and the literature on these phenomena is immensely large. As far as I can see, the expert not working psycho-analytically or not exclusively so, nevertheless takes proper account of the pioneering work carried out by Freud and his faithful or otherwise followers in the fields of neurosis and anxiety. This is, for example, directly evident if we read the definition of the concept "neurosis in the narrower sense" given by Rümke in the first volume of his *Psychiatrie*. The Utrecht professor can definitely not be called a blind adept of Freud, but all his material concerning concepts in these matters is derived from psycho-analysis.[4]

One may judge for oneself:

This syndrome can be defined as follows: a disturbance in the development of the organisation of the libido and a disturbance in the development of

[4] This phenomenon is found again and again in literature relating to anxiety. The most important works in which Freud treated the problem of anxiety are: "Vorlesungen zur Einführung in die Psychoanalyse", *Gesammelte Schriften* (Leipzig-Vienna-Zürich, 1925–34), Vol. VII. "Hemmung, Symptom und Angst", *Ges. Schr.*, Vol. XI. "Neue Folge der Vorlesungen zur Einführung in die Psychoanalyse", *Ges. Schr.*, Vol. XII. Concerning the development of the concept of "anxiety" in Freud's work, see A. C. Oerlemans, *Development of Freud's Concept of Anxiety*. Thesis (Amsterdam, 1949).

the "ego" with a fixation in one of the stages of development; a struggle between immature aspirations of the "id" under the direction of the "super-ego". There arise on this soil phenomena which can partly be considered as "veiled" or "symbolised" expressions of aspirations suppressed from the consciousness or of those which have never been allowed into the "ego"-consciousness, and partly as the expression of the defence against these aspirations; to this, anxiety is added, this having arisen either through the "ego" being threatened to become overwhelmed by the rejected aspiration or passion, or through the fear, if the aspiration or passion breaks out, of losing the love of those with whom the prohibitions initially originated. Finally, part of the phenomena arises secondarily through the flight from this anxiety.[5]

Everyone who has studied the problem of neurotic anxiety, even if only superficially, will see how flexible, comprehensive and well-considered this definition is. It would show little self-knowledge and would extend the limits of this study unnecessarily if I were to attempt to elucidate or even judge critically each of the conceptual indications used here. The interested reader may refer to the work in question by Rümke and the further relevant literature.[6] It is adequate for our purpose at the moment to summarise in a somewhat popular manner the last lines about the origin of anxiety.

According to Rümke and many others, anxiety arises if a conflict occurs between various factors in the soul. There can be expressed in anxiety an anti-social desire which has remained unconscious, e.g., a criminal or sexual tendency which is rejected by the "ego", or also – being the opposite – the satisfaction of a forbidden desire which leads to anxiety for punishment or loss of love. Think of the "free" life of someone who has discarded the religious or moral commandments of his youth, but in whom the anxiety for a – consciously denied – higher power suddenly arises again. There is a feeling of guilt in both cases.

---

[5] H. C. Rümke, *Psychiatrie* (Amsterdam, 1954), I, p. 270.
[6] A book I consider to be very important, and which has a large bibliography, is: Juliette Boutonier, *L'angoisse* (Paris, Presses universitaires de France, 1949). Apart from the works already mentioned, the following were also used: S. Kierkegaard, *Le concept de l'angoisse*, translated from Danish by Knud Ferlov and Jean J. Gateau (Paris, 1935). Arnold Künzli, *Die Angst als abendländische Krankheit* (Zürich, 1948). Wilh. Stekel, *Nervöse Angstzustände und ihre Behandlung*, 4th edition (Vienna, 1924). P. Janet, *De l'angoisse à l'extase* (Paris, 1928). M. Loosli-Usteri, "De l'anxiété enfantine", *Schweizerische Zeitschrift für Psychologie*, 1943, Beiheft No. 3. C. G. Jung, *Psychologie und Religion* (Zürich-Leipzig, 1940). Paul H. Hoch and Joseph Zubin, *Anxiety* (New York, 1950). J. H. Plokker, S. Dresden, K. Baschwitz, W. Banning, *Angst en Crisis der Moraal* (The Hague, 1949). O. Pfister, *Das Christentum und die Angst* (Zürich, 1944). Edm. Rochedieu, *Angoisse et Religion* (Geneva, 1952). E. Krijgers Janzen, *De justificatie*, Utrecht thesis (Amsterdam, 1940).

Anxiety itself may also not become manifest, but be "shifted", e.g. to a phobia. The "ridiculous" object of the phobia can be lived with as long as it can easily be avoided, but behind it hides another anxiety with a completely different object of which one should not become aware. Probably more numerous than phobias are the physical symptoms behind which anxiety hides – affections of the heart, stomach etc.[7]

In my opinion, the broad distinctions used here are fairly generally recognised, independently of the theoretical opinion one holds about the phenomena. It is of course not my intention to pass judgment on the various theories of anxiety. It will have become evident from what has been said above that the psycho-analytical theory appears to me to promise the best results.

We shall meet various forms of anxiety in Gogol's life and also in his work. We may wish that we were better informed about his earliest development and that Gogol's letters, which have been preserved in such large numbers, gave us a better insight into his character.

We shall attempt as far as possible to avoid an error in method, namely to form a picture of Gogol's personality from his work and then to explain his work from that picture. His work, which in the first place we wish to learn to understand on its own, will certainly be able to help us, as an expression of spiritual life, to approach the writer's soul. A lot more could be said about this from the theoretical point of view which nevertheless seems to me to be unnecessary in this case. It must after all appear from the result of our considerations whether anything has been added to our knowledge, or whether the facts have merely been grouped in a different way.

Gogol's mother was eighteen when she gave birth to Nicolay Vasilyevich. She had been married at the age of fourteen and had already brought two still-born children into the world. She awaited the arrival of this third child with anxiety and prayers which had a magical side to them. If the child should live and be a boy, it was to be called Nicholas after the worker of miracles who was the saint of the church in Dikanka. It is not surprising that this child, who was weak at birth and remained sickly for a long time, was surrounded by great concern. It is certainly not rash to assume that Gogol took from this parental home, where also his father was far from robust, the habit of paying particular attention to his health.

[7] A large number of examples of all these possibilities are found in Wilh. Stekel, *op. cit.*

Let us choose from the few facts concerning his earliest youth the two memories which undoubtedly derive from Gogol himself. There is the horrible story of how the five-year-old Gogol killed a kitten. It has come to us twice from the same source. Mrs. Smirnov recorded it in her memoires which were first published in 1929 (what were known as such previously were a forgery). The same story occurs in Viskovatov's version. He is said to have taken it down from her own words. The stories differ considerably in details. According to Mrs. Smirnov, Gogol was lying outside on a warm, quiet day at the height of summer. To judge from the punctuation, she is quoting Gogol's words as follows:

The sun was burning hot. The quietness had something solemn about it, it was as if I heard the ticking of time, which was passing away into eternity. A kitten was miaowing plaintively, I became melancholy, I stood up and succeeded in seizing it by the tail and throwing it into the well near the stream. People began looking for the poor kitten, I confessed that I had drowned it, began to be sorry and reproached myself that I had robbed one of God's creatures from enjoying this life.

Mrs. Smirnov adds: "He did that in his fifth year. What a depth of feeling." [8]

According to Viskovatov, who tells the whole story in the first person, the boy was at home alone in the twilight and heard the ticking of the clock.

Believe me, then it appeared to me as if the ticking of the pendulum were the ticking of time, which passed away into eternity. [He became afraid when he saw the kitten and the green fire in its eyes, he threw it outside into the pond and pushed it back with a stick when it tried to get out.] I was afraid, I was trembling, and at the same time I felt a sort of satisfaction, perhaps it was revenge because it had frightened me. But when it was drowned and the last rings had died away on the water — complete peace and quiet reigned again – I suddenly felt terribly sorry for the kitten. I felt the pricking of my conscience. It seemed to me that I had drowned a human being. I cried terribly and calmed down only when father, to whom I had confessed what I had done, had thrashed me. [9]

It does not appear to me to be easy to discover which version approaches Gogol's own story more closely, and not even which is the earlier. Mrs. Smirnov presumably wrote that section of her memoires

---

[8] A. O. Smirnova-Rosset. *Avtobiografiya* (Moscow, 1931), pp. 309, 310.

[9] P. A. Viskovatov, "Iz rasskazov A. O. Smirnovoy o Gogole" in *Russkaya Starina*, (1902), p. 486. Quoted according to V. Veresayev, *Gogol v zhizni* (Moscow-Leningrad, 1933), p. 19.

in which this passage occurs at the end of her life.[10] The story, as told by Viskovatov, appears more "literary", although Mrs. Smirnov's is also not without a literary connection. It is, in fact, quite conceivable that she consciously connected this event with the well-known passage in "Old-fashioned Land-owners", in which Gogol confesses that a sudden anxiety could come upon him precisely on a bright, quiet summer's day while, in addition, a kitten is the messenger of death in this story.[11] Be this as it may, both versions have features in common. Quietness, a vague realisation of time, sudden oppression, then aggressiveness and repentance. (In Viskovatov's version we could also clearly point to a sadistic trait and a need for punishment, but we must leave these facts on one side as being uncertain.)

Another event mentioned in every biography must date from about the same period. In a letter of 2nd October 1833, Gogol reminds his mother what an egocentric child he was, a child that looked at the whole world with indifferent eyes, as if it had been made for him. Even regular attendance at church did not arouse any impressions, except boredom and aversion.

But on one occasion – I remember it as vividly as if it had happened to-day – I asked you to tell me about the last judgment. And you told me, small boy that I was, so well, so intelligibly, so movingly about the bliss which awaits people after a virtuous life, and so strikingly, so terribly did you describe the eternal torments of sinners that this shocked and aroused my whole inner life, this later giving rise to and developing in me the most sublime thoughts.[12]

We shall not discuss here what *religious* significance matters had for Gogol. The letter in question is intended as an instruction for bringing up a younger sister. The child should never be alone with the servants, must always have something to do, must be well aware that God sees her all the time and must also have a vivid idea of the rewards and punishments in the hereafter. Gogol says plainly that he himself was brought up badly – apart from that one impressive story. Did idleness and association with a personnel of serfs have bad consequences for him? In his memory they apparently did.

The fact which mainly interests us is that here again anxiety and the feeling of guilt occur, aroused on this occasion by his mother, the only person whom, in his own words, he loved at that time.

[10] See A. O. Smirnova-Rosset, *op. cit.*, p. 14.
[11] See p. 124 below.
[12] *P.*, I, 260.

What was the mother like who in this strange way aroused the inner life of her son with a start? Very young, very beautiful, extremely sentimental, childishly religious, with a strong tendency towards the superstitious, poorly educated, unpractical, pessimistic and brooding.

The marriage with her husband, who was thirteen years her senior, appears to have been happy. Gogol's father was much better educated than she and was an author on a modest scale. He too was a sentimental man, in permanent bad health. He was probably suffering from tuberculosis. His literary work certainly had some influence on that of his son. We hardly know what he contributed to the formation of his son's character. It is, in my opinion, not possible to discover whether he suffered from a psychosis, which may or may not have been organically conditioned, and even less whether his son inherited it from him, assuming that it were possible to diagnose the disease of the young Gogol.[13]

His younger brother, by one year, with whom Gogol went to Poltava when he was nine in order to be prepared for the grammar school, died about one year later. Did his death make a deep impression on Gogol? There are biographers who mention it.[14]

The twelve-year-old who entered the grammar school at Nezhin was not a very attractive boy, being sallow in complexion and scrofulous. Opinions differ concerning his stay there. It was probably not the "hell" of which Lyubich Romanovich [15] (who could not stand Gogol) speaks. Gogol, who learnt moderately well and was initially not liked, certainly made some friends, attracted admiration through his talent as a mimic and kept his enemies at bay through his sharp tongue.

It would take us too far to weigh up the rather conflicting accounts. The most important thing for us are his letters written during these years. It is not that they form pleasant reading, the earliest being no doubt dictated or at least corrected thoroughly. They did not, however, become natural and detached in tone as time went on. The style, in most cases, is conventionally rhetorical, sometimes excessively tender or passionate. It would be possible to ascribe all this to poor instruction in style, if these features did not persist in Gogol's whole correspond-

---

[13]　Terebinsky considered this possible. He came to the conclusion that it was hereditary tabes dorsalis. See V. I. Terebinsky, "O bolezni Gogolya" in *Russky vrach v Chekhoslovakii*, 1939, Nos. 1, 2 and 4.

[14]　Thus Kulish, *Zapiski*, I, p. 17 and G. P. Danilevsky, *Sobr. soch.*, XIV, p. 121.

[15]　V. I. Lyubich-Romanovich, "Gogol v Nezhinskom litseye" in *Istorichesky Vestnik*, 1892, 2, pp. 548–60.

ence up to his death. This was not however the case to all his corre-
spondents. It has already been pointed out that Gogol considered more
than is customary the impression which his letters could make on their
readers and that he projected into them the personality he wished to
appear as with regard to their recipients. This is not the whole story
however. It would seem that Gogol soon found in the dry or stilted
choice of words of the epistolary form he was taught a useful means
by which to conceal himself. I know, for example, of no single letter
to his mother which is, as a whole, simple and cordial, in which the
love which he undoubtedly felt for her flows naturally. His letters to
her are cool and business-like or they contain so many superlatives
that we begin to doubt the genuineness of the feeling the writer wants
to express.

There is only one category of persons to whom Gogol writes naturally,
they being those with whom he laughed about the same things – old
school-fellows, such as Danilevsky, or later friends, such as Maksimovich – people to whom he did not have to prove anything of his
importance as a person and writer.[16]

It is possible that the veneration in which his mother soon began to
hold him was an oppression that always forced him to appear differently
from what he was, although that was not always something more: he
did not wish to be worshipped by her as a literary genius, knowing
after all that she lacked any discernment.[17] We shall consequently be
prepared seldom to find in Gogol's letters a direct expression of emotion. It becomes all the more important to investigate how this young
letter-writer wanted to present himself. The drama which a person
produces with himself in the centre is always interesting, even if he
does not for our taste often enough act out of character.

The illness about which the boy writes, shortly after entering
boarding-school, the complaint with which he lay awake crying at night,
was probably home-sickness.[18] Nevertheless, the pain in his chest, as a

---

[16] Changes occur in the relationship with Danilevsky and Prokopovich in about
1845, as a result of which there is also an end to the friendly tone of the letters.
[17] See e.g. the letter of 9th August 1833, *P.*, I, 255 and the letter of 2nd
October 1833, *P.*, I, 261, 262.
[18] See the letter of 14th August 1821 from Nezhin. "After the holiday I am so
sullen that my tears flow every day that God gives, and I myself don't know why,
and particularly when I think of you, then I cry my eyes out. And I have such a
pain in my chest that I cannot even write much. (. . .) Also, do not forget my good
Simon who does his best for me so that no night passes in which, dear parents,
he does not exhort me not to cry, and sometimes he sits the whole night with me."
On 26th August there is a short letter with no word about the illness. It was

result of which he found such difficulty in breathing, is notable, bearing in mind that his father was in fact consumptive. We might see in this a trace of imitation, probably also a symptom of anxiety.

Gogol's father died when the boy was sixteen. His mother, who had just given birth to her twelfth child, was not present at his death nor did she write to her eldest son. He heard the sad and unexpected news from the principal of the boarding-school at Nezhin. The beginning of the letter which he wrote straight afterwards to his mother deserves to be quoted.

Do not be alarmed, dearest mother. I have endured this blow with the strength of a true Christian. It is true that I was at first terribly upset by this news; I did not however let anyone see that I was distressed. Yet, when I was alone, I succumbed to the full power of complete despair. I even wanted to die by my own hand, but God dissuaded me from this; and towards evening I perceived only sadness in myself; it was, however, no longer tempestuous and finally passed into a slight, scarcely perceptible melancholy, mixed with a pious respect for the Almighty. I bless you, oh holy faith! In you alone, do I find a source of consolation and relief for my sorrow. And so, dearest mother, I am now calm, although I cannot be happy, since I have lost the best father, the truest friend, everything that was dear to my heart. Yet do I not still have a sensitive, affectionate and virtuous mother who can for me replace my father and friend and everything that is dear and precious? Yes, I still have you and have not yet been deserted by fate.[19]

We are inclined to take offence at these lines in which no word rings true. We do not really believe in that outburst concerning suicide, a somewhat unusual reaction in a boy who has lost his father. But that does not release us from asking a few questions. Why could not Gogol write simply and cordially to his mother whom he really loved? Why this miserable observation of himself, not only carried out but also reproduced? Why did Gogol, even if he had not seriously thought of

---

presumably dictated, as witness the second and last sentence: "Oh, how I hope that you may be enjoying perfect health and well-being, may God fulfil your son's hope, who for always remains with sincere respect and affection for always (sic) your humble and obedient son, Nikolay Gogol-Yanovsky". – The following letter of 6th September contains an apology about the thoughtless one of 14th August, in addition to the following: "When I had arrived at Nezhin, I contracted a pain in my chest the following day. At night it hurt so much that I could not breathe freely. It was somewhat better in the morning, but my chest was still sore and I was therefore afraid it was something serious and was also very sad because you are so far away. But now everything has passed, thank goodness, and I am healthy and happy." P., I, 10, 11.
[19] P., I, 26.

taking his own life, apparently consider that this would have been a suitable reaction?

There is in this too great a concentration on himself. It is strange that Gogol the moralist already appears here, for the passage quoted is merely the first half of the letter, which ends with an adjuration to his mother to moderate her sorrow, as he had done his own and, like himself, to seek her refuge with the Almighty.

I shall dedicate the whole of my life to you. I shall sweeten all your moments. [In a second P.S. he nevertheless asks for ten roubles.]

Yet, apart from this, there is aggressiveness in the thought of suicide, aggressiveness directed against himself. Is it too premature to presume a feeling of guilt on the basis of this?

The tone of Gogol's letters to his mother becomes more normal as time goes on. There is sometimes genuine tenderness in them and a loyalty which he did not renounce up to his death. Yet, the later letters also often contain something overwrought. His father is very rarely mentioned in this correspondence, and then only casually. Yet once, two years later, he speaks about him in greater detail, first in conventional terms – "My friend, benefactor, comforter . . . I do not know what I shall call that heavenly angel."

It then appears that a complete identification is desired.

This pure, exalted being, that inspires me on my difficult path and encourages me, presents me with the gift of *feeling myself* and often penetrates inside me like a heavenly flame in moments of sorrow and illuminates the sombre cloud of my thoughts. It is sweet for me to be with him at such a time; I cast my glances into him, *that is into myself,* as into the heart of a friend, I feel in me the strength to undertake a momentous, noble task, for the salvation of my native country, for the happiness of its citizens, for the welfare of my fellow-men and I, who was for so long uncertain and (rightly) without trust in myself, am kindled in the fire of a proud *self-confidence,* and my soul, as it were, sees that angel that has appeared to me and that firmly and unmovedly continues to point to the goal of my ardent searching . . . In a year's time I shall enter the public service . . .[20]

As far as I know, it has not previously been pointed out that Gogol expressed the thought of his vocation for the first time in this way – as an assignment from a heavenly image of his father. Belief in a mission on the scale of world history can serve to give proof of a brilliant talent. It can, however, at the same time be the path along which a

[20] *P.,* I, 68. The italics are mine (F. D.).

person hopes to be freed of his feelings of guilt. The future will, after all, make good all that has happened! Without for a moment excluding the first possibility, the second definitely seems to me to be present here. That same belief in fact occurred again with Gogol towards the end of his life and even in a similar form. It never disappears and continues to have this form, namely that a mission is being held onto at the cost of the past. There is literally not one of his works that Gogol did not repudiate or belittle referring to the future. That applies even to the first part of "Dead Souls" and to the "Selected Passages".

The letters quoted here have already shown a certain degree of narcissism. This began to become evident in details. Gogol's tendency to dandyism, known from his later life, already became visible in these years.[21] Narcissism is however also seen in direct relation to his great mission.

There was a cold perspiration on my face at the thought that I should perhaps have to die without having made my name known through one glorious deed: it seemed appalling to me to be in the world and not to show anything of my existence.[22]

We know how St. Petersburg received the young man who dreamt of a glorious life amongst friends sharing the same ideas as his own, at the same time a grandiose life, in which the twenty-year-old, prepared by some general lessons on natural right and international law, was about to apply himself to reforming the administration of justice. The capital had nothing to offer him except a clerical post at a starvation wage.

Then came the first grab at fame which turned out to be a mistake: "Hans Küchelgarten", Gogol's lyrical epic poem, which appeared under a pseudonym. It was quickly and indifferently slated in a few short criticisms. His shame could only be blotted out in one way, namely by destroying the work. Gogol had all the unsold copies collected from the bookseller and burnt them. Then he fled abroad.

The famous letter in which he informed his mother of this flight (not of his literary failure) has been quoted and analysed on innumer-

---

[21] In a letter of 26th July to G. Vysotsky, a former grammar-school pupil, who was already working in St. Petersburg, he asked him whether it would be possible to order a fashionable coat there from a good tailor. He is also anxious to know what materials are in fashion for waistcoats and trousers. (The distance from St. Petersburg to Nezhin is more than 600 miles. The tailor would therefore have to obtain the measurements from Vysotsky, while Gogol wanted to order the material in Nezhin!) *P.*, I, 79, 80.
[22] *P.*, I, 89.

able occasions. I nevertheless consider that we shall do well to look again at this strange epistle and the letters which follow it.

We must first of all put on record that the thought, not of a major journey, but of a prolonged stay outside Russia had already occupied his mind during his school-years. To the same uncle, P. P. Kosyarovsky, to whom he had confided how unbearable an ordinary career seemed to him, he had written a year later:

I am definitely going to St. Petersburg at the beginning of the winter, and heaven knows where I shall end up after that. It may very well be that I shall come to rest in foreign countries, that nothing will be heard of me for a few years." [23]

Two months before he decided to leave, he had written to his mother about an unsuccessful plan for a foreign journey.

When it came to it, and he had used for the cost of the journey the money his mother had sent him for paying off the interest on a mortgage, the reasons he listed were many.

First of all, God's hand is there, now raised chastisingly because he had resisted God's will by remaining in St. Petersburg.

Lunatic that I was, I wanted to resist those longings that can never be silenced which only God had put in my heart (. . .). He showed me the way to a new country, to learn there to master my passions in silence and solitude, in the roar of uninterrupted work and activity, so that I should raise myself by stages to a higher level, from where I should be in a position to spread blessing and to work for the welfare of the world.

In order to please his mother, he had not obeyed God. Yet now the punishment had come, a frightful one, namely love. Then follows the description of the divine woman who had sparked off this passion in him. It is customary to stress the ridiculous nature of this portrayal. It is perhaps more desirable to read it very attentively.

But I have seen her . . . no, I shall not mention her name . . . she is too exalted for everyone, not only for me. I should like to call her an angel, but that expression is commonplace and does not become her: an angel is a being which has neither virtues nor vices, which has no character, because it is not a person and lives alone with its thoughts in heaven. But no, I am talking nonsense, I cannot express her nature, she is a deity, yet gently swathed in human passions.[24] A face which instantaneously makes an indeli-

---

[23]   P., I, 105.
[24]   Shenrok did not publish Gogol's letters faultlessly. It is not always clear whether something has been left out and, if so, why. Sometimes we can find the

ble impression on the heart through its blinding beauty; eyes which quickly penetrate to the soul; but no mortal can endure their burning radiation which passes through everything. Oh, if you had seen me then! – it is true, I succeeded in hiding myself from everyone, but did I hide from myself? An infernal sorrow with all conceivable tortures raged in my heart. Oh, what a horrible state! If hell is prepared for sinners, then I don't think it is as painful. No, that was not love, I at least have never heard of such a love. Carried along in a storm of frenzy and the most terrible torments of the soul, I yearned, I longed to refresh myself by one look, I thirsted for one look alone. To behold her once again was my only craving which became stronger and stronger with an inexpressibly gnawing desire. With horror I became aware of myself, and surveyed my frightful condition. Absolutely everything in the world was strange to me at that moment, life and death were equally unbearable to me, and my soul did not realise what was taking place in it. I felt that I had to flee from myself if I wanted to save my life and to obtain even the slightest trace of inward peace in my tormented mind.

I recognised with emotion the invisible hand of God which was looking after me, and I blessed the path which had been pointed to me so clearly. No, that being that He sent to rob me of my tranquility, to cause my shakily built world to collapse, was not a woman. If she had been a woman, then she would not have been able to cause such appalling and unspeakable impressions with all the force of her charms. It was a deity, created by Him, a part of Himself. But, for God's sake, do not ask me her name. She is much too exalted, too exalted! [. . .]

Do not be distressed, dear, unforgettable mother! This change is unavoidable for me. I am undoubtedly being moulded in this school, I have a bad character, a corrupt and spoilt mind (I admit that with all my heart), idleness and staying here, which is like death to me, would certainly have permanently consolidated these qualities. No, I must reform myself, become reborn, live again with a new life, develop my strength of mind by continuous work and activity, and if I cannot be happy (no, I shall never be happy myself; that divine creature has taken the tranquility from my heart and has left me), then I shall at least dedicate my whole life to the happiness and welfare of my fellow-men.[25]

---

suppressed material in one of the (extremely inconveniently arranged) appendices to the last volume of the edition. In this case, everything has been omitted from the letter between "does not suit her" and "she is a deity". The letter is always quoted in this way and quite an incorrect impression is given. It seems as if the name "angel" is not yet exalted enough. It is precisely these omitted words which, in my opinion, point to the existence of an actual woman. They are found in IV, 457. – When Kulish published the letter he perhaps omitted the passage in question because it was not desirable in 1856 to speak so disrespectfully about angels. In Shenrok's edition and also in that of the Academy of Sciences all improper expressions in the field of digestion and sexuality are also omitted, this being very inconvenient for our study.
[25] P., I, 123–29.

He intended to stay away for two or three years. Six days at sea, amongst strangers, had a sobering effect. Immediately he arrived in Lübeck, he wrote to his mother in quite a different tone.

Only now, when I am alone in the midst of immense waves, have I discovered what separation from you, my inestimable mother, means in these solemn, terrible hours of my life, when I have run away from myself, when I have tried to forget everything around me, and the thought of *what I have in this way done to you* has descended like a heavy stone onto my heart, and in vain have I tried to convince myself that I had, from sheer necessity, to subject myself to Him who rules us from heaven. No, I cannot part from you, my generous friend, my guardian angel![26]

It is all rather childish. Let us not forget, however, that it is the letter of a twenty-year-old provincial, for whom life had become unbearable in inhospitable St. Petersburg, and who had now, nevertheless, passed from the frying-pan into the fire.

Remember one thing, however: our separation will not last long. I am not intending to stay here long, although life here is more tolerable and cheaper than in St. Petersburg. I think I have forgotten to write to you about the main reason why I have just now gone to Lübeck. I had been ill for almost the whole spring and summer in St. Petersburg; although I am now well again, I have a severe rash on my face and hands. The doctors have told me that this is a result of scrofula and that my blood is thoroughly vitiated, that I have to take a blood-purifying potion, and they have advised me to take baths in Travemünde, a small town about 11 miles from Lübeck. I need not stay for more than two weeks for this. If you wish, you have merely to bid me leave Lübeck and I shall leave immediately, the sooner the better, since I cannot be settled so far away from you, particularly now the thought of you alone fills my mind, now that I look forward only to the opportunity of pleasing you alone, which I have so far, unfortunately, not succeeded in doing.[27]

We know that Maria Ivanovna Gogol combined the two facts, namely woman and affection of the skin; in other words venereal disease. Gogol has always been reproached as having, through his lies, been the cause of this misunderstanding. Why really? It cannot be proved in any way what basis of truth lies hidden in all these confused stories, any more than that they are based solely on fantasy. We must, I think, in the first place bear in mind that we are dealing with the crisis of a very youthful person.

The nineteen-year-old who came to St. Petersburg from a provincial

[26] *P.,* I, 129.
[27] *P.,* I, 130.

town was, on the one hand, a vulnerable, suspicious boy who had suffered enough humiliations to adopt a certain reserve towards his fellow-men; [28] on the other hand he was the opposite of worldly-wise.[29] Within seven months, he was inwardly bankrupt. It would be unreasonable to assert that he had not done everything to escape from it. In that half year he had managed to have "Hans Küchelgarten" published. He had experienced what poverty and loneliness mean. His dream about the magnificent northern metropolis turned to a dislike which he never again completely lost. He also refused to accept the first post which came along. The above-mentioned narcissism undoubtedly played a part in this refusal. Should he, the gifted one, destined for great deeds, have to be satisfied with work that any fool with legible handwriting could do just as well, for a salary which would just prevent him from dying of starvation, but which offered him no possibility of enjoying the culture of the capital?

There is, however, at the same time a very correct insight. If he had resigned himself to the position, he would have had to give up his mission. Sticking to his belief of having been selected, gave him the strength for his desperate attempt to escape, and also thereafter for an incessant search as to how he was to make his name known, how he could come to the fore. Even before he fled, he had conceived the idea of writing Ukrainian tales and he asked his mother for material on folklore.

Apart from the reasons which Gogol mentions, we now see as the causes for his flight a few facts which can be put on record objectively. These are failure in a social sense and failure as a writer. From Gogol's point of view, they were proof that he was not taking the correct path for following his mission. This accounted for his anxiety.

What is the position with the motives he lists to his mother? The first, namely that God's hand is punishing him, fits in completely with Gogol's train of thought. The second, namely the illness, is something which accompanied his anxiety throughout his life. We have referred to it in his first letters from Nezhin. It also occurs later in his school-years: "I have been lying ill for a whole week and was very seriously ill, even despairing of my recovery." This is a sentence from a letter

[28] "No, I know people too well to be a dreamer", *P.*, I, 98 (to his mother, 1st March 1828).
[29] To P. P. Kosyarovsky he writes that he shall possibly be able to manage abroad. "I know a few trades: I am a good tailor, I can paint walls al fresco quite well, I work in the kitchen and know quite a bit about catering." 1st September 1828. *P.*, I, 107.

to an old school-friend, dated 19th March, 1827.[30] There is no evidence of a critical illness in other letters dating from the same period. The long letter in which the above words occur by its contents contradicts this statement. Was it a lie? Probably not, but a dramatic exaggeration in order to appear interesting. At the beginning of his first letter from St. Petersburg to his mother, we find these sentences:

I am subject to a heavy melancholy or something of that sort, and I have been sitting for a whole week with my arms crossed and am doing nothing. It is probably a result of the setbacks which have made me completely indifferent to everything.[31]

The pain in his chest and difficulties with breathing are precisely what the small boy in Nezhin had complained of. Is it so strange that he felt himself just as small and lonely in St. Petersburg? The rash was probably not so serious that a journey abroad was necessary for it. We must nevertheless bear in mind how important Gogol's external appearance was to him.

And now we come to love. It is all too easy to dismiss this with a reference to the stilted style in which Gogol describes the lady, to shrug our shoulders at his exclamations about the torments of hell and all the rest, to smile meaningly when he keeps on repeating to his inquisitive mother: "Don't ask me her name." It has never become quite clear to me why Gogol should not have conceived a romantic veneration for a lady whom he scarcely knew and should not have considered this for a moment as a fatal passion. With an eye to what is to follow later in this chapter, it is not so unlikely that the woman in question would have been "too exalted" for him. On the contrary, we may presume that he was predestined to fall in love exclusively with a beauty who could not be approached.

Yet, even if we do not wish to believe one word of the story, there still remains the fact that Gogol, just twenty years old, did not succeed in thinking of any severer punishment from heaven than to feel attracted to a woman who was unattainable because of her elevated nature. It has been supposed that all this was a speculation based on his mother's romantic fantasies. This is not completely inconceivable. Gogol had, as appears from her answer, then certainly blundered greatly. It is not very likely however: the *femme fatale* depicted by her son was, in any case, not a figure of the type which inhabited Maria

[30] *P.*, I, 63 (to Vysotsky).
[31] *P.*, I, 114.

Ivanovna's Arcadian imagination.[32] She will likewise not have disappeared from Gogol's thoughts for some time to come.

"A product of Hades!" These are the first words of the first piece which Gogol dared to publish under his own name in January 1831. It is entitled "Woman".[33] According to Telecles, Plato's pupil, who is speaking here, Zeus has concentrated all the poison of the earth in one drop and has, in his rage, tainted creation with it. "You have created woman!"

Plato tries to calm Telecles and asks him whether he knows what loving is. Telecles answers:

Ask Zeus whether he can cause the earth to quake by knitting his brows. Ask Phidias whether he can make marble glow in feeling and can give form to life in dead stone. If blood does not seethe in my veins, but a fierce flame, if all feelings, all thoughts, if my whole being is transformed into sounds, if those sounds burn and my soul only resounds with love, if my words are a storm, my breath fire... No, no, I cannot love! But tell me then, where is that strange mortal who has that feeling? Has perhaps the all-wise Pythia discovered that wonder amongst men?

Plato answers this frenzy with words that are certainly somewhat calmer, but not much clearer. He knows that Telecles is being deceived by the beautiful Alcinoë and yet he defends woman and love.

What is woman? The language of the gods. We admire the serene, clear face of man; but we do not behold in him the image of the gods: we see in him woman, we admire in him woman and only in her do we admire the gods. She is poetry! She is thought, we are only her incarnation in reality.

And furthermore:

What is love? The spiritual home of the soul, the beautiful longing of man for what is past, where the innocent beginning of life has taken place, where there has remained on all things a trace of innocent childhood which cannot be described or obliterated, where everything is native soil. And when the soul sinks into the ethereal bosom of a feminine soul, when it finds in it its father – the eternal God, its brothers – feelings and visions so far inexpressible for the earth, – what happens to it then? It then repeats previous sounds in itself, a previous life in paradise at God's bosom, and develops it into infinity...

---

[32] The way in which her husband had at the time sued for her hand had been extremely poetic. See *Mat.*, I, 42.
[33] *Soch.*, V, 60–65. The piece appeared in *Literaturnaya Gazeta* of 16th January 1831.

The appearance of Alcinoë puts an end to this dissertation. I shall not quote the whole description of this figure with the "marble arm, through which the blue veins shone (sic) full of heavenly ambrosia", and would merely draw attention to its close:

Her carelessly thrown-back locks, dark as a night full of inspiration, fell over her lily-white forehead and flowed down in a sombre waterfall onto her shining shoulders. The lightning of her eyes caused the whole soul to be kindled . . . No, even the queen of love was never so beautiful, not even at the moment when she was born so miraculously from the foam of the virgin waves! . . .

Helplessness, undoubtedly. The strangest thing is, however, that Gogol was never to get *this* subject, namely ideal beauty, in his power. If we consider the last effort he made in his life to give shape to his feminine ideal, then we find the same strings of conventional attributes, the same helpless hyperboles.

"Rome" is a fragment from the time in which "Dead Souls" and "The Overcoat" appeared. It is, in other words, a work by Russia's greatest writer of prose of those years. It begins thus:

Try to look at the lightning when it glitters unbearably in a flood of light as it splits the pitch-black clouds. Such are the eyes of the Alban Annunciata. Everything in it reminds one of classical times when marble came to life and the chisels of the sculptors sparkled. The compact pitch of her hair was raised in heavy, doubly wound plaits on her head and fell in four long locks along her neck. Wherever she turns the sparkling snow of her face, her whole figure impresses itself into the soul. (. . .) Yet the strangest thing is when she looks straight at you, eye to eye, and fills your heart with cold and oppression. Her powerful voice sounds like bronze.

No lithe panther can be compared with her in speed, power and pride of movement.[34]

This glance at a certain, weak side of Gogol's work was necessary in order to make it clear that the letter to his mother could not have been written differently. It is, in my opinion, difficult to over-estimate the fact that he first appeared unmasked on the literary stage with "Woman". Gogol makes a mistake here which he was to repeat until his death. After having keyed himself up to a certain degree of seriousness and having overstrained his tone, he considers that he will speak great words and will be listened to as the scholar, philosopher or prophet as which he wishes to pose. If we disregard the philosophical meaning

[34] *Soch.*, II, 130.

which we shall seek in vain in "Woman", we nevertheless still learn much about the author from it.

It deals with the same subject as that on which he had written to his mother. The piece is apparently the fruit of a renewed effort to come to terms with himself. The fateful woman shows the same grandeur, arouses the same passion, the same question is asked: is this passion in fact love? The definition of this feeling is also significant. Words are apparently borrowed from Plato which can point to the pre-existence of the soul. In my opinion, the writer nevertheless had quite different things in mind. Gogol never became an abstract thinker, and there is nothing of it in this youthful work. We obtain the same feeling as with the argumentative passages from "Arabesques": Gogol thinks in images, and when a link in his thoughts is missing, an image appears through association. The peculiar definition of love acquires a completely new meaning if we bear this in mind; in other words, if we do not take the key words as abstracts, but as vague indications of concrete images. Love is then a return to one's spiritual home, to innocent childhood, the rediscovery of a father who is divine, the renewed experiencing of indescribable youthful memories, finding oneself again in a lost state of paradise. Summarising: love is an infinite perpetuation of youth. In a different meaning from Plato (the Greek, not the Russian of Gogol), it is homesickness. This view is placed opposite Telecles' violent passion. It is however obvious that the fatal woman cannot arouse such feelings of love.

Yet, why is this inaccessible one ever escaping even the artist's depiction? The answer has already been given by Gogol's first biographer, Kulish, who has said that Gogol's sole passion applied to his mother.[35] If we consider this possibility for a moment, then we probably remember the youthful portrait which has been preserved of Maria Ivanovna Gogol. We see again the marble-pale face with the dark eyes, framed by raven-black hair. We begin to ask ourselves whether the image of his mother had not obscured that of all other women for Gogol. I consider that the answer to this question must be in the affirmative. If we assume an excessively strong bond to his mother, then a whole series of phenomena from both his work and his life suddenly becomes clear. We see why no single love affair of Gogol is known, and why in Gogol's works woman is always devalued sexually. Gesemann already referred to this a long time ago.[36] Now we

[35] Quoted by Shenrok, *Mat.*, I, 182.
[36] Gerhard Gesemann, "Grundlagen einer Charakterologie Gogols" in *Jahrbuch*

can also understand why the phenomenon of love has two aspects for Gogol, namely the passionate desire which is forbidden and the longing for "the spiritual home of the soul" which is lost. Both are directed at his mother. A question I should merely like to put and which I dare not answer is this: is it not conceivable that Gogol in the last resort fled from his mother and unconsciously desired to cut through the bond attaching him to her?

When discussing Gogol's relation to woman, there is a letter which should be considered and which has given rise to misunderstanding. It is that of 20th December 1832 to Danilevsky, Gogol's former school-friend, who had lost his heart to an exceptionally beautiful girl in the Caucasus who could never be his wife.[37] Insufficient account has been taken of this latter point, namely the hopeless nature of Danilevsky's love, by V. Bryusov who used a particular passage from this letter to illustrate his opinion about the tragedy of Gogol's life. He even borrowed the title for his subsequently famous oration at the Gogol celebrations in Moscow in 1909 from an expression in this passage, namely "The person burnt to ashes".[38] However much truth and originality this may contain and however willingly I acknowledge that I owe much to it for clarifying my own view, I consider that Bryusov's conclusions in this respect are nevertheless based on an incorrect interpretation of Gogol's words and on a garbled quotation. According to Bryusov, Gogol is said to have written the following to Danilevsky:

I understand and feel your state of mind very well, although I do not myself, thanks to my stars, know it from experience. I say "thanks to" because that flame would have burnt me to ashes in a moment. To my salvation a strong will restrained me from the desire to look into the abyss.[39]

---

der Charakterologie, I (1924). I had known of this study for some time. Gesemann himself drew my attention to it 20 years ago, adding warning that I should not attach great value to it. Unfortunately, I took this warning to heart and only re-read his article when I had written this chapter. Apart from a somewhat too great manipulation with Kretschmer's typology and a view of Gogol's illness as a psychosis (schizophrenia), to which I should like to object, Gesemann's article in my opinion contains very much that is valuable – it has definitely influenced my work without me being aware of the fact. – See also G. Gesemann: "Der Träumer und der Andere" in Dostojevsky-Studien, collected and edited by D. Chizhevsky (Reichenberg, 1931).

[37]   Emilia Aleksandrovna Verzilina. See Mat., I, 352 ff.

[38]   V. Bryusov, "Ispepelenny". Speech given on 27th April 1909. Printed in Gogolevskiye dni v Moskve (Moscow, 1909), p. 157 ff. Also appeared separately (Moscow 1909) and printed once again in Vesy, 1909. (The title is not given in the anniversary volume, but at the head of the other editions mentioned).

[39]   Bryusov, Gogolevskiye dni v Moskve, p. 178.

Quoted in this way, Gogol's words seem to mean that he had felt the power of attraction of love as being sucked towards an abyss. Bryusov sees in this an example of the immoderate and excessive tension of all Gogol's feelings.

There is however something else and something more which is not in agreement with Bryusov's view. After the sentence which ends with the words "in a moment", Gogol in fact continues:

I should not be able to enjoy the past, I should try to convert it into the present and should myself become the victim of that attempt. And therefore I possess, to my salvation, a strong will which has twice restrained me from the desire to look into the abyss. You are lucky, you have been allowed to enjoy the highest pleasure on earth, love, but I . . .[40]

The first sentence omitted by Bryusov seems obscure only of we do not know that Danilevsky's love was without prospects or could, at least, never lead to marriage. The difference in station between the young lieutenant and the girl from the fashionable world was an obstacle thereto. Danilevsky would consequently have to be content with a beautiful memory. Gogol says nothing more than that he would in such a case not be able to restrain himself from desiring the ultimate, which could merely become fatal to him.

While, therefore, the general drift which Bryusov imparts to Gogol's words must be dropped, the story of the flight appears in a different light. Danilevsky's beloved was also "too exalted" for him. Gogol writes to him that he has seen that situation looming up *on two occasions* and that he has escaped from it by his strong will. That would consequently agree with his explanations to his mother. We must, in my opinion, doubt only the "strong will" – "strong anxiety" would probably be more correct. If the assumption of an Oedipal attachment to his mother put forward above contains any truth, it is then obvious that the object of Gogol's love had eo ipso to be chosen as being "too exalted".[41]

[40] *P.*, I, 232. It must be mentioned that Gogol was not in such a dignified mood to prevent there being a very crude story at the end of the letter (the essential point of which is naturally omitted in Shenrok's edition).

[41] "Too exalted", of course not specially in the social sense. It is perhaps not superfluous to note that love was mentioned here continually. We can, I think, assume that Gogol had had sexual intercourse. See *Mat.*, IV, 855. The doctor, Tarasenkov, relates how he had treated Gogol shortly before the latter's death: ". . . he had not had intercourse with women for some time and he himself admitted that he had no need thereof and had never felt special satisfaction thereat; he was also not addicted to masturbation."

In this way the consideration of Gogol's flight in 1829 led us to consider the problem of Gogol's disturbed erotic life. The results are relatively meagre and we have not advanced much beyond establishing a mother fixation which had already been suspected. There is still a large gap. We are, as a result of the scarcity of data concerning Gogol's youth, not in a position to name the event which acted as the trauma, although we must naturally assume that there was such a trauma. Nevertheless, the material indicated above is not yet completely exhausted. There is still the question of the part which Gogol's father played in all this. We have seen that the awakening of Gogol's self-assertion coincided with an appeal to his father and we have even spoken of a father identification which first appears from the sentences quoted, but which may date from an earlier period. Consequently, there was not exclusively aggressiveness towards his father. If, with this in mind, we read again the words of Gogol's Plato about the nature of woman, we are struck by the fact that there is in them such a peculiar reference to man. The divine element is never directly beheld in man, but is witnessed only through the image of woman, of which man is the bearer. In other words, according to Gogol, one loves the feminine in man. This supposition gains support if we read in the following paragraph the opposite – if the soul sinks into the bosom of a female soul it finds its father there. If we apply this to Gogol's relationship with his parents, it would follow that there is also an erotic relationship with his father and that Gogol saw the feminine in him. We should then have to presume a homoerotic component in Gogol's relationship with his father. It is necessary here to point out with the greatest possible stress that this component must have been unconscious and that it would be an unwarranted simplification of the hypothesis stated here to call Gogol homosexual. I am thinking merely of the possibility that the power of the homoerotic element which exists in every person and through which, for example, friendship becomes possible for persons of the same sex, was fairly strong in Gogol. A new light then falls on his cool attitude towards women.

Are there other facts than these which can serve to render the above hypothesis more likely? I shall name two. We know about the conflict between Gogol and Pogodin in 1840 which assumed such sharp forms after Gogol had been living in Pogodin's house. All sorts of objective causes can be advanced for it: Pogodin did not suffer from an excess of sensitiveness and wanted to force Gogol to hand over work for his own journal at a time when Gogol was not in a position to supply it.

Anyhow, a state of irritation remained and finally found expression from Gogol's side in a particularly unpleasant passage in "Selected Passages", as a result of which Pogodin justly felt greatly offended, and which all Gogol's friends rightly took great exception to.[42] Gogol himself was never able to give proper account of this, for him, very unusual act. It is striking that Gogol's whole correspondence never reached the degree of intimacy which his letters to Pogodin show just before the conflict broke out. Clearest in this respect is the letter of 4th November 1839.[43] Pogodin had conceived the idea of publishing a literary daily. Gogol found this a desperate undertaking and tried to dissuade him from it. He addresses Pogodin as "my soul and my life" and says:

I shall implore you on my knees, I shall throw myself at your feet, my soul and my life, you know that you are dear to me, that you are my life itself. I swear to you, you will have no success with your undertaking and I shall not be able to bear seeing your failure.

I shall quote these few short sentences from the close of the letter:

Farewell my angel. (. . .) I kiss and embrace you a thousand times, my angel, Keep well and may heaven protect you in everything. My dear one [*dusha moya*] I cannot stand it here without you.

We must bear in mind here that expressions such as "my angel", "my soul", "my little heart" flow more easily from the pen of a Russian than from our own. Gogol is nevertheless for the rest very sparing with accumulations of such terms.

I should like to repeat once again that there should be no question of concluding from this material that there was a homosexual relationship between Gogol and Pogodin.

A last indication I want to add to the above is contained in the piece "Nights at a (Roman) Villa", which was not published during Gogol's lifetime, but which came to light amongst Pogodin's papers. It is an autobiographical fragment, written on note-paper, of which only the first and last pages have been preserved. It contains reminiscences of his nocturnal watches with the twenty-three year-old Count Velgorsky who died in Gogol's arms in Rome on 21st May 1839. This death made an indelible impression on Gogol. The fragment is not literature and cannot have been intended for publication in this

---

[42] The passage is in the essay: "What the word means" ("O tom, chto takoe slovo"), *Soch.*, IV, 19.

[43] *P.*, II, 18, 19.

form because of the contemptuous statement about the Tsar which occurs in it. There is every reason to assume that the overwrought feelings expressed in the piece are genuine in origin. Apart from the final passage, the style is different from everything Gogol wrote. The sentences are short and panting. His contempt for the benefactions of his imperial protector is not in contradiction with the eagerness with which he sought these benefits. Essentially, it is self-contempt, coupled with contempt for the whole of mankind.

The final passage is, in my opinion, very important. This whole experience was for Gogol nothing but the repetition of an episode from his youth, not his very earliest, it is true, but rather that dating from the boarding-school at Nezhin. We can, of course, then think only of male objects for his feelings of love and can presume that he had in those tender youthful friendships experienced again an erotic desire which had its origin even further in the past.

To these unusual things can be added a last one which is for me decisive, namely the tone of tenderness. This is not so strongly expressed in any of his letters, not even in those to Pogodin. If we were to replace the male names by female ones, no-one would doubt that it was here a question of an amorous relationship. This, however, may be a dangerous test. It is also possible to consider the piece simply as an unsuccessful preamble to a literary outpouring and to view the exaggeration as strange, but not as the expression of unusual feelings. In order to allow the reader to form his own opinion, I have added the completely translated fragment.[44]

If from these data one reaches the conclusion I have suggested, then the role which his dead father continued to play in his life has become much clearer. Gogol felt himself closely attached to him and, at the same time, guilty. The mission to fulfil which he had received from his father unconsciously took on the value of a penance and at the same time unconscious aspirations were warded off. If we assume the homoerotic component, then we see Gogol's fate as being even more tragic and his sense of isolation as being even greater. Even if we do not however decide on this, and if his repressed aspiration were to be merely an Oedipal inclination towards his mother, while the tender feelings for his father mean exclusively reconciliation with the avenger of the incest, there is reason enough to find the development of anxiety understandable.

[44]   *Soch.*, V. 530–32 and 671–73. See below, the "Appendix" p. 230 ff.

We must certainly assume that after his flight the feeling of disillusion continued for a period, being disappointment about St. Petersburg and particularly about himself. The clash with reality shook his faith in God's guidance. It is oppressive to see how Gogol, after his first misfortune pleads almost word for word the same excuses as after his last – the publication of "Selected Passages".

Compare:

Only now and again, as if prompted by God himself, there arises in me the thought as to whether all this has taken place for a purpose; perhaps we are visited by sadness solely so that we can later enjoy our life in repose and happiness. (25th August 1829, to his mother).[45]

... only my proud youthful ideas, nevertheless emanating from a pure source, only from the fiery desire to be useful, but not moderated by reason, have carried me along too far. (. . .) God has brought down my pride, his sacred will be done! (24th September 1829, to his mother).[46]

Longing and desire for what is good, and not pride, forced me to publish my book, but when it had appeared, I saw precisely in it that I am suffering from pride and infatuation. (. . .) – But my book does not spring from a bad intention, my foolishness is to blame for everything, God also having punished me for it. (. . .) But how merciful the punishment is! Through the punishment he gives me the grace to feel humble, this being the best thing I can receive. (9th May 1847, to Father Matvey).[47]

Faith in his mission did not however die, and it seems as if Gogol is now really being guided in his search. At the end of 1829 he found a post in a department which he was able to change for a better one in April 1830. In the meantime, he was writing his Ukrainian stories in order to dispel his melancholy. He was introduced into literary circles and had in the end the inestimable privilege of making the acquaintance of the greatest figures in the Russian literary world, such as Zhukovsky (beginning of 1831) and Pushkin (end of May 1831). Beside this there pales into insignificance the fact that in February 1831 he was able to bid farewell to the hated life in the department and could appear as an assistant teacher at an institute for noble young ladies.

His pride must have been not a little flattered when it turned out that even these greatest amongst the great paid him recognition and

45 *P.*, I, 134.
46 *P.*, I, 136.
47 *P.*, III, 458, 459.

made him party to their plans. In November 1831 he wrote to Danilevsky concerning the previous summer:

Almost every evening we were together, Zhukovsky, Pushkin and I. Oh, if you only knew how much that is beautiful flows from the pen of these men! [48]

"Zhukovsky, Pushkin and I", these are words from a letter which is probably not free from bumptiousness. It is however our object to look with Gogol's eyes at the scene he himself was staging.

What did the two men, whose names Gogol places alongside his own, mean to him? It is not difficult to say as far as Zhukovsky is concerned. He also played the part of patron with regard to Gogol and in later years, a genuine friendship arose between him and the much younger writer, which depended partly on a large degree of agreement in their religious views. We nevertheless gain the impression that Gogol behaved unassumingly towards this older person, in spite of all the similarity in their views and also maintained a certain respect for his sobriety and sense of humour.

Matters were different between Pushkin and Gogol.[49] It is certain that Pushkin soon recognised and encouraged the talent of the strange *khokhol*.[50] Pushkin's enthusiasm about the "Evenings in a Village near Dikanka" certainly did more than anything else towards the rapid growth of Gogol's fame. There was with Pushkin evidently also a strong feeling of responsibility towards the young genius who, without guidance, was running the danger of losing himself in details. Pushkin conferred a dual benefit on Gogol by strengthening him in his faith in his mission and making clear to him what path he should follow with his ability. It is however highly unlikely that there was ever more than a literary friendship between these two. Pushkin moved in quite

---

[48] *P.,* I, 196.
[49] See M. Speransky, "O vzaimootnosheniyach Pushkina i Gogolya" in *Dnevnik A. S. Pushkina (1833–1835)* (Moscow-Leningrad, 1923). Remarks by Modzalevsky in another edition of Pushkin's diary: *Dnevnik Pushkina 1833–1835.* Pod red. (. . .) B. L. Modzalevskogo (Moscow-Petersburg, 1923). Pushkin's correspondence should also be consulted, *Sochineniya A. S. Pushkina,* izd. Imp. Ak. Nauk, *Perepiska,* pod red. i s primech. V. I. Saitova, 3 vols. (St. Petersburg, 1906–11). Gippius gave a very good review of the available material. See V. Gippius: "Literaturnoye obshcheniye Gogolya s Pushkinym" in *Uchenye Zapiski Permskogo gos. univ.,* otd. obshchestvennych nauk, vyp. 2 (Perm', 1931). – The first to strike a blow on scientific grounds at the legend of the intimate friendship between Pushkin and Gogol was V. Kallash, see his "Zametki o Gogole" in *Golos minuvshego,* 9, (1913), 234 ff.
[50] *Khokhol* – derisive name for a Ukrainian.

a different milieu from Gogol, but perhaps the difference in their character was an even greater obstacle to the formation of warm, personal relations. The difference in age, although less than between Gogol and Zhukovsky, was certainly also important. In 1831, when they met, Pushkin who developed phenomenally early, already had a series of masterpieces to his name, including "Eugen Onegin" and "Boris Godunov". The problems of life with which he was struggling were quite different from those of Gogol. The master of Russian literature had nothing to learn from Gogol while Gogol had everything to learn from him.

It seems to me that the feeling of respect which Gogol always maintained towards Pushkin was an extremely important and beneficial element in their relationship. What Gogol the artist found in Pushkin can be stated in very few words: "the measure of all things". What an inestimable significance such an experience can have, appears from the confession of a poet.

"It was the most difficult moment of my life when I understood that from then on I should have to discover for myself whether my poems were good or bad." [51] These words are by Albert Verwey. They form the introduction to a very sober-minded dissertation and are to be taken literally. Verwey survived this moment as an artist, which Gogol did not. After Pushkin's death, Gogol drafted nothing further of literary value. The first part of "Dead Souls", the last great work of art he completed, was begun on Pushkin's advice and under his auspices. The idea for "The Government Inspector" was also due to him.

What has been established here is very old. An effort has, of course, also been made to idealise the relationship between Gogol and Pushkin, but an estimation of Pushkin's importance as an artist for his younger contemporary is already found in the work of Gogol's first biographer. In 1856, Kulish wrote the, in my opinion, very correct words:

We should remember now in what rapid succession works such as "Taras Bulba", "The Government Inspector" and the first part of "Dead Souls" were written, at the same time as other less important works, and then we see what Gogol did after Pushkin's death. He wrote and burnt. He had no authority that gave him strength, no brilliant artist of his format who could show him the right path for his poetic activity. In a word, Pushkin's death formed just as sharp a dividing line in the life of Gogol as the move from the Ukraine to the capital. After Pushkin's death, Gogol was a completely different person from before.

[51] Albert Verwey, "Het beoordelen van Gedichten", in *Proza*, IV (Amsterdam, 1921), 229.

In a note on the same page, Kulish then relates how he had found to his surprise the same view, but in an even stronger form, in the manuscript of S. T. Aksakov's "History of my friendship with Gogol". Aksakov says:

It is known from Gogol's own letters what a crushing blow this loss was for him. Gogol became ill in body and soul. I would add that, in my opinion, he never completely recovered and that Pushkin's death was one of the causes of all the morbid symptoms of his mind.[52]

It seems to me that Aksakov, who observed Gogol very acutely, here makes too simple a causal connection. Certain quotations from Gogol's letter after Pushkin's death nevertheless show what Gogol lost in Pushkin.

I never undertook anything without his advice, I did not write one line without having his image before my eyes. 'What will he say, what observations will he make, why will he laugh, about what will he express his unswerving approval?' Only that kept me going and again and again gave me new strength. The mysterious vibration of an ecstasy unknown on earth came over my soul . . . (To Pletnyov, 28th March 1837).[53]

My life, that which was my highest joy, has died with him. The light moments in my life were those in which I was creatively active. Whenever I was working, I saw only Pushkin before me. All idle chatter meant nothing to me. I looked down upon that contemptible mob which is known by the name public. Of sole value to me was his eternal and immutable word. I never undertook anything, never wrote anything without his advice. Everything that is good in my work I owe to him. My present work is also his creation.[54] He made me swear I would write it, and not a line of it was written without him appearing to me while I was writing. I consoled myself with the thought of how satisfied he should be, I tried to guess what would please him, and that was my highest and foremost reward. Now that reward is no longer on the horizon! What is my work now? What is my life now?" (To Pogodin, 30th March 1837).[55]

The great man is no more. My whole life is poisoned. Write to me in God's name. Remind me as much as possible that everything is not yet dead for me in Russia, that begins to appear to me like a grave which is mercilessly engulfing everything that is dear to my heart. (To Prokopovich, the same day).[56]

---

[52] *Zapiski o zhizni N. V. Gogolya,* I (1856), 194.
[53] *P.,* I, 432.
[54] "Dead Souls".
[55] *P.,* I, 434.
[56] *P.,* I, 436.

Rhetoric and exaggeration can be observed even in the passages just quoted – Bryusov has pointed out that the rest of the letters from which they are taken are relatively sober and that Gogol did in the end continue to work. In my view, this is merely further proof of the agreement with the situation opposite his father. Gogol undoubtedly also had feelings of guilt with regard to Pushkin to whom he had not said good-bye before his departure from Russia. It seems to me not impossible that Pushkin had offended Gogol without meaning to, and that this sense of injury had led to feelings with which Gogol later reproached himself and which he disguised.[57]

His father had called him, Pushkin had made his mission clear to him and had given him for a period, irresolute as he was, the belief that he could trust himself as long as the positive person with infallible judgment did so. Psychologically speaking, I think I can say that a father image was revived and died in Pushkin. After his death, Gogol no longer sought any "eternal and immutable word" from people, he sought it from God alone. His tragedy lies in that he sought spasmodically and listened anxiously to the voice in him which sometimes seemed to speak with a dependable certainty, but which he later suddenly recognised as his own voice, or even worse – as that of the devil.[58]

The years in St. Petersburg, the period of Gogol's greatest creative intensity, were far from tranquil. His illness was for the time being still only a means in order to be interesting to himself. To Gogol's friends it appeared ridiculous. We see however for the first time complaints about digestive upsets, which showed themselves often crudely and jeeringly in his letters, taking on the character of genuine anxiety. In 1832, he wrote a letter to Pogodin from Vasilevka from which it appeared that his first act after arriving at his parent's home had been visiting all the doctors in the district.

Sometimes it seems to me as if I feel a slight pain in my liver and in my back; sometimes I have a pain in my head, sometimes in the chest.[59]

---

[57] Although that cannot be proved, it seems to me very probable that Gogol was hurt when Pushkin did not completely approve of Gogol's essay on Russian journalism in the first number of *Sovremennik*. See Yu. Oksman, "Pismo k izdatelyu" in *Ateney*, 1924, I, p. 6 ff. Compare however A. Stepanov, "Gogol-publitsist" in *Gogol, Stati i Materialy* (Leningrad, 1954), p. 39 ff. In my opinion, Stepanov has not proved that Pushkin "was unconditionally in agreement with Gogol", *op. cit.*, p. 67.

[58] Compare the letter to Father Matvey on 12th January 1848. *P.*, IV, 151 ff., in particular p. 152.

[59] *P.*, I, 220.

Yet Dyadkovsky, the Moscow doctor whom he had consulted on his way through, still had authority enough to put his mind at rest.

Gogol made a last attempt to find social recognition by mounting a public platform – he sought and obtained a professorship in history. It was a wretched failure. Two things should, however, be noted. Gogol had wanted a chair in Kiev where he would have been back in his native country and could have become absorbed in its history. Dream and mission would then have been combined. In reality, he obtained a place as assistant-professor in hated St. Petersburg. The genius he had invoked so ecstatically in his fragment "1834" had not taken pity on him.

In the second place, Vengerov has shown in detail that Gogol, poorly prepared as he was, did not by any means have occasion to cut a bad figure amongst his often less than mediocre colleagues. The requirements which he placed on himself were nevertheless so high that he must definitely have felt his powerlessness compared with them.[60] In other words, Gogol caused his failure himself, he himself unconsciously prevented the success of his mission.

After his departure from the university, there followed feverish working on "The Government Inspector", the performance of which was the cause of his second flight from Russia. If we consider this matter objectively, Gogol appears to have had as much success with his piece as any reasonable person could have hoped. That was, however, not enough. He took greater exception to the unfavourable judgment of his enemies than he was pleased at the applause of the public that filled the halls and the admiration of those whose opinion he should have prized. What was lacking was, in my opinion, the unanimous recognition of his greatness, necessary to silence his own uncertainty. On 6th June 1836, he left for foreign parts.

And the justification? It is fairly similar to that of his first flight.

A prophet finds no honour in his own country. (. . .) But I am not going to foreign parts because I should not be able to endure these unpleasant experiences. I want to seek recovery of my health, diversion and recreation and then, once I have chosen more or less permanent quarters, to consider thoroughly my future work. (To Pogodin, 10th May 1836).[61]

Everything that has happened to me has been beneficial to me. All the injuries, all the unpleasant experiences have been sent to me by high providence in order to mould me. Now too I feel that a supernatural will is

[60]   S. A. Vengerov, *Pisatel-grazhdanin* (St. Petersburg, 1913), pp. 35–50.
[61]   *P.*, I, 370, 371.

guiding my path. This journey is obviously essential for me. (To the same, 15th May 1836).[62]

Having come to this point, it is necessary that we should look back for a moment and form a clear idea of what we have found. It will not be possible to treat the last part of Gogol's life in detail. It is also superfluous to do so. If what we have established so far is for the most part true, then the rest of this life cannot be anything but a further development of a disposition we have already described. Putting together our various conclusions, we obtain the following picture.

A sickly, probably spoilt child, who very soon began to suffer from anxiety, which showed itself through aggressiveness, arrived at the beginning of puberty in strange surroundings which were experienced as being hostile. We can at the moment assume with a high degree of probability the existence of an Oedipal mother fixation, accompanied by the customary feelings of guilt. There was possibly also a more than normally strong bond with his father, which can be explained as identification with the father aggressor. The child adapted itself to its new surroundings, found friends, but kept its distance – a calm social contact appeared difficult. His father died – the reaction was the appearance of excessive sorrow, coupled with feelings of guilt and (probably feigned, but considered as desirable) aggression against himself. The feeling of having a mission arose – the mission originated with the father.

The narcissism which was already present became intensified, the sense of having been selected began to become something very special. (Achievements were moderate.) With his first failures in St. Petersburg melancholy appeared which can be seen as a phenomenon of anxiety. A number of reasons was given for the flight, the actual correctness of which cannot be verified. The strangest was a menacing declaration of love to a woman who was "too exalted", i.e. represented his mother. In the youth's fantasy his mother still seemed to appear as an idyllic figure from a youthful paradise. Another means of justification was illness – in the form of tightness of the chest already known from his early youth, and in the new form of a skin affection (not repeated later). Finally, and embracing both, God's hand was guiding him. Faith in understanding this guidance was still unstable.

Pushkin helped Gogol in the choice between the two possibilities he

[62]   P., I, 378.

saw for fulfilling his mission: he was not to speak to Russia as a
statesman, but as a writer.

The first great word was spoken: "The Government Inspector". It
was not experienced as a shock throughout the whole of Russia. Consequently "everyone is against him", and Gogol left the country.

Justifications: there was no place for a writer with his aggressive
talent, illness, God's guidance.

We may, after this short summary, draw a conclusion to which I
alluded at the beginning of this chapter: we are concerned with an
abnormally strong self-dramatisation. Connected with this fact, we
find another: it is extremely likely that pity with himself was very
important in this drama. I am not alluding here to a common human
weakness, but to that stupendous force which, according to the psy-
chiatrist Arndt,[63] is the agent through which a traumatic situation can
change into a neurosis and the reason why people adhere so obstinately
to a neurosis. No-one in the world is of course prepared to offer us so
constantly and to such a great extent the cherishing given to us by
this pity.

Accepting all this, the further development of Gogol's anxiety is no
longer difficult to understand. He was now abroad with his commission, Pushkin's commission, namely "Dead Souls". Pushkin died, there
was wavering again, for a moment, but he entrusted himself to God's
guidance. These words have already been used a few times with a
certain amount of irony, and an explanation is now due. The position
is, in my opinion, that there was with Gogol no question of a permanent religious trust which supported him. In fact, God began more and
more to assume the role of the father image, Gogol also felt an in-
explicable guilt with regard to Him. This feeling was not a deep
realisation of sin. We certainly find bouts of feelings of rejection, but
never of repentance. On the other hand, we constantly see attempts
to rise above his own unworthiness by means which cannot be construed
as anything but magic. It is, therefore, completely incorrect to call
Gogol's religious feelings mystical. Part of his tragedy in fact lies in
that his religious life was a "private religion" in Freud's sense, a
defence against anxiety, which always conjures up new anxiety. For
the inexorable God whom Gogol had created for himself can never be
satisfied, precisely because he is a creation of anxiety; genuine contact
can naturally not occur.

[63]   J. L. Arndt, "Autopsychodrama. Een bijdrage tot het neurosebegrip" in
Geneeskundige Bladen, 46th series (1954), p. 201 ff.

Let us now consider some more facts. The illness grew and assumed varying forms. This expression is not figurative. Gogol himself would have agreed with it. He has also suggested to us a name: hypochondria. This term which was in the course of falling into discredit in medical circles is now being used again and, without making any diagnosis, we may note that it fits in well, as a summary of a group of symptoms, with the phenomena. I quote one sentence from the paragraph which Rümke devotes to hypochondria:

... in decided hypochondria the world has shrunk to one's own corporality, in most cases only a part of it; the image – an often very primitive image – plays a part here." [64]

We could fill a small volume with quotations from Gogol's letters about his health. One complaint which he contracted in St. Petersburg was haemorrhoids. It is obvious that Gogol's attention should consequently have been directed particularly towards the digestive process. Initially, this was still done jokingly, namely in the Petersburg years themselves, but when abroad it was in bitter and sometimes tragicomic earnest. There is also the point that Gogol was a large eater and even a gourmet. The way in which he now met his need of punishment resulting from his feeling of guilt, consisted in that his stomach rendered eating impossible.[65] Things did not however stop at intestinal symptoms. Direct attacks of anxiety also occurred which affected his chest and head. Yes, the symptoms went even further. His circulation became sluggish, he could scarcely keep his extremities warm any more. This was of course all connected with his great commission, in fact with his work on "Dead Souls".

Since the references are so very numerous and sometimes so long, it is difficult to make a choice and to quote extensively. The composition of the above-mentioned volume would indeed form the most convincing proof of my assertions. I must, however, restrict myself to quoting or paraphrasing a few very striking utterances only.

12th November 1836 (to Zhukovsky, from Paris). Work on "Dead Souls" was not proceeding smoothly.

The doctor has found that I have symptoms of hypochondria, resulting from haemorrhoids.[66]

---

[64] H. C. Rümke, *op. cit.*, p. 247.
[65] An apparently quite common way in which to punish oneself. Cf. Wilh. Stekel, *op. cit.*, chapter IX, "Religion und Magenleiden", p. 187 ff.
[66] *P.*, I, 414.

19th September 1837 (to Prokopovich, from Geneva). Gogol had fled
from Rome to escape cholera, but was pursued by his hypochondria.
His stomach was not working, although he was eating moderately.
Haemorrhoids appeared again, together with heavy pressure in his
head. A cure in Baden-Baden did nothing to help.[67]

25th June 1838 (to Vyazemsky, from Rome).

My health is poor. Every activity, even the very lightest, causes heaviness
in my head. Italy, the beautiful, my beloved Italy has lengthened my life,
but it is powerless to rid me of the illness which has penetrated like a despot
into my system and has come to be second nature. What shall I do if I do
not complete my work? Oh, away with that terrible thought. It contains a
veritable hell full of tortures which God may not inflict upon any mortal.[68]

31st December 1838 (to Danilevsky, from Rome). His health was becoming worse and worse. It seemed as if a devil were in his stomach,
– the same image, still jokingly, occurred in a subsequent letter to
Danilevsky from Rome (5th February 1839).[69]

Thus it went on steadily. Gogol received a serious shock when he
made the acquaintance of death at close quarters, through that of the
young Count Velgorsky. That impression is to be blamed, at least
for a while, for strange symptoms in Gogol himself. After a time, he
was afraid he had tuberculosis, this being the illness from which
Velgorsky had died. Annenkov, who knew him in Rome in 1841,
also mentions that, just as Velgorsky, he no longer dared go properly
to bed, but spent a large part of the night sleeping in his chair.[70]

A great crisis followed a stay in Russia in 1840. On the way back
from Italy Gogol had worked hard in Vienna during a short period of
inspiration. In general, travelling was the best medicine he knew. It
also helped to arouse his dormant zest for work. It was summer, and
Gogol did not lose the opportunity of taking a further mineral-water
cure while working.

There now follows a quotation from a letter dated 17th October
1840 (to Pogodin, from Rome).

... suddenly my nervous excitement passed into a nervous irritation. All
at once, I had a violent tightness on my chest. I was frightened. I did not

[67]   P., I, 454.
[68]   P., I, 514.
[69]   P., I, 563.
[70]   Quoted according to Veresayev, op. cit., p. 264, 265. Veresayev also has
the story of how Gogol was afraid to visit in Rome a fellow-countryman who
had suddenly become ill and even got a nervous attack or simulated it on the
day before the burial.

understand my condition myself. I stopped working, thought that it was a
result of a lack of movement coupled with the taking of mineral water and
my sedentary life. I began to walk and take exercise in order to tire myself
and it became even worse. The disorder and irritation of my nervous system
increased greatly, a heaviness in my chest and a pressure, such as I had
never before felt, became greater and greater. Fortunately, the doctors found
that I did not yet have consumption, that it was a stomach upset, as a result
of which digestion had stopped, and an unusual nervous irritation. That
was not much use to me, for the treatment was quite dangerous: what helped
the stomach had a fatal effect on my nerves as did my nerves in turn
on my stomach. There was also a morbid depression which cannot be
described. I got into such a state that I really no longer knew where to
hide myself, what to cling to. I could not remain in a quiet state for two
minutes on end, neither in bed, nor in a chair, nor on my feet. Oh, it was
terrible, it was that same depression and that appalling uneasiness I had
seen in poor Velgorsky during the last moments of his life. Imagine, I
became worse and worse every day. Finally, the doctor could give me no
further hope either.[71]

After all this, the remedy was surprising. Gogol went and sat in a
stage-coach and was driven as quickly as possible to Italy!

This attack however made a deep impression on his travelling-
companion Botkin. There seems to be mention of visions, about which
Gogol spoke only to Botkin. This event has been seen as the point at
which a religious change is said to have taken place in Gogol. He himself never gave support to such a view and always denied any abrupt
change in his religious life. Rightly so, in my opinion. We are concerned with a sudden break-through of anxiety which was to be
repeated on various occasions.

It is quite understandable that people have also sought a purely
physical explanation of all this suffering and it is just as comprehen-
sible that it is difficult to find one which fits in with all these symptoms. As a non-medical man, I can merely say that none of the diag-
noses made by doctors appears obvious to me. It is certain that in the
literature about Gogol they are mentioned merely after the manner of
curiosities which are then pushed aside. I think that one would for
the time being be well-advised to assume not more than a possibly
hereditary predisposition. The body was for Gogol the means by which
he expressed his inner conflicts.

The crisis we have just mentioned forms an example of it. 1839 was
a difficult year for Gogol. He had returned to Russia in quite a differ-

71   *P.*, II, 81.

ent state from what he had imagined, namely empty-handed. Aksakov understood very well how painful it must have been for him when every former acquaintance asked after the first meeting: "And, Nikolay Vasilyevich, what have you brought for us?" [72] He had not wanted to return to Russia, but had to in order to take steps concerning the education of his sisters. When he departed again, he felt happy; travelling always had a salutary effect on the eternal fugitive in those years.

A cure with Marienbader water in Vienna helped for the first time, and there came at the same time a powerful creative urge. Gogol responded to this, without sparing himself. His nervous tension rose until there was a relapse. There is consequently a direct connection between his work and the nervous crisis, and it would seem that the crisis was not the primary factor, but the tension about his work and mission.

Thus we see it again at the beginning of 1842. The first part of "Dead Souls" was finally finished. Gogol was in Moscow to supervise its publication. There were however painful complications regarding censorship. The manuscript could not be found for weeks on end. Gogol also felt lonely amongst people, although he was overwhelmed with kind acts. He complained about exhaustion and nervousness. He had the feeling that he had lost contact with the world. There was a new attack of anxiety, described in detail in a letter to M. P. Balabina, dated 17th February 1842. [73]

I have been ill, very ill, and am still ill inside. My illness reveals itself through attacks, stranger than I have ever had before. I found to be most terrible however that condition which reminded me of my dreadful illness in Vienna, particularly when I felt that tension coming over my heart, as a result of which every image which came fleetingly into my thoughts assumed huge dimensions and every trivial and pleasant sensation passed into such frightful mirth that no human nature could endure it, while every despondent feeling changed into pain, heavy, tormenting pain. There then followed fainting-fits and finally a condition of complete somnambulism. And on top of it all, while my illness was unbearable, I had to suffer further unpleasant experiences which would have unbalanced even a healthy person. I had to summon all my strength of mind to endure it! And I did endure it. I keep on, as much as I can, I even go out. I do not complain or let anyone notice that I am ill, although that very often requires my utmost powers.

[72] Quoted according to Veresayev, *op. cit.*, p. 210.
[73] *P.*, II, 147, 148. Shenrok's dating appears vaguer. He gives "February". In the *Soch. A.N.*, XII, 36 we find "(17th February 1842)". The reason for this guess is not given.

Impressive as the description is, the last sentence nevertheless causes us once again to doubt its complete genuineness. Our doubts are increased when, a little later, Gogol appears to write to Dondukov-Korsakov about his illness which had kept him in his room for two to three weeks "in an almost immobile state".[74]

All this misery came to an end when, on 5th June, Gogol left again for foreign parts, the first part of "Dead Souls" having appeared. There followed a short period of calm and self-confidence. Read the letter to Zhukovsky of 26th June 1842, in which he described how glorious and grateful he felt.

I shall only say this, that my soul is becoming lighter and more festive every day, every hour, that they have not been without purpose and significance, these journeys, this withdrawal and retirement from the world, that the development of my soul has taken place invisibly during them, that I have become an infinitely better person. [Work on the education of his soul was not yet at an end.] My soul must be purer than mountain-snow and lighter than the heavens, and only then will I find the strength to perform deeds and begin a noble career, then only will the riddle of my existence be solved.[75]

He had of course to begin with the denial of his last great deed, the first part of "Dead Souls" was nothing special.

I have largely rewritten the book since I read the first chapters to you, but I still see its insignificance, compared with the other parts which are to follow. In relation thereto, it seems to me continually just like a porch which a provincial architect hastily ran up for a palace of colossal dimensions which is still to be built.

This giant work was the commission under which Gogol was to collapse. For the time being, the mission was itself adequate to give him a notion of worthiness. The letter to Zhukovsky we have just quoted is merely a poor example of the rhetoric tone which Gogol began to use more and more and of the furtive pride which sounds through it.

Gogol began to educate himself to be a calm, wise hermit who smiles about earthly matters. He became the spiritual leader of a number of ladies from the highest circles who poured out their hearts to him. For a long time he had felt himself the superior of his mother and be-

---

[74] Shenrok gives as the date "about 4th March". *P.*, I, 153. *Soch. A.N.* has "between 24th February and 4th March", without giving the reason. *Soch. A.N.*, XII, 41.
[75] *P.*, II, 184. Compare with this some remarks from a much earlier period. For example, "Really, everyone finds me a riddle, no-one has completely fathomed me". To his mother, 1st March 1828 (*P.*, I, 98).

gan to send her more and more instructions, while the tone of his letters to his sisters became unbearable. Again and again the impression is created that Gogol wanted to play the part of a saint. We sometimes even think – not of an imitation, but of a copying of Christ.[76] Gogol repressed his aggressiveness more and more and irritated those friends who did not wish to submit to his authority. The faithful Sergey Timofeyevich Aksakov was worried and sometimes angry. Worse still was the fact that he could also no longer express his aggressiveness in his work: the second part of "Dead Souls" was to form the entrance to a temple. The building was however never completed. In 1845 he burnt the manuscript. Tikhonravov considers that it was for the second time.[77] This year was dreadful. Gogol had lost his self-confidence and his illness occupied him completely. Frankfurt, Homburg, Berlin, Dresden, Karlsbad, Gräfenberg – everywhere he consulted doctors, never did he follow their advice and he broke off every course of treatment.

I have to pass over many notable things, but one of them must be mentioned. On this occasion there again occurred as a great rarity, a mention of his father. Nothing further need be said about its significance after my quotation.

But I do still know one thing, namely that at a certain stage I did myself a serious injury in that I wanted to compel myself by force to write, while my soul was not prepared and I should have subjected myself to God's will. Be that as it may, my illness takes its natural course. It is a decline of strength. I could not in any case have been able to live long. My father also had a weak constitution and died young, he was extinguished because his strength was used up and not as the result of one or other illness. (5th June 1845, to Yazykov).[78]

Reading all these melancholy letters with their complaints, helpless pride and modest requests for intercession once again creates the impression of unreality, although we also feel that Gogol's suffering must have been terrible.

---

[76] There occurs, as early as 1841, the following curious passage in a letter to Yazykov: "And if, upon our departure, upon our handshake, a spark of fortitude does not pass over into your soul, then that means you do not love me. And if sadness overcomes you and you think of me and are not in a state to master it, then that means you do not love me; and if a temporary illness makes you melancholy and depresses your spirit, that means that you do not love me." 27th September 1841 (*P.*, II, 118).

[77] See *Soch.*, III, 536 ff. Tikhonravov bases himself largely on statements by P. Annenkov who considered that the first burning took place in 1843.

[78] *P.*, III, 64.

That letter of one line to the priest Bazarov appears to be an exception. "Come and bring me the sacraments, I am dying." [79] But Bazarov has described how he came and found a sick man who was walking up and down his room and with whom nothing serious was wrong.[80]

The illness became a magnificent gift of God. To Mrs. Smirnov he wrote on 11th May:

I see from your letter that you are at present suffering from a fairly serious nervous crisis. Let us begin by thanking God for it. (. . .) Blessed are the chosen whom God visits before others! [81]

The idea for "Selected Passages" was born during this year. The great word to Russia was to be spoken after all. While writing, he began to feel better. He thought it must have been God's grace which was enlightening him. We know how the book was received. This time they were really "all against him". It was not the razor-edged criticism of Belinsky which destroyed Gogol. It was the surprise and aversion of his best friends who had discerned the poorly masked pride and the false tone of the book.

The long desired journey to Jerusalem in 1848 brought no release, although Gogol's requests for prayers at fixed times and even at precisely indicated places in Russia were certainly fulfilled. On the contrary, the serious crises were absent, but Gogol began to complain more and more about his hardness and apathy to deep religious impressions.

In 1847 there appeared for the first time in his correspondence the name of Father Matvey Konstantinovsky, to whom such a disastrous influence on Gogol has been ascribed. Nevertheless, Matvey, a last menacing father image in Gogol's life, could not do anything but strengthen tendencies which had already clearly shown themselves. Gogol sought personal contact with him when he was back in Russia (April 1848), and it is certain that this passionate popular preacher with his hard, coarse language and his blindness to all culture will have contributed little to Gogol's inner peace. Sometimes we imagine we hear his voice when Gogol speaks about himself in terms such as:

. . . if I have not yet become completely immersed in the pool of my iniquities, if I am not yet completely, from head to foot, a rotting corpse, then this is thanks to the prayers of those who pray for me.[82]

[79]   *P.*, III, 58.
[80]   See Veresayev, *op. cit.*, 334, 335.
[81]   *P.*, III, 56.
[82]   *P.*, IV, 271 (to Count A. P. Tolstoy, undated, probably July 1849).

Gogol began to trust more and more in the prayers and advice of the pious. It was a sort of defence magic. Yet, with the growth of the realisation of sin, the evil element also began to assume more and more tangible forms. The devil, with whom Gogol had played in his stories, began to appear more often in his letters.

The second part of "Dead Souls" was again nearing completion. Gogol was however always oppressed by the thought that he would have to give account above for every word he wrote on earth.[83]

"My work is proceeding very unevenly", is a sentence from his last letter to Aksakov, which Shenrok places at the beginning of 1852.[84]

Mrs. Khomyakov, a dear friend, died on 26th January. Whether it was the cause, no-one knows, but it certainly resulted in Gogol once again being seized by anxiety. The thought of his own death never left him. The description of the last days of Gogol's life has been given on innumerable occasions, so that I consider it unnecessary to repeat it here.

I should merely like to draw attention to a few points. However acutely and soundly Gippius has demonstrated the contrary,[85] it seems to me inconceivable that Gogol should not have known what manuscript he was burning on the night of 12th February. When the papers showed no inclination to burn, he himself undid the ribbon holding them and spread them out better. Would Gogol, who cherished his manuscripts as his most valued treasures, not have recognised this dearest of all, namely that of "Dead Souls"? It occurs to me that, even if he had not seen what he was doing, he must have had the feeling that something fatal was being repeated.

He crossed himself before turning away from the extinguished fire. The following morning he informed Count Tolstoy in tears that the devil had caused him to commit the fatal mistake.

---

[83] "Naturally I should have money at my disposal if I decided to publish my work unfinished and incomplete. I shall, however, never decide to do this. Thank God I have a conscience which will not permit me to do this, even if I were to be in the direst need. Every person must fulfil his vocation on earth conscientiously and honestly. Since, with the passage of the years, I feel more and more that I shall have to justify *there* every word that is written *here,* I have to consider my works with much more critical sense and wariness than a writer who is young and has not yet been tested by life." – This same thought naturally also occurred earlier. Cf. for example the essay from "Selected Passages" quoted in note 42. Here, however, there is more thought of posterity than of God's own judgment (*Soch.*, IV, 18 ff).

[84] *P.*, IV, 421.

[85] V. Gippius, *op. cit.*, 217 ff.

Gogol used his magic for the last time against the evil powers. He fasted, punished himself in the old way, which had become more and more familiar to him during these ascetic years. No doctor, no official priest could induce him to take food once he considered his death as inevitable.

An ancient image also looms up before us for the last time. Gogol imagined that he recognised his complaint: "The illness of my father" was what he called it.[86]

He died on 21st February 1852.

[86] P. Tarasenkov in *Mat.*, IV, 852. Psycho-analytical studies of Gogol's mental illness have also been written by O. Kaus, *Der Fall Gogol (Schriften des Vereins für psychoanalyt. Forschung)* (Munich, 1912) and I. Yermakov, *Ocherki po analizu tvorchestva N. V. Gogolya* (Moscow-St. Petersburg, 1924). Both works are worthless because of lack of knowledge of Gogol's life.

CHAPTER II

EVENINGS IN A VILLAGE NEAR DIKANKA

PART 1

The whole of the first part should really have been omitted entirely: it consists of a pupil's first experiments which are not worth the close attention of the reader; yet when I wrote them, I felt the first sweet moments of a youthful inspiration and I considered it a pity to omit them, just as it is a pity to banish from memory the first youthful games which are never to return. The sympathetic reader can skip the whole of the first part and begin reading at the second.[1]

These are the final words of Gogol's introduction to the edition of his collected works which appeared in 1842. They are of course meant to be taken as a joke: Gogol was certain that no-one would follow his advice; when he looked at that first part with youthful experiments, he remembered not only his earliest inspiration, but also his first successes. The joke does not however exclude seriousness; these lines certainly contain thoroughly sincere and valuable information.

Gogol still felt that first fame somewhat as destiny. He knew that he had, through his work, been stamped as a light-hearted joker in many people's eyes, and that this view, unreasonable with regard to the youthful work itself, stood in the way of an understanding of his maturer creations. It was against this that his plea was directed. This is only of historical interest for the present-day reader. He is interested in where Gogol himself drew the line between the experiments of the pupil and the work of the man. This consequently lies at the end of a volume which contains the "Evenings in a Village near Dikanka".[2]

[1] *Soch.*, I, p. XXV, XXVI.
[2] There were originally two collections. The first appeared in 1831, the second in 1832. The Russian title is *Vechera na khutore bliz Dikanki*. The word *khutor* is, following the most common meaning, often translated by "farm" or the like. This is not in accordance with Gogol's intention as appears from the explanatory

Gogol calls the stories collected here "trials", "experiments" and what is more obvious than to start viewing them as such? All sorts of things have been attempted here, both consciously and unconsciously, and the "Evenings" thus confront us with a number of widely varying problems. That regarding the material is extremely interesting. Gogol borrowed directly and indirectly from popular literature, but just as much from German romanticism.

At least as interesting is the language which this Ukrainian, who wrote in Russian, used for his popular tales, his deliberate or otherwise use of Ukrainianisms, his conscious creation of new words, his unusual use of certain syntactic means.[3]

This leads us directly to the question of how a style is in this way formed, in which archaisms, neologisms and vulgarisms occur side by side, how the writer tries to combine elements which had been kept separate in literature prior to his time, to an initially somewhat motley whole, the expression of heterogeneous states of mind.

One may also see the writer as the representative of a certain social class and try to approach certain peculiarities of this work by stating the problem sociologically. Moreover, there are the classical questions about the place which this work occupies in the writer's output and about its position in the literature of his time.

Answers have been given to all these questions, being of a more or less detailed nature. The investigation has however in a few respects only led to a definite result.[4] The following observations will, in part, form a summary of the results of earlier investigations. An attempt will, in particular, be made to see these stories as experiments in the technique of composition. This has so far not been done systematically. I have not attempted to achieve completeness. It was possible for Paul Zincke to devote a fairly comprehensive work to one short story by Paul Heyse.[5] It would certainly be very feasible to write a book in several volumes about these slender collections of stories. I have, for the most part, restricted myself to their composition and have also preferred to give a detailed discussion of a few short stories rather than a super-

---

list of words he had printed at the end of the volume. He gives *khutor* as being *nebolshaya derevushka*, "small village" (*Soch.*, I, 506).

[3] See I. Mandelshtam, *O kharaktere Gogolevskogo stilya* (St. Petersburg, 1902), p. 73, 74.

[4] Gogol is one of the most disputed Russian authors. Almost every new work concerned with literature or literary movements led to a new theory concerning his work.

[5] Paul Zincke, *Paul Heyses Novellentechnik* (Karlsruhe, no date).

ficial characterisation of all of them. The examples have, however, been chosen in such a way that, in my opinion, a fairly complete picture of Gogol's method of composition is formed.

Kulish in his "Notes on the life of Gogol" made an important statement concerning the origin of the "Evenings" as a collection.[6] He relates that Gogol had certain stories ready in 1831 and turned for advice about possible publication to the well-known man of letters Pletnyov. Kulish then goes on:

Pletnyov wanted to protect the young man against the influences of literary parties and, at the same time, to save the stories from the preconceived opinions of people who knew Gogol (personally or from his first experiments) and had not gained a high opinion of him. He therefore advised Gogol to assume a very strict incognito for the time being and thought up a title for his stories which would arouse the public's curiosity. Thus the "Stories" appeared as having been edited by the bee-keeper Rudy Panko, who was supposed to live near Dikanka, which belonged to the Prince Kochubey.

It follows from these words that the stories were not conceived within a framework. The title thought up by Pletnyov however apparently helped Gogol to the idea of placing them within a framework. This also seems to have been much more than a light-hearted fantasy for perpetuating the illusion aroused by the title: the fiction which Pletnyov presented to Gogol offered him the opportunity of imagining the stories from the first of the two collections as being told by various narrators. It is conceivable that Pletnyov also suggested this to him. This suggestion nevertheless coincided very well with the fact that the four stories from the first collection belong together in pairs as far as the technique of composition is concerned.

Pletnyov's invention was certainly doubly pleasant to Gogol, since he could now erect a double entrenchment between his work and the world. The romantic fashion of a pseudonym must have been more welcome to him than to most.

"What oddity is this: *Evenings in a village near Dikanka?* What sort of *Evenings* have we here? And thrust into the world by a bee-keeper!"

That's what people will say, Panko imagines. They will ask whether perhaps enough geese have not been robbed of their feathers, not enough rags turned into paper, not enough fingers covered with ink-

---

[6] (P. A. Kulish), *Zapiski o zhizni Nikolaya Vasilyevicha Gogolya* (St. Petersburg, 1856), I, p. 90, 91.

stains that such a villager should now poke his nose out of his hole.

Rudy Panko had predicted all that more than a month ago, but he had a modest defence ready. He will just tell the city-folk precisely what he means by his "evenings". When autumn comes and the peasant climbs onto the stove in order to rest, then as it becomes dark you see a little light shining here and there in the village street, you hear singing and the twang of the balalaika, talking, laughing, noise and you know: there is an "evening party". Such a gathering certainly has something of a city-ball, only people do not come in order to move their legs and to yawn behind their hands. On the contrary. Girls gather in a peasant cottage in order to spin and that goes well for a time. Then the boys come, there are games, dancing and all sorts of pranks are played. Such an evening is however best when someone begins to tell stories. And nowhere is that done so magnificently as at the bee-keeper's, red-headed Panko. The narrators are not ordinary peasants. There are amongst them also those who would feel at home in the finest company. There is the sacristan of Dikanka, Foma Grigoryevich. He's a fine one! Don't ask what the material of his blouse cost. His boots never smell of bacon, he polishes them with the best fat which many would willingly put into their porridge. He never wipes his nose with anything but a nice handkerchief which he carries folded into twelve parts. Another of the guests, that was such a fine gentleman, you would take him as an assessor. "Sometimes he would hold up his finger, and looking at the tip of it, begin telling a story – as choicely and cleverly as though it were printed in a book! Sometimes you listen and listen and begin to be puzzled. You can't make head or tail of it, not if you were to hang for it. Where did he pick up such words?" Foma Grigoryevich sometimes teased him about his learning and the little gentleman in his pea-green coat mumbled something about pearls before swine. Yet all ended well and there was no quarrel.

And then there is another story-teller who knows such terrible stories, the bee-keeper does not want to frighten people by them. He will perhaps tell one of them in another part. Maybe he will then tell one himself as well.

He does not however. Rudy Panko remains in his role. His house is merely the meeting-point for the story-tellers and he is a listener. That is his interest in the composition; the reader sees the stories not merely as produced by, but also for a given setting.[7]

[7]   V. Vinogradov, *Etyudy o stile Gogolya* (Leningrad, 1926). Vinogradov has suggested a connection between Rudy Panko and the narrator in Walter Scott's

Have the "Evenings" now become a "story within a framework"?
Certainly not. There is no question of a framework even in the literal
sense. The bee-keeper certainly introduces the book, but does not
finish it.[8] Also, no single evening is described at which a story arises
from a general conversation. One essential element of the framework
story is however present: each story has its own narrator, provisionally
characterised by Rudy Panko in his external appearance and whose
inner nature is to be recognised through style and composition
from the stories themselves. If the reader is all the time conscious of
the narrator's listeners, then this creates the condition for a double
understanding, for "naïvety" (as a "listener"), for "comprehension" (as
an "outsider"). The combination of these possibilities leads to that
strange humoristic mood which Gogol asks of his readers.

Thus, Gogol goes a significant step further than Pushkin did in
his "Belkin Stories". Pushkin also characterises the small landowner
Belkin in detail. He also mentions from whom Belkin had heard the
stories, but the narrators mentioned casually in a note have little to do
with the form of Belkin's stories.

The sketchy indication of a framework consequently served Gogol
in creating a general atmosphere in which we can imagine the stories
and the mention must help the reader to be prepared for a special
atmosphere in each of them. Too little notice has so far been taken in
serious literature about Gogol's indications. An attempt will be made
in the following observations to discover something new with the help
of these indications.

As mentioned above, the four stories in the first part of the "Evenings" are to be ascribed to two narrators and they also belong together
in pairs in their method of composition.[9] It will therefore be sufficient
to discuss one story from each pair. As the first I have chosen the
story which opens the book: "The Fair at Sorochintsy".

1. *The Fair at Sorochintsy*

I shall first give the content of the story, taking into account the limits
of the various short chapters into which it is divided.

"Old Mortality". The relationship between the work of Scott and that of Gogol
is however still very obscure.

[8] This was somewhat different in the first edition of the first part. The errata
are introduced by Rudy Panko with a talk in which he apologises for all the
misprints, blaming them on his old eyes.

[9] See below, page 74.

I. Cherevik is going to the fair at Sorochintsy, accompanied by his ugly wife and the beautiful daughter from his first marriage. Having almost arrived there, they meet a group of youths, one of which, dressed in a white *svitka*,[10] expresses his admiration for the girl and his dislike of her stepmother. The latter swears back at him, and the youth replies not only with words, but also with street-refuse.

II. The next day, at the fair, the young people renew their acquaintance.

III. Cherevik is giving all his attention to a story he hears about the devil who has been seen at the fair and who is walking about there looking for a red *svitka*. Just as he turns around, he sees his daughter in the youth's arms. He makes his acquaintance, the youth turns out to be the son of one of his friends. The father gives his permission for the marriage.

IV. His wife is furious on hearing that her stepchild's suitor is the same person who has insulted her. She forbids the marriage.

V. Grytsko, the youth in question, pours out his troubles to a gypsy who promises to help him if Grytsko will sell his oxen cheaply.

VI. Cherevik's wife is having a love affair with a priest's son in the house of her husband's *kum* [11] where the family is staying. Their wooing is interrupted by the return of her husband in company with the *kum* and a few others. The priest's son hides himself on a few loose boards under the ceiling.

VII. The guests drink and the *kum* tells the story of the red *svitka:* A devil who had been chased out of hell, made merry at Sorochintsy, but finally, because of lack of money, had to pawn his red *svitka* with a Jew, on the condition that the latter would not sell the *svitka*. This of course nevertheless happened, and the devil's blouse, which appeared to bring misfortune, had already passed from hand to hand and had even been cut to bits. The devil murdered the Jew and now came once a year to look for his property, on this occasion precisely during the fair. He now had all the pieces, except one sleeve. When the *kum* has reached this stage in his story, the panes rattle and a terrible pig's face looks in.

VIII. Horror and flight in all directions. Cherevik runs outside with a pot on his head. He hears steps behind him and doubles his speed. Finally, he collapses, something pounces upon him and he loses consciousness.

---

[10]   A *svitka* is a sort of blouse.
[11]   *Kum* is the name which parents use for the godfather of one of their children.

IX. Gypsies bring him to, his wife is sitting on him.

X. The following morning he is sent out by his wife to sell his horse. When he wants to dry his face on the rag she throws to him, it turns out to be a sleeve from a red *svitka*. On the way to the market, he is stopped by a gypsy who asks him what he is leading along. He turns around and sees on the reins not the old mare, but the red sleeve of a *svitka*. He runs away.

XI. He is caught – as a horse-stealer, and a little later the *kum* – as an accomplice.

XII. The two whining prisoners are set free at the request of the lover who suddenly turns up.

XIII. The girl and the youth start the wedding-feast with the father. Before the mother can intervene the wedding is over.

My method of summarising is not to be blamed for the fact that the reader has probably gained the impression of being confronted with the outline for an operetta libretto. The story is constructed very much on the lines of a scenario, and the bonds which also link it genetically with the stage are quite strong.

The whole scene with the old woman and the priest's son is based on a play by Gogol's father who no doubt incorporated popular literature in it.[12]

The trick with the reins was probably likewise taken by Gogol from the lost comedy by his father "Sobaka-Vivtsia". The latter had however in his turn dipped into popular literature for it, particularly into the *vertep,* the Ukrainian puppet theatre.

Can we in all this brusque and burlesque piece recognise something of a well-devised construction and, if so, is it anything but schematic and does its linear course indicate an idea? I think I can show that this is, in fact, the case.

The centre of this love-story is not an amorous scene. On the contrary, it is the story of the devil's red blouse. This also stands formally precisely in the centre, in the seventh of the thirteen chapters, which is, at the same time, the longest, if we leave out of consideration I and XIII, about which we shall speak in a moment. Only in the last chapter is the theme of love resumed. The girl had disappeared from the stage

---

[12] This piece *Prostak* in its turn shows a similarity with I. P. Kotlyarevsky's *Moskal-Charivnyk*. See N. I. Petrov, *Ocherki istoriyi ukrainskoy literatury XIX stoletiya* (Kiev, 1884), pages 79, 80.

in III, the youth in V. He appears again only in XII, she at the beginning of XIII.[13]

The centre of gravity consequently lies with the red *svitka,* that is to
say, a demoniac principle. Of course, the devil does not exist, not even
for the narrator. The fact that he can nevertheless appear, depends on
the belief in demons of the people taking part and that point was not
invented by Gogol. That the devil's property brings misfortune, that
the devil demands his possession back, that red is the devil's col-
lour, these are all motifs which are very widely spread in Ukrainian
popular literature.[14] Gogol was to use them more than once; in the
story to be discussed after this, we find a clear and tragic example
thereof, and they occur again even in a much later work such as "The
Portrait".

The demoniac element occurs here in a concrete form and an *object*
is the bearer thereof, namely the red *svitka.* We are quite justified in
calling this a symbol. It occurs in III, VII and X.

Has love a corresponding symbol as the counterpart? No. There is
however something else. When the youth enters for the first time,
he is not mentioned by name, but as the youth "with the white *svitka*".
He also appears in this guise in II, not in III, which is a continuation
of II and where the red *svitka* first occurs, but in V and VIII, not
however in VII, where the young man frees Cherevik.[15] This means
that every time the youth enters as a lover, he is accompanied by the
image of the white *svitka.* This itself has no function in the story and
always appears very modestly and, as if casually. The word "symbol"
would be too ponderous, but we may certainly speak here of a "Leitmotiv" in the sense in which Walzel uses this term.[16]

Just as the demoniac element is the pivot of the action, love is the
centre of the story. These two act together: the lover has to thank the
possession of his beloved to the mock-devil. They are rendered concrete
in an analogous manner, love in the white, demonism in the red *svitka.*

There is however another devilish figure in the story and, at the same
time, one of the most real, and this works against the joining of the
lovers: the stepmother. When the youth sees the girl for the first time,

---

[13] Her presence is indicated once very much in passing in VII.
[14] See note 49.
[15] In IV Cherevik, in front of his wife, calls the *svitka* something that has more
value than her beautiful clothes.
[16] See O. Walzel, "Leitmotive in Dichtungen" in *Das dichterische Kunstwerk*
(Leipzig, 1926), p. 5, and the chapter of the same name in his *Gehalt und Gestalt
im Kunstwerk des Dichters* (Berlin, 1923), p. 358 ff.

sitting on the waggon, he exclaims: "A fine girl! I'd give all I have to kiss her. And there's a devil sitting in front!"

When the gypsies find Cherevik, who thinks that the devil is sitting on his back, and they discover that it is a woman, one of them says: "Oh, well, then that's the devil!"

The stepmother is consequently intended as a contrast to the girl, "devil" as opposed to "angel" and her lovelife as opposed to that of the young couple. Thus, the scene with the priest's son gains significance as a contrast. We could assume of this last scene, borrowed from a comedy by Gogol's father, that it is not connected enough with the rest of the action. Gogol nevertheless consolidated the bond by a masterly indication in the final chapter which has a very clear symbolic value.[17]

The girl is thinking about her lover; she is happy that she will soon, as a married woman, no longer have to show any respect to her stepmother. She is wondering how her cap will look and she decides to try on her stepmother's cap.

Then she got up, holding the looking-glass in her hand and bending her head down to it, walked in excitement about the room, as though in dread of falling, seeing below her, instead of the floor, the ceiling with the boards laid on the rafters from which the priest's son had so lately dropped, and the shelves set with pots. "Why, I am like a child," she cried, "afraid to take a step!" And she began tapping with her feet – growing bolder as she went on.

Here we have a *picture* of the relationship in which we must imagine the love-life of the stepmother and stepdaughter. These two are one another's opposite. The reversal has taken place here in the literal sense and with what charm, and at the same time with what irony. The child is after all wearing as a sign of her future married life her stepmother's head-dress, the floor on which she is moving consists of the boards from which the priest's son had fallen. Things which are purely one another's mirror-image, are after all identical.

This grotesque is introduced and concluded in the most surprising way. The first chapter begins thus:

How intoxicating, how magnificent is a summer day in Little Russia! How luxuriously warm the hours when midday glitters in stillness and sultry

---

[17] The situation occurs precisely in this way in "Prostak". I shall refrain from giving a psycho-analytical explanation, although this would be possible.

heat and the blue fathomless ocean arching like a voluptuous cupola over the plain seems to be slumbering, bathed in languor, clasping the fair earth and holding it close in its ethereal embrace! Upon it, not a cloud; in the plain, not a sound. Everything might be dead; only above in the heavenly depths a lark is trilling and from the airy heights the silvery notes drop down upon adoring earth, and from time no time the cry of a gull or the ringing note of a quail sounds in the steppe.

That is true eroticism; here there forces itself to the front, in descriptions which, however conventional they may seem if they are viewed in the abstract, a feeling which is nothing more than playing material in the story.

The erotic element is expressed in the most usual way, namely in lyricism. The lyrical introduction to this mad grotesque is striking. We can from the outset see how normal the combination of the lyrical and the epic, even the epic-dramatic was for Gogol. No more than was later to be the case with the strange lyrical passages from "Dead Souls", does the lyricism here harmonise with the "main point". No more than there, is such a harmony intended. In both cases the lyricism gives the basic mood of the writer which contrasts with the nature of what is being described.

The contrast is romantic. Gogol sought contrast with a certain preference during his first period. We shall find many examples of it. The lyrical element is in this case, however, not a direct outpouring, as in "Dead Souls", but it has the form of a description. It is also as such a good specimen of what the "Evenings" have to offer in this genre. The Dnieper passage from "A Terrible Revenge" forms the outstanding example thereof. Kotlyarevsky [18] is correct when crying it down, he finds that Gogol's Dnieper shows no resemblance to the real one, any more indeed than the landscape described here does to any landscape in the world. It is not described realistically, it is celebrated in song. Gogol's adjectives do not graphically suggest a reality, but musically a mood.[19]

What we have just quoted is merely the beginning of a passage which closes with the words: "how full of voluptuousness and languor is the Little Russian summer!" There then follows a comic-realistic description of the travellers on their way to the fair. The emotional atmosphere

---

[18] Nestor Kotlyarevsky, *Nikolay Vasilyevich Gogol*, 4th edition (Petrograd, 1915), p. 98.
[19] Every translation of Gogol I know falls short in this respect. A very creditable Dutch translation has appeared by W. Huisman, *N. W. Gogolj, De Jaarmarkt te Sorotsjintsy* (Amsterdam, Wereldbibliotheekvereniging, 1952).

of the beginning nevertheless returns when Gogol begins to depict the small river, the Psyol as a capricious beauty with bared bosom and shoulders. It is not only for the sake of brevity that I am not quoting anything of it. The description is not completely successful, unity of vision is sometimes missing, while the erotic element predominates. Thereafter, the actual story really begins.

The last chapter forms a counterpart to this one. It begins with the depiction of the girl in love, thinking about her lover, and this scene makes us think back to the description of the Psyol just referred to. One could speak about magnificent details in this section, but I should like to limit myself to a consideration of the end of this chapter.

The wedding has begun. At the first sounds from the violin everyone obeys, as if forced by a magic force, the call of the dance. An observer would have been overcome by a strange feeling, says Gogol, upon seeing the general will-less submission to that impulse.

Everything was heaving, everything was dancing. But an even stranger and more enigmatic feeling would have been stirred in the heart at the sight of old women, whose ancient faces breathed the indifference of the tomb, shoving their way between the young, laughing, living human beings. Caring for nothing, without the joy of childhood, without a gleam of fellow-feeling, nothing but drink, like an engineer with a lifeless machine, makes them perform actions that seem human; yet they slowly wag their drunken heads, dancing after the rejoicing crowd, not casting one glance at the young couple.

Here is the other side of the picture, no lyricism, but the reflection of an observer who is looking at his own puppets. The strange, enigmatic feeling in his chest is not happiness, it is fear of a world which has turned into something rigidly mechanical. We all know how characteristic that feeling is for the romanticist. Read the beautiful pages devoted by Franz Schultz to the symbol of the puppet.[20] We also know, and shall be mentioning it again, how strong this horror of mechanical numbness became for Gogol. We should, however, here beware of too far-reaching conclusions. It is not the real world which is spoken of in this story, but the world of play. The same applies to the ending.

Is it not thus that joy, lovely and inconstant guest, flies from us? In vain the last solitary note tries to express gaiety. In its own echo it hears melancholy and emptiness and listens to it, bewildered. Is it not thus that those who have been sportive friends in free and stormy youth, one by one stray,

[20]   Franz Schultz, *Klassik und Romantik der Deutschen* (Stuttgart, 1935), I, p. 46.

lost, about the world and leave their old comrade lonely and forlorn at last? Sad is the lot of one left behind! Heavy and sorrowful is his heart and naught can aid him.

That is indeed again lyricism, with loneliness as its basic mood, with melancholy as its final sound.

Gogol's last Ukrainian tale, the story of the two Ivans from "Mirgorod" ends with a similar tirade. The difference is however just about as great as the similarity. In the later, mature work, the tragic note of the final passage suddenly gives a new meaning to the whole. Here there is no tragedy, only sentimentality. The foregoing was, after all, a play beyond reality, and the player is sad that it is over.

And now it is time for the question: "Who was really the narrator?" This could be decided by elimination, even if Gogol had not given any indication at the beginning of the following story.[21] If we compare the material in the prefaces to the first and second part of the "Evenings" and the introductions and titles of various short stories from these collections, then it appears that the narrator cannot be anyone but the gentleman with the pea-green coat, the man who could narrate in such an affected manner that even a Moscovite would scarcely follow it. This means a figure who stood above or outside the events, in contrast to the sacristan Foma Grigoryevich, who could, while relating, identify himself with his heroes, or could at least rank with them. It follows from this that Gogol could put lyric poetry into the mouth of the *panich*,[22] could make him the spectator of a landscape of which the sacristan himself was too much an inhabitant ever to observe it as a miracle. The same applies to the contemplations at the end, the tone and manner of observation of which would be inconceivable for a figure who could possibly form part of such a dancing group.

It follows at the same time that the possibilities are limited as regards form. If the *panich* set to work purely epically, then there would have to be a conflict between the narrator and the milieu of the "Evenings" or a discrepancy between the narrator and the story. After all, if he narrated objectively, as if he himself viewed the events as reality, then he would have to be another Foma Grigoryevich. If he were to assume a subjective attitude towards what was narrated, then little more would remain for him than irony, but this would render the story unacceptable to his listeners, to Rudy Panko and the sacristan. The only

---

[21]   "... that gentleman with the pea-green coat ... by whom you, I think, have already read a story." *Soch.*, I, 36.
[22]   Panich – approximately "dandy".

possibility which remains is the dramatic or rather the scenic. As soon as the action begins, the persons speak their own language, direct speech is used everywhere, and the ironical attitude is left to the reader. And what about the lyricism? Yes, those are the passages in which Rudy Panko and Foma must doubt the reason of the *panich*.

This explains the division into short chapters, each of which contains one scene. The narrator is objectively most clearly present in the first and the last, and this is where we consequently find lyricism; it is lacking in the others. He also comes forward a little at the beginning of II, but then also ironically. Gogol takes care that the irony has just enough emphasis that the reader cannot be mistaken, but that the illusion of the *panich's* listeners is not disturbed.

It is now quite clear whom Gogol meant by the gentleman from Poltava. The man who stands outside, for whom this cheerful world is a play, of which he can, with homesickness and anxiety, be only the observer, the man who is neither *moskal*[23] nor *khokhol*, who else should it be but Gogol himself?

One manuscript has been preserved of this story, which differs so much from the printed text that Georgiyevsky, who published it,[24] came to assume a second version, preceding the printed one.[25] A second manuscript is, however, unknown. Two editings can also be distinguished in the first: Gogol was in the habit of recasting a draft repeatedly and thoroughly.

We are consequently in a position to investigate in what respects the sketch differs from the completed work and on what principles the recasting was based. The results are very clear. Careless slips were of course removed, often repeated words were replaced by their synonyms, etc. There is however equally much proof of artistic revision in a certain direction.

The first principle which guided Gogol was the effort towards giving concrete form. I have chosen two examples, to which a more general observation can be added. Cherevik's *kum* has in the first version no name, in the last he is called "Tsybulya", which means "onion". Names had a great significance for Gogol, they characterise the bearer, not only

---

[23] *Moskal* – derisive term for a Russian (in Ukraine and Poland).
[24] *Gogolevskiye teksty* izdany G. P. Georgiyevskym (St. Petersburg, 1910).
[25] Tikhonravov, who supervised the 10th edition of Gogol's complete works certainly knew the manuscript, but he published the variants in a very incomplete form. Shenrok, who completed the edition after Tikhonravov's death, introduced no improvement in this.

and principally through their meaning, but primarily through their sound
and the associations this suggests. A Russian could not possibly be
called "Luk" (onion), whereas the Ukrainian "Tsybulya" does not
sound bad. The word could be pronounced with dignity or heartiness,
if only it had no meaning.[26] When discussing "The Overcoat" we shall
have more to say about Gogol's playing with names and his persistent
searching until he had found the correct combination of foolish sound
and direct or indirect associations.[27] The stylistic aid serves here to
accentuate the grotesque character of the story.

This same tendency towards the concrete is also found in a wider
scale. In X the gypsy cuts through the reins of Cherevik's horse. In the
first version, the animal occurs only in this chapter. But when Gogol
was working on the manuscript, he added in I a touch to the description
of Cherevik and his ox-waggon. Above the lines there is added: "At
the rear of the waggon and tied to it walked a mare". This addition
gave Gogol a new idea during the last stage of revision. The manuscript
characterises the relationship of Cherevik and his wife thus: "She
understood the art of managing him as easily as a gypsy does the reins
of his pole-horse."[28] In the printed text we find that she managed him
as easily "as he drove his old mare, now as a reward for long years
of service being taken to be sold."[29]

In this way, originally disjointed ideas have been "organised". The
image of the horse has become more concrete, the joke about Cherevik's suppression becomes wittier through it and the fabric of the story
has also been strengthened by an extra thread.

A second tendency we note is the effort on the part of the writer to
make his language and style more "literary". Gogol did not avoid any
Ukrainian expressions, they gave local colour. He was nevertheless
aware how much moderation was dictated in the use of the dialect.
The last version is, in this respect, more sober than the first.[30] A crude
expression, provided it was juicy enough, Gogol shunned least of all.
The curses which Cherevik's wife pours forth over the head of her
future son-in-law have been extended and increased in the last version

---

[26]   This applies even more strongly to a name such as Golopupenko ("little bare
navel"), which looks genuinely Ukrainian because of its ending. It is the name
of a hero!

[27]   A. Bely has devoted great attention to the personal names in Gogol's works.
Masterstvo Gogolya (Moscow-Leningrad, 1934), p. 215, 216.

[28]   Georgiyevsky, *op. cit.*, p. 37.

[29]   *Soch.*, I, 11.

[30]   E.g. Georgiyevsky, *op. cit.*, p. 49: *ne do penka vyskochiv*. On the other hand
Soch., I, 31: *obmanyvay drugikh etim* (see also *Soch.*, I, 513 ff).

to a small fantasy about his family. On the other hand, a joke about someone who has to go outside in order to relieve himself, but who dares not for fear of the devil, disappears.[31] Naturalness does not always gain through this effort. In the manuscript the *kum* maintains that he has never stolen anything: "except a patty with cooked cabbage". In the printed text the word "except" is replaced by "perhaps with the exception of".[32]

Finally, I should like to discuss two further changes which refer, more than the above, to the atmosphere of the work. The quasi-lyrical introduction to II originally began as follows:

Who has never seen, who has not found himself sometime in the whirlpool of a noisy fair ...

Above it is written:

Have you ever heard the rushing of a distant waterfall, when you imagine you hear indistinct sounds in the distance ...

In the printed edition the irony is much heavier, the opening lines being:

You have no doubt heard a rushing waterfall when everything is quivering and filled with uproar, and a chaos of strange vague sounds floats like a whirlwind round you. Are you not instantly overcome by the same feelings in the turmoil of the village fair ...

A magnificent preparation for the immediately following parallel:

Noise, swearing, bellowing, bleating, roaring – all blend into one discordant uproar.

This must really be combined in turn with the epigraph, the comic effect of which unfortunately cannot be reproduced.

By far the most interesting thing is however the changes made at the end of the last chapter. They confirm what has been said above concerning the abhorrence of what is mechanical, which is, in my opinion, the basic mood of this section. When Gogol has described the dancing of the old people, there follows in the first version:

Also on a ruin and a tomb-stone moss turns green and becomes attached, as if destruction itself can smile. The crowd marched on in a long line and disappeared like the shadows of a magic lantern.

Gogol rightly rejected the first sentence, probably because of its sentimental rhetoric. Why did he do this with the second? I don't know – were shadows, after all, too immaterial for him? Did he find his intention expressed too barely by them? The last supposition seems to me very plausible.

[31] Cf. Georgiyevsky, *op. cit.*, p. 29 and *Soch.*, I, 12.
[32] Georgiyevsky, *op. cit.*, p. 51: *krome*; *Soch.*, I, 31: *vyklyuchaya razve*.

Summarising, we can now identify this grotesque as a play of contrasts. A puppet theatre, in which the devil is given the role of the
servant of love, occupies the central position. The amorous and demoniac elements are both unreal. The first half of the fable is allocated
to love, which serves really only to create the entanglement. It is
striking that the heroine is the person who is characterised to the least
extent, the girl having almost a silent role. The dénouement is brought
about by the fantasy-devil in a very rapid tempo, the action first acquiring speed in the middle of the story. As a counterpart to this
abstract love and the mock-demon, there is the marriage of Cherevik to
his certainly real, fiendish vixen, and Gogol suggests that the love play
of the young people will end in the same way. The frame to these
dramatic scenes is formed by lyricism and outpouring with hidden
eroticism and anxiety. The manner of narration and the style are in the
central section realistic and concrete, which has led to misunderstanding and the search for realism in the content as well.[33] The tone is
lyrically musical or pathetically contemplative in the framework. The
narrator is kept hidden, yet seems to wear the pea-green coat of the
gentleman from Poltava, Gogol's most transparent disguise in this
collection.

Gogol uses all sorts of motifs in this story which are to recur in his
later work in bitter earnest. He plays with them here. The "popular
tale" is the fantasy of a St. Petersburg official suffering from home-
sickness, his direct utterances are hyperbolical or sentimental. The
conflict between dream and reality is here held within the sphere of the
aesthetic play.

"The Fair at Sorochintsy" is a magnificent example of a grotesque.[34]
The grotesque recurs again and again in Gogol's work, both in the
comic and in the tragic. We shall be meeting it repeatedly.

2. *Saint John's Eve*

The second story in the collection has the title "Saint John's Eve". In
many respects it is the contrary of the preceding one, this following
directly from the fact that it is, to a certain extent, placed in a framework and has a narrator: Foma Grigoryevich, the sacristan, whose

---

[33] Kulish did this in his criticism which has already been mentioned. The
remark that things were in reality different in the Ukraine lacks any purpose in
this context.
[34] For a definition see Ya. Zundelovich, "Poetika groteska" in *Problemy poetiki,
Sbornik statey,* pod red. V. Bryusova (Moscow-Leningrad, 1925), p. 63 ff.

story is once again introduced by an anecdote by Rudy Panko which we shall discuss further in a moment. Its content also shows quite a different character from that of the previous story.

Petro, a young Cossack, is a workman in the service of the rich Korzh and is in love with his daughter. When the father surprises the young couple while they are embracing, he almost chokes with rage and throws Petro out, for he has marked out Pidorka, his daughter, for a rich Pole.

The desperate Petro enters into an alliance with Basavryuk, a mysterious figure, who is rightly suspected by the villagers of being the devil in human form. He gives Petro the strange commission of picking for him the flower of the bracken in the middle of St. John's Eve. He will then make Petro extremely rich. The youth sets off into the night. When he has picked the flower, Basavryuk appears and with him a witch, who orders Petro to throw away the flower. It describes a long path and where it finally comes to rest a treasure lies hidden. Dig as Petro will however, the treasure sinks deeper and deeper into the ground. Human blood has to be shed if he is to get it into his hands. The witch brings a child, which turns out to be little Ivan, Pidorka's young brother. Petro shrinks back, but when the ground becomes transparent and he sees the precious stones piled up below his feet, he strikes. The blood streams out of the boy's neck. A devilish laughter resounds from all sides and the witch drinks the blood like a wolf.

The following day Petro has forgotten everything. Two sacks with gold are standing in his hut. Korzh now accepts him willingly as a son-in-law and he marries Pidorka. He is however terribly tormented by the vague feeling that he has to remember something, something horrible that has happened to him and which has disappeared completely from his memory. He begins to languish under this pressure, his sombreness begins to resemble madness. At her wit's end Pidorka goes to enlist the help of a witch, it once again being St. John's Eve. When the witch enters, Petro wakes up, rises and suddenly remembers everything. He grabs an axe, strikes at the old woman with it, but she has disappeared. In the middle of the room stands a child, a cloth over its head, its body covered with blood.

Pidorka flees. When she returns, she finds only a heap of ash where Petro had been standing.

"St. John's Eve" is the only story from the collection which had already appeared in a periodical, namely in *Otechestvennye Zapiski* for

1830. There is had the title "Basavryuk, or St. John's Eve. A Ukrainian story (based on a popular legend), told by the sacristan of the Church of Our Lady". In the edition of the "Evenings" the full title is: "St. John's Eve. A true story told by the sacristan of the *** church".

Much was changed in the reprint.[35] Gogol made many cuts, re-wrote the end completely, and also here and there restored the original version, where Svinin, the editor of the journal, had been "improving".

The reason for this was not, as Tikhonravov assumed, that Gogol got to know Tieck's "Liebeszauber" (The Magic of Love) in the period between the two editions and, struck by the similarity between his work and that of Tieck, adapted "St. John's Eve" even more to "Liebeszauber". The great Gogol authority started from the incorrect assumption that Gogol could not have read Tieck's story in the original edition because of his faulty knowledge of German, and that the first Russian edition is said to have appeared at about the same time as "St. John's Eve".[36]

V. Gippius has now shown that Tikhonravov's last and strongest argument must be disposed of. A translation of Tieck's short story had already appeared in 1827.[37] Whatever may have been the position as to Gogol's knowledge of German, and this was probably not as bad as was once assumed, he could also have read Tieck's work in Russian before he wrote "St. John's Eve". There is certainly no-one who doubts that this happened. Attention had already been drawn in 1831 to the similarity between the two short stories.[38] The only surprising thing is that Tikhonravov can have supposed that the most important similarities, which the two stories immediately showed, were not founded on dependence.[39] The only change, through which the second edition of "St. John's Eve" draws somewhat nearer to "Liebeszauber" is that Gogol stressed to a greater extent Petro's fruitless attempt to re-member (for this motif was certainly present quite clearly in the first edition). On the other hand, he no longer speaks about Petro's greed when he is rich. How unimportant these details nevertheless are, com-

[35] Tikhonravov does not say accurately how much precisely (see *Soch.*, I, 516 ff). He quotes large sections from the first version, but gives no exact collation of the two texts. I was unable to consult the journal.

[36] *Soch.*, I, 527. He means the publication in *Galateya* of 1830.

[37] V. Gippius, *Gogol* (Leningrad, 1924), p. 224. The translation appeared in the *Slavyanin*.

[38] By Nadezhdin in *Teleskop*.

[39] Tikhonravov ascribed the similarities to borrowing from related popular literature on the part of both authors.

pared with the many other similarities, will appear from a résumé of the content of "Liebeszauber".

The hero is in love with his neighbour over the way, but too timid to confess to her his love. The girl in question is, however, no less in love with him and, at her wit's end, enlists the help of a witch, who demands human blood and, here too, the small brother of the bride to be is the victim. Emil, the lover, sees the terrible deed take place from his window. Just as Petro, he loses his memory. He suddenly regains it on his wedding-day, when he sees his friend appear in the costume of the witch at a masquerade. He kills his bride in an attack of frenzy and commits suicide.

We see that, with all the differences, there are great similarities in the outline of the stories. What does not, however, appear from this short résumé, are the parallels in small details which are at least equally important for the question as to whether Tieck influenced Gogol. Since this question was answered in the affirmative a long time ago,[40] I shall leave it on one side and shall attempt to arrive at a characterisation of both short stories while drawing comparisons. This will show how wilfully Gogol handled his model and how greatly "St. John's Eve" differs from "Liebeszauber".

Tieck's story forms part of the large, hybrid collection "Phantasus".[41] "Liebeszauber" is also set in a framework and Tieck gave a far greater significance to this than Gogol. A group of young people has collected in a country-house. The men all have at least one manuscript in their pockets which is read out, the women merely joining in the criticism thereof. After the reading of "Liebeszauber", one of the ladies announces her disapproval. She finds the story too horrible. She has become so frightened that she suspects the presence of a monster in every bush or arbour. She is afraid that the dearest and best-known figures can suddenly change into spectres,

and one is and remains foolish, and listens, allows oneself to be enticed further and further by words, until we are suddenly seized by the most monstrous horror, which violently engulfs all previous sensations as if in a whirlpool.[42]

[40] G. I. Chudakov, "Otnosheniye tvorchestva Gogolya k zapadno-yevropeyskim literaturam", *Universitetskiye Izvestiya* (Kiev), 1907, 7, 1908, 3, 8, 10.
[41] I am quoting on all occasions the Berlin edition of 1828, *Ludwig Tiecks Schriften*, Vol. IV.
[42] "und man ist und bleibt thöricht, und hört zu, läszt sich von den Worten

The answer is given by Manfred: "But your reality"[43] – it is not only horrible, but also lacks the comforting shape of art, the idea of fate is often not even recognised in it.

"This distress of the world can however in such fabulous inventions enter only as if refracted by many joyful colours, and I would think that even an eye which was not strong should be able to endure it in this way." "And even if you were right", said Clara, "I should still remain inexorable!"[44]

She was, of course, quite right. Her attack reproduces Tieck's own feeling and Manfred's words form a not very brilliant attempt to give the matter a reasonable appearance. What of "shape of art", "fate", "joyful colours"! No, the kernel of this story and of so much else that Tieck produced consists in the idea that fiendish spirits slumber in the lightest of landscapes, that the most serene countenance can be the mask of a demon. Clara's attack was as sharp as Manfred's defence was weak: "One allows oneself to be enticed further and further by words". "By words": that is Tieck's weak point. While reading Tieck, we can often not escape the feeling that he was trying to intoxicate himself with his own words. This is also the case with "Liebeszauber" which contains more fantasy than suggestion. It was written to establish one idea, yet lacks a taut line of tension, so that the magnificent conclusion thereby loses much of its effect.

One idea is allegorised in "Liebeszauber" (to use one of Tieck's own terms), for which the writer started from one stimulus to the fantasy. In Munich, he had been able to watch from his room, through a chink in the shutter, a young girl with a child, and there then arose in him the thought of writing a story in which death approaches someone through such a chink. An idea that is also theoretically closely linked with his later theory about the short story as a form, a school example of a "turning-point short story" (Wendepunktnovelle), also taking "turning-point" (Wendepunkt) in the specific Tieckian sense: the intervention of a strange, hostile power, against which no protection is possible.

---

immer weiter und weiter verlocken, bis das ungeheuerste Grauen uns plötzlich erfaszt, und alle vorigen Empfindungen wie in einem Strudel gewaltthätig verschlingt." *Op. cit.*, p. 283.

[43]   "Aber Eure Wirklichkeit."

[44]   "In dergleichen märchenhaften Erfindungen aber kann ja dieses Elend der Welt nur wie von vielen muntern Farben gebrochen hineinspielen, und ich dächte, auch ein nicht starkes Auge müszte es auf diese Weise ertragen können." "Und wenn du auch Recht hättest," sagte Clara, "so bleibe ich doch unerbittlich!" *Op. cit.*, p. 287.

After these general observations, we must investigate in what way Tieck embodies this idea.

His hero, Emil, is a dreamer fearing life, love and the insanity which can at any moment destroy his balance. Music is a symbol of this to him, and he fears it in every form. He is already predestined to his fate before the spell begins.

His opponent is his friend Roderich, who is just as much an extrovert as Emil is an introvert and who lives in a completely "extempore" manner. This figure serves, from the point of view of composition, mainly as a background for Emil. He is not clearly connected with the action.[44a] Only at the end of the story does he bring about the dénouement through his masquerade, and it is with Roderich's dagger that Emil commits the murder. Furthermore, all the comic elements in the short story are connected with his person. He yields to all whims and repeatedly clashes with Emil, and thanks to this figure, the misery of the world must appear to us "as if refracted by many joyful colours".

The other effect of contrast which Tieck uses does not lie in the comic field. It is brought about by the episode of a peasant wedding, of the marriage between two poor creatures. A half-idiotic farmhand is, on Emil's wedding-day, being married to an ugly old maid whom he has seduced, and Emil meets the procession. He is moved to tears: "'Life disgusts me,' he sobbed, deeply moved, 'I cannot be happy, I do not want to be.'"[45]

We can attempt to consider from one point of view the way in which Gogol varied his theme. It is here just as easily possible to start from the form as from the content, and I have chosen the first possibility.

The great difference which immediately springs to mind is the absence of the narrator with Tieck, while the way in which the short story is told in Gogol's case determines its nature to a large extent. With Tieck the story is read aloud, and the so-called maker has to endure the attacks of the fair sex. It is, as already mentioned, in a framework, and in a stricter sense than Gogol's story. Nowhere however does the so-called writer push himself as "I" between his delivery and his listeners, nowhere does it appear that the style coincides with

---

[44a] Tikhonravov seems to have considered that he is an accomplice of the witch, which would however have made the similarity with "St. John's Eve" even more striking.

[45] "'Mir ekelt das Leben', schluchzte er in tiefer Bewegung, 'ich kann nicht glücklich sein, ich will es nicht.'"

his character. Nothing appears more clearly from the disputation after the reading than that the writer is identical with that of "Phantasus".

"St. John's Eve" presents quite a different picture. The narrator is the sacristan of the Church of Our Lady, who is not relating his own fabrication but a story by his grandfather. This is a state of affairs which occurs on two further occasions in the "Evenings", namely in "The Lost Letter" and "A Place Bewitched", two stories concerning the devil in which, however, the comic element predominates. Gogol has certainly used this figure of the sacristan as a stylistic aid, there being something similar in the tone of the three stories. Lyricism is practically missing and the story is interrupted again and again by the digressions of an old man.

The contrast with "The Fair at Sorochintsy" is complete. Just as the grotesque was set between two lyrically pathetic pieces, this tale of terror is placed in a comic frame.

To begin with, there is the preface from the second version, in which Gogol quasi-nonchalantly achieves a twofold purpose. For us, the least important point is that he pulls the leg of Svinin, who had off his own bat, "improved" the first version, and at the same time jokingly defends his own amendments in the new edition. It is however interesting that, while doing this, he introduces his narrator.

It was a special peculiarity of Foma Grigoryevich's that he had a mortal aversion for repeating the same story.

Such a city gentleman, evidently a publisher of those thin, monthly volumes, had succeeded in squeezing a story out of him. Foma himself had long since forgotten this. The gentleman with the pea-green coat had brought it with him from Poltava, and the bee-keeper read it to Foma. Suddenly the sacristan asked what he was reading, and when Rudy Panko, somewhat taken aback answered that they were his own words, that it even said "told by such and such a sacristan", then Foma Grigoryevich could no longer contain himself. "Hang the fellow who printed that! He's lying, the cur!"

And he began to relate again as follows:

"My grandfather (the kingdom of Heaven be his! May he have nothing but rolls made of fine wheat and poppy-cakes with honey to eat in the other world!) was a great hand at telling stories."

He was a past master at telling blood-curdling stories.

"But the chief thing about my grandad's stories was that he never in his life told a lie and everything he told us had really happened."

In the present-day incredulous world there are all sorts of free-thinkers. There are even, it would seem, wind-bags who do not believe in witches. Foma has nevertheless seen terrible unbelievers in his long years "who would tell a lie at confession as easily as I'd take a pinch of snuff, but even they made the sign of the cross in terror of witches".

Not only are the narrators characterised comically and is the expectation of a comic tale aroused, but Gogol playfully shatters as much as possible the illusion that a true story is to follow. It will in fact be a masterpiece, to arouse after all a sensation of anxiety. It is however as if Gogol wants to produce precisely that masterpiece. He lets Foma speak all the time. Basavryuk is introduced as follows:

Why he came and where he came from nobody knew. He drank and made merry and then vanished, as though he had sunk into the water.

Do we think in a similar case of the devil in human guise? Just as comically as on his first appearance he keeps on appearing when the devilish game is at an end and Petro has already vanished from the face of the earth. He is recognised in all sorts of guises, for example, in a roast ram by the peasants, in a glass of vodka which bows by an old sexton, in a dancing baker's trough by Foma's aunt, who also often heard him clattering on the roof and scratching at the walls.[46] Finally Foma himself relates that he still remembers how a respectable person could no longer pass by the ruins of the tavern which had belonged to his late great-aunt and which the devils had for a long time run on their own behalf.

Smoke came out in clouds from the grimy chimney and, rising so high that one's cap dropped off if one looked at it, scattered hot embers all over the steppe, and the devil – no need to mention him, son of a cur – used to sob so plaintively in his hole that the frightened rooks rose up in flocks from the forest near and scattered with wild cries over the sky.

Compare this with Tieck's ending. The whole last act of the drama has taken place at a furious tempo.

Roderich took the dying man in his arms. He had found him in his wife's room playing with the dagger. She was almost dressed when he entered; upon seeing the loathsome red garment his memory had revived, the terrible picture of that night had appeared before his senses; gnashing his teeth, he had sprung at the trembling, imploring bride in order to punish the murder and her devilish feat. While dying the old woman confirmed

---

[46] Compare the end of "The Overcoat".

the crime which had been committed, and the whole house had suddenly been transformed into sorrow, tears and horror.[47]

With Tieck the bare horror, with Gogol a subdued ironic laugh. Roderich, who has until the last retained his comic role, is the tool of fate and holds his dying friend in his arms. Gogol's cruel devil disappears like a phantasm of superstitious country people. In Tieck's case, the comic element was connected with one of the dramatis personae, in Gogol's case, it is solely a trait of the narrator.

Gogol also ensures that Foma makes his presence felt at every decisive moment. He always makes a remark at a climax in the action which does not break the tension, but allays it. With a very clear feeling for moderation, Gogol succeeds in limiting these reflections to a minimum, if necessary. Thus, at the moment when Petro has plucked the bracken:

Everything was hushed. Basavryuk, looking blue like a corpse, appeared sitting on a stump. He did not stir a finger. His eyes were fastened on something which only he could see; his mouth was half open, and no answer came from it. Nothing stirred all round. Ugh, it was terrible! ...

There then again comes a rise in the tension which was interrupted by the last four words.

These examples could be multiplied, but the conclusion can already be drawn. This short story shows to a high degree that peculiarity which Walzel, not quite correctly, wanted to ascribe to the whole art of telling short stories, namely that of epic indirection. There thus arose a continuous hovering of the mood, a humour which Tieck also tried to achieve in a different manner, namely by slowing up his story and by inserting passages which are not directly connected with the action, e.g. the peasant wedding. Tieck nevertheless achieved nothing except that the tension is missing for pages on end. Only at the end, are the main features of the story concentrated to give a blood-red focal point, while they are intentionally made to diverge in Gogol's case.

This difference in construction is coupled with a great difference in the delineation of the characters. Gogol's heroes are firm and straight

---

[47] "Roderich nahm den Sterbenden in seine Arme. Mit dem Dolche spielend hatte er ihn im Zimmer seiner Gattin gefunden. Sie war fast angekleidet bei seinem Eintreten; beim Anblick des rothen widrigen Kleides hatte sich seine Erinnerung belebt, das Schreckbild jener Nacht war vor seine Sinne getreten; knirschend war er auf die zitternde, flehende Braut zugesprungen, um den Mord und ihr teuflisches Kunststück zu bestrafen. Die Alte bestätigte sterbend den verübten Frevel, und das ganze Haus war plötzlich in Leid, Tränen und Entsetzen verwandelt worden."

as Tieck's main figure remains vague and unstable in his emotions. Compared with "Liebeszauber", "St. John's Eve" has a staggering degree of concreteness. If the timid Emil had crossed the street and tapped at the shutter, instead of writing verses and peeping through the chink, nothing would have happened. He is an anaemic dreamer, predestined to succumb to longing for love.

Petro is a nimble Cossack, who has already come to blows before the father of his adored one shows him the door. He is just on the point of going as a privateer to the Crimea in order not to have to come to Korzh empty-handed, when the news of Pidorka's forthcoming marriage to the Pole reaches him.

The motivations are poles apart: anxiety concerning life and love in Tieck's case – in Gogol's an angry father-in-law.

In the same way, everything is given a concrete form in Gogol's case. Emil's beloved immediately receives the fulfilment of her desire for love through devilish arts – Petro receives two bags of gold. With Tieck, the demoniac principle is personified in an old witch, with Gogol the devil himself is also present as such, being very terrible and sinful: he drinks vodka like the best of them.

Tieck's Emil perceives how a dragon's mouth suddenly darts out and laps up the blood. Struck by a green ray from the dragon's eye, he falls down unconscious. With Gogol it is the witch, whom Petro has already seen before, who laps up the blood. This brings us to a new aspect of the matter. Gogol suggests that this witch is *baba-yaga*,[48] the curious witch-figure who occurs in Russian fairy-tales; her regular attribute is not lacking. There is consequently a connection with popular literature and this is not the only one. The disastrous devil's property, the search for a treasure, the bracken, which bears its red flower on St. John's Eve only, these are all motifs taken from the world of the fairy-tale and popular belief.[49] In this way the fantastic element gets a region of its own, a region where it can appear to its full advantage. This however coincides with that of a bygone world of the Cossacks, which certainly never existed in that way, but which acquires an appearance

[48] He lets Basavryuk speak of a *yaga*. She lives in the well-known "house on chickens' legs".
[49] See G. I. Chudakov, "Otrazheniye motivov narodnoy slovesnosti v proizvedeniyakh N. V. Gogolya", *Universitetskiye Izvestiya* (Kiev), 1906, 12. K. Nevirova, "Motyvy ukrainskoyi demonologiyi v 'Vecherakh' ta 'Myrhorodi' Hoholya", in *Zap. Ukr. Nauk. Tov. v Kyyivi*, 1909, p. 27 ff. These motifs are also well known in the West, see N. Bächtold-Stäubli, *Handwörterbuch des deutschen Aberglaubens*, under "Johannes der Täufer" and "Farn".

of reality through the detailed nature of its description. Gogol used as much ethnographic material as possible, in order to give his story local colour (his mother provided him with descriptions, noted down from the mouths of old people having the requisite knowledge) and applied it, inter alia in the description of the wedding of Petro and Pidorka.

Just as in the previous story, Gogol here makes moderate use of Ukrainian words. In one of the above quotations I used the term "rolls made of fine wheat". This is not a "translation" of the Ukrainian *bukhantsy*, which was also unintelligible to Gogol's Russian readers and which was translated by him in a glossary as "small white loaf". It would be easy to mention a large number of such expressions.

Emil's songs, sung from love and despair, also have their equivalent in "St. John's Eve". But while his are highly individualistic, those of Petro and Pidorka are very close to popular poetry.[50]

We must, on the other hand, be very careful in ascribing such motifs all too exclusively to folklore. It is certain that, in the final analysis, they have their origin in it, and it is with this that Gogol wanted intentionally to connect them. Did he however know them *solely* from there? I should dare to doubt it. We are still too unacquainted with what Gogol liked to read in his youth. It is, however, certain that he knew Tieck and Hoffmann, even if we cannot check precisely what works by them he had read.

The motif of St. John's Eve occurs in both authors. In Tieck's "Karl von Berneck"[51] as the night of fate, and here again twice, with a year in between. The fable of this play shows for the rest no similarity to that of Gogol's short story.

Yet in Hoffmann's "Bergwerke von Falun"[52] the similarity is somewhat greater. There the young man meets his death on St. John's day and is also found again on St. John's day. Moreover, we find here the motif of the earth, in which the most magnificent treasures lie hidden, becoming transparent. This short story was in turn inspired by Tieck's "Runenberg" . . . Enough to consider the literary borrowing of popular motifs as not out of the question. Although I am convinced of not having supplied proof of this borrowing, the possibility of literary influencing will have to be taken fully into account at this stage of

[50]   Shenrok, *Mat.*, III, 533 quotes a parallel between the words of the lovers on hearing of the forced marriage with the Pole and those of a folksong with a similar content.
[51]   *Schriften,* Vol. XI, p. 1–144. The piece was written in 1795.
[52]   Written in 1818.

Gogol's activity as well, the more so since Hoffmann was very popular in Russia.

The borrowing of one feature for "St. John's Eve" from Tieck, namely the red colour, is quite likely.[53] After the murder Petro sees everything in a red tint, his whole surroundings have taken on the colour of blood. In "Liebeszauber" the setting sun before the masquerade gives everything a blood-red tint, and it is the horrible red of the old witch's jacket which brings back Emil's memory.

Is it not however possible to presume that this red garment, this symbol of the devil, also influenced "The Fair at Sorochintsy"? There would then even be a genetic relationship between these two stories, the bonds between which are to me certain on other grounds. They are in tenor, composition, style so completely one another's antitheses, while the central motifs, namely the devil as the servant of love and goods of the devil which bring disaster, are so very similar in nature that I cannot conceive of this contrast being other than deliberate.

This brings us back to the difference between Gogol and Tieck. Tieck's "Liebeszauber" is, after all, deadly serious and has a direct bearing on Tieck's view of life. "The Fair at Sorochintsy" and "St. John's Eve" are both examples of playing. If we were to strip the last story of everything that connects it with the sacristan, we should have something left, just as horrible and suggestive as the strangest blossomings of German romanticism. Gogol did not however want this. Yet demonism and love are very close to one another in this short story. It is but one step to make them coincide in essence. Gogol was to take that step, but only years later.

It would certainly be worthwhile to investigate the composition of the other stories in this first collection. I must make do with mentioning that they may be regarded as variations in the technique of composition based on the other two.

"A May Night" is certainly by the gentleman in the pea-green coat. Once again we have the short chapters, lyricism and drama, but in this case distributed differently.[54] The material also shows some similarity with that of "The Fair at Sorochintsy". Here it is the father of the lover who stands in the way of the uniting of the lovers. Once again help comes from a non-human quarter. There is however no doubt here

[53] Tikhonravov pointed this out in *Soch.*, I, 534, 535.
[54] A fine parallel with the beginning of the "Fair" is formed by the beginning of Chapter II of "A May Night": "Do you know the Ukrainian night?" etc.

as to whether we must imagine the *rusalka*[55] who rescues the hero as real. She hands him a document which remains when her apparition disappears. There is once again performance by the devil, but in a genuine disguise which is seen through as such. The great difference between this story and "The Fair" lies in the fact that in "A May Night" love is taken seriously. The hero and heroine are idealised and speak rhythmically.

"The Lost Letter" is told by the sacristan and once again contains a genuine story of the devil. This time it is without love and with a happy ending. Once again, it is a true story experienced by Foma Grigoryevich's grandfather. Here too, Foma's manner of narration dominates the short story, but the comic element predominates, all that is gruesome being dispelled by his tone.

Thus, in the end, the first part of the "Evenings" also appears to show a clear composition as a book. It includes, alternately, stories by two narrators. The first and the second are complete contrasts, the third treats a theme, which is related to that of the first two but, in contrast to both, love is here an extremely exalted matter. The last is just as humorous as the first, has many grotesque features, but differs greatly from it through its composition.

The collection could consequently be defined as a play of contrasts, very strong emphasis being laid on the word "play".

PART 2

The second part of the "Evenings" shows a looser connection than the first as regards composition.

In Rudy Panko's introduction, Gogol makes fun of himself and his readers. The bee-keeper solemnly assures us that he is really very old — he does not himself know precisely how old, for the priest who baptised him has already been dead for a long time! — that he now has stories by new narrators, with the exception of the last which is by Foma Grigoryevich, and that the row with the gentleman in the pea-green coat has at last broken out. Just fancy, he imagined that he knew better how to preserve apples than Rudy's wife who had turned grey in the kitchen. Finally the *panich* became so angry that he spat on the floor, picked up his cap and went away for good. Yet even without him, a book has nevertheless appeared. — There is little point in seeking a

[55]   *Rusalka* – a sort of water-nymph.

deeper meaning behind Gogol's ridicule with his own masks. We must merely put on record that "Christmas Eve" is a story which, solely through its tone, the reference to places known to the reader and a single person (Foma Grigoryevich), creates the impression of being by a narrator from Dikanka, although that narrator is not named. The next story "A Terrible Revenge" stands completely outside the sphere, just as much as the strange history of "Ivan Fyodorovich Shponka and his Aunt", although Rudy Panko describes its author accurately.

Only "A Place Bewitched", which is said to be told by the sacristan who is familiar to us, brings us completely into the familiar sphere. It is, like "St. John's Eve", a devil's tale, it also comes from Foma Grigoryevich's grandfather, who besides plays the main part in it. It is also about digging for treasure. It is however completely comically grotesque, so much so that we even begin to think of a parody of "St. John's Eve".

It seems to me important for following Gogol's development to consider the two stories which differ most in content and technique from their predecessors in the first collection.

1. *A Terrible Revenge*

If we wish to gain some impression of the construction of this short story, a survey is desirable in which the division into chapters is clearly indicated. That is why this division has been strictly maintained when giving an account of its contents.

I. The *yesaul* [56] Gorobets had arranged a huge wedding-feast for his son. Also present were Danilo Burulbash with his young wife Katerina and their child who was only a year old. Katerina's father, who had shortly before returned from foreign parts, did not accompany them.

When Gorobets lifted up the holy ikons for benediction, there was suddenly a startling change in a young Cossack in the company. His nose grew longer and twisted to one side, his eyes took on a green sparkle, a long canine tooth glistened between his bluish lips, his figure became hunch-backed. "It is he, the wizard", cried the guests. Gnashing his teeth, he had however already departed, and the feast continued.

II. The following night, Danilo and his family returned to their distant dwelling on the far side of the Dnieper. Katerina was afraid because of the stories she had heard about the wizard. Danilo laughed at

[56] *Yesaul* – Cossack leader of lower rank.

her apprehension. In the meantime they passed the castle where the wizard was said to live. A graveyard became visible. Danilo thought he heard a cry. Then a corpse gradually raised itself from its grave. Its face twisted with unbearable pain and it groaned: "I am stifling, stifling". Once again a grave opened, then another. The third corpse was the most terrible. Its beard hung down to its feet, its long fingers pierced into the ground and it shrieked as if it felt a saw in its yellow bones. The child began to cry. Suddenly, everything was normal again.

During the rest of the journey, Danilo told his wife that her father was not a good Cossack. Danilo could not bring himself to speak out openly against him.

III. The following day Katerina's father paid a visit to Danilo's house. Both men were gruff and irritated. A fight soon ensued which would have ended in the death of Danilo if Katerina had not come between them with her child. Danilo asked his father-in-law's forgiveness without being aware of his own guilt. Katerina shuddered under the glittering look of her father when he kissed her.

IV. Katerina told her husband about a horrible dream in which her father had suggested to her that she should become his wife. Danilo, who was more concerned about an attack by the Poles, repeated that his father-in-law was not a Cossack and probably not a Christian, this being confirmed by his behaviour when he appeared on the scene and scorned the Cossack fare.

In the evening Danilo became aware of a suspicious light in the wizard's castle. He stole there, climbed a tree and looked in. In a chamber in the castle he saw his father-in-law who was conjuring up Katerina's soul by means of devilish incantations. She appeared as a white figure in a rose-coloured light. Katerina's soul rebelled against her father's shameful wishes and assured him that she would remain true to her husband under all circumstances. When the wizard, following Katerina's gaze, looked outside, Danilo fled.

V. At home he found Katerina awakened from a horrible dream, which agreed completely with what Danilo had seen. Only Katerina was aware of less than Danilo knew. He considered her father to be an "antichrist", and Katerina disowned him. "You are my father", were the words with which she expressed her allegiance to Danilo.

VI. The wizard was awaiting his execution in an underground chamber, not because of his sorcery, but because of betrayal to the Poles. He nevertheless succeeded in mollifying Katerina with an appeal to her dead mother and swore to her that he would live a holy life if she freed him. She helped him to escape, but immediately regretted having done so.

VII. Danilo threatened the wizard's confederate with the most terrible of punishments. Katerina whispered involuntarily: "And if I . . ." "I would sew you up in a sack and drown you in the mid-Dnieper . . .!", was his answer.

VIII. A band of Poles entered the country.

IX. Danilo felt that death was approaching him and ordered Katerina to take care of their son. The Poles suddenly appeared: they gave battle. Danilo fell, by a bullet from his father-in-law's musket. His last thoughts were devoted to his child. In a frenzy Katerina fell on his dead body. Then Gorobets' auxiliaries appeared.

X. A description of the Dnieper in still weather passes gradually into the portrayal of a storm raging over the river. A boat crossed the river during that storm and moored near the wizard's castle. It was he himself who stepped ashore and again tried to conjure up his daughter's soul. In place of this, a face appeared which was unknown to the wizard, but which struck deadly terror into him. Suddenly it disappeared.

XI. Katerina was in Kiev with Gorobets. Once again her father had appeared to her in a dream and with the same desire. If Katerina did not meet his demand her child would die. Gorobets tried to calm her, the child stretched its hands smilingly towards a pipe the Cossack was holding at it. In the middle of the night Katerina awoke with a start and rushed to the cradle. Her son was dead.

XII. Far from the Ukraine, beyond Poland, are the Carpathian Mountains. A giant figure in armour rode there through the mountains, as if asleep.

With a child behind him on his horse, he continued until the highest peak, the Krivan, was reached. There the horse stopped and the figure became invisible in the clouds.

XIII. Katerina, having gone out of her mind, was wandering through the woods and seeking her father in order to take revenge. An unknown companion in arms of Danilo appeared at Gorobets' house. Katerina listened, for the first time again with a glimmer of interest, to his stories. Yet, when the guest related how Danilo had charged him to take Katerina as his wife if Danilo should fall, she fell upon her father. After a short struggle, she was stabbed by her own knife.

XIV. To the astonished inhabitants of Kiev there appeared a strange phenomenon. The horizon disappeared into the distance and remote regions became visible, even as far as the Carpathians. When the clouds rose from their highest peak, the people saw another marvel: a horseman was standing there in full armour, his eyes closed.

Suddenly, one of the onlookers leapt onto his horse and fled as if death were at his heels. It was the wizard who had recognised the horseman's face, being the same one that had appeared to him after Danilo's death.

On the way home, his horse suddenly stopped, turned its head and it seemed to the wizard that it was laughing, that its curled lips were distorted into a sneer along its glistening teeth. Screaming he again urged his horse towards Kiev, and on the way it seemed to him that everything was grasping at him, as if the trees wanted to strangle him with their foliage, the stars were racing ahead of him and pointing to him and even the road seemed to be pursuing him.

XV. A hermit in his cell had just closed his holy book when a stranger rushed in and pleaded for his intercession. The hermit opened his prayer-book, but saw to his alarm that the letters appeared to be drenched in blood. He refused to pray for such a terrible sinner, and while he was speaking, the wizard imagined he saw a laugh on his lips. In a frenzy he stabbed the old man. Something moaned; behind the forest thin hands with long nails rose up. In a whirl, the wizard fled, but he could no longer guide his horse. It led him, against his will, further and further from his house until he was standing opposite the giant figure of the sleeping horseman on the Krivan. The wizard felt as if everything inside him stiffened. The horseman opened his eyes, and his laugh rolled like a clap of thunder through the mountains. He seized the wizard and lifted him up. The wretched man died instantly, but opened his eyes again, as a dead man, and with those dead eyes he saw on all sides, in Kiev, in Galicia, in the Carpathians, corpses rising up out of the ground, all of whom were exactly like him. They formed a circle around the horseman who laughed once again and then threw his victim into the abyss. The dead leapt onto it and fastened their teeth into the wizard's corpse. One of the dead men wanted to rise from the ground, but was powerless to raise his mighty body out of the earth. When he moved, the ground quaked.

XVI. A blind *bandurist*[57] was telling a breathless crowd the story of the Cossacks Ivan and Petro who served the King of Transylvania

---

[57] *Bandurist* – popular singer, who accompanies himself on the *bandura,* a plucked instrument with several strings.

in very ancient times. They lived as brothers and together shared their booty, yet, after a daring venture, when all the king's reward went to Ivan, Petro was consumed with envy, although Ivan, as before, had honestly given him his share. On a journey through the Carpathians Petro pushed Ivan and his child into an abyss. Ivan, who had been able to hold onto a branch, prayed in vain for his son's life. Petro laughed and pushed both of them with his lance into the ravine.

After Petro's death, God did not know of any punishment for him and allowed Ivan to determine what it should be. Ivan's demand was terrible. Petro's whole progeny was to be laden with a curse and his last descendant was to be a criminal, the like of whom the world had never seen before. Each of his atrocities was to startle his forefathers out of the peace of death, so that, tormented, they would rise up from their graves. Only the Judas, Petro would lack the strength for this and would writhe under the earth like one possessed.

And when the measure of the misdeeds of this last betrayer was full, then God might allow Ivan to rise from his grave and place him by that same abyss. Then the criminal should come to him and be thrown by Ivan into the abyss, and all his ancestors would gnaw his body, all except Petro. He would not be able to raise himself, even if he wanted to, but would grow larger and larger under the earth and gnaw at himself. "For there is no greater torture for a man than to long for revenge and be unable to take it." God found the punishment so terrible that he condemned Ivan to sit there on his horse for ever. So it was all fulfilled. That strange horseman is still standing there on the Krivan and revels in the gnawing by the dead at a corpse; under him, the great sufferer is still growing and makes the earth quake from his unbearable tortures.

Upon a first quick look at the composition, we are immediately struck by the division into two parts. The sixteenth chapter gives an unexpected explanation of all the riddles which had remained unsolved in the remaining fifteen. It forms a contrast with them in character, it has something of a saga about it, while the first part resembles a "tale of mystery".

As the action proceeds, the gloom becomes greater. It is at its darkest at the end of XV. As a result of the *bandurist*'s tale we all at once see everything that has gone before in a different light. The facts re-group themselves. It is as if everything falls into place. We become aware that motifs from the tragedy of Ivan and Petro continually appear through the drama of Katerina and her father, initially as details which one can easily overlook, but later becoming clearer and clearer, and finally beginning to dominate the action until another mystery has taken the place of that of the wizard.

If we examine various points in detail, then the story turns out to be a masterpiece of composition, and it is almost inconceivable that there are investigators who have not realised that we are here dealing with one of the summits amongst Gogol's work.[58] Both the construction of the parts taken separately and their combination and relation to one another show a balance which cannot have been due to a single moment of inspiration alone, but to the work of a mind which calculated each artistic effect very clearly.

The following survey will perhaps create the impression of being too detailed. This can however hardly be avoided if we wish to give any proof for what has just been stated.

Chapters I, II and III initially lack a clear connection. Each confronts the reader with one or more problems which appear to be related only when we come to IV. These chapters also represent a crescendo which reaches its climax in IV. Katerina and Danilo become more and more closely concerned in the action. In I they see the wizard in the company of all the wedding guests. Their own reactions are not mentioned. The corpses in II appear to both Katerina and Danilo and their servants without addressing themselves to them and without any accountable reason. The conflict between Danilo and his father-in-law in III takes place without witnesses in Danilo's own house.

I raises the question as to who the wizard can be, II, whether he is in league with the Poles, who the corpses are, what is peculiar about Katerina's father, III, unmysterious as it may be, nevertheless confronts us with two new questions: what moves Katerina's father and what moves Danilo? His anger is just as unreasoned as the irritation of his father-in-law. We cannot understand why this has to lead to a fight for life or death. In IV, Katerina's father turns out to be identical with the wizard. It was his unnatural desire which resulted in his attitude, while Danilo's reaction to it can now be explained as an instinctive dislike to the man in whom he unconsciously suspects this sinful tendency. In the meantime, Katerina has completely unwillingly become the pivot of the action.

Armed with the knowledge of the *bandurist's* story, we see something more in this exposition. I shows how a strange, demoniac force can

[58]   E.g. V. Nabokov, *N. Gogol* (Norfolk, Conn., 1944), p. 31, 32.

penetrate into the closed world of the Cossacks, II how the "terrible revenge" already shows itself at the beginning of the other story. The dead do not rise up at the behest of the wizard, as Danilo thinks, but in order to testify against him. The crying of the child also has a deeper meaning. It is the last Ivan who is to fall victim to the last descendant of Petro.

The wizard's fear of being laughed at, which Katerina mentions to Danilo, likewise forms a reference to the finish. The blood-lust and incestuous tendency of Katerina's father are now seen rather as his fate than as his will.

Gogol's mastery with composition is even clearer when we consider the construction of the separate chapters and pay special attention to the manner in which they are begun, finished and connected.[59]

The first chapter begins heavily and powerfully, almost like a poem:

Shumit, gremit, konéts Kíeva "... a bustle and uproar in a quarter of Kiev."

Thus begins the detailed description of the feast, interrupted only by the appearance of the uninvited guest. Then the dance continues, and the close is calm and broad: "wherever the tipplers stumbled there the Cossacks lay, snoring for the whole of Kiev to hear." The closed nature of the Cossack world is expressed perfectly in this way.

Just as calm, but infinitely more gentle, is the beginning of the following chapter:

There was a soft light all over the earth: the moon had come up from behind the mountain.

Just as the heavy breathing of the Cossacks sounded "over the whole of Kiev", so the pale moonlight falls "all over the earth", over the unreal landscape of the Dnieper, over the mysterious river on which Danilo's boat is floating. This whole chapter is however dominated by anxiety and menace. The appearance of the dead brings even the Cossacks under its spell. It ends as follows:

A thatched roof came into sight behind the mountain: it was Danilo's ancestral home. Beyond it was another mountain, and then the open plain, and there you might travel a hundred miles and not see a single Cossack.

The limit of the Cossacks' world has been reached.

[59] Andrey Bely has done that in his manner in *Masterstvo Gogolya* (Moscow-Leningrad, 1934), pp. 57–68. It is not possible here to discuss details of his view on the subject.

How much it was Gogol's intention to focus attention on this, appears from the first words of III:

Pan[60] Danilo's house lay between two mountains in a narrow valley that ran down to the Dnieper.

Nothing would have been simpler than to combine the two sentences we have quoted. Now however, the first forms a climax, the second a new calm beginning.

The close of III forms a dissonance:

Katerina shuddered faintly: the kiss and the strange glitter seemed uncanny to her. She leaned her elbows on the table, at which Danilo was bandaging his wounded hand, while he mused that he had acted ill and unlike a Cossack in asking pardon when he had done no wrong.

The sombre premonitions aroused by this ending are intensified at the beginning of IV, which by its form suggests an epic song:

The day broke, but without sunshine: the sky was overcast and a fine rain was falling on the plains, on the forest and on the broad Dnieper. *Pani*[61] Katerina woke up, but not joyfully: her eyes were tear-stained, and she was restless and uneasy.[62]

In this chapter, in which Katerina's soul is conjured up by her father, the tension continues to rise until just before the end, when it is subdued again, first by the words:

"Terrible, terrible!" he murmured to himself, feeling a thrill of fear in his Cossack heart, and he rapidly crossed his courtyard, in which the Cossacks slept as soundly as ever, all but one who sat on guard smoking a pipe.

There then follows the pure counterpart of the sentence with which the chapter had begun, which at the same time suggests the peace and impassiveness of surrounding nature: "The sky was all spangled with stars."

The three following chapters once again form a unit. The elements of the drama of fate seemingly recede into the background, a new sin is, however, added to those of the wizard: his being in league with the Poles. He is, as appears from VI, a prisoner because of this. This sixth central chapter from the group, is surrounded by the short, stirring dialogues of V and VII, which are contrasted: V ends with the supreme surrender of Katerina to Danilo, while in VI she denies her

[60]   *Pan* – "Lord".
[61]   *Pani* – "Lady".
[62]   For a similar parallelism in Ukrainian popular literature, see Shenrok, *Mat.*, II, 68.

husband, whom she has called her father, by freeing her own father, the wizard. VII is dominated by her mortal fear of him whom she loves above all else, namely Danilo.

"How glad I am you have awakened me!" is the abrupt beginning of V. The dialogue reaches its climax with Katerina's words: "No, do not call him my father!"

The beginning of VI is set much lower:

In a deep underground cellar at Lord Danilo's the wizard lay bound in iron chains and locked in with three locks.

There now follows the story of how Katerina, who first forbids him to call her his daughter, finally yields to his prayers, in the hope of still being able to save his soul. Her horror at the thought of having betrayed her husband is expressed at the end:

"Someone is coming! It is he! my husband!" she uttered a desperate shriek and fell senseless on the ground.

"It is I, my daughter! It is I, my darling" are the opening words of VII. They come – not from Danilo – but from a trusty old woman. The tension is broken for a moment, but all too quickly Danilo does in fact appear. No threat is terrible enough for the guilty one:

"And if it had been I?" Katerina could not resist saying, and she stopped, panic-stricken. "If you had done it, you would be no wife to me. I would sew you up in a sack and drown you in mid-Dnieper . . . !" Katerina could hardly breathe and she felt the hair stand up on her head.

V and VII which, as we have said, form a framework for VI, are not only just as long, consist not only both of dialogue, but are also connected by their clearly contrasting ending. The relationship between Danilo and Katerina is objectified in this contrast.

V and VII however have another function. V is also the repeated expression of what Katerina's soul had already said in IV, it is, in other words, reinforcement of IV.

The close of VII is not only set against that of V, but is also parallel to that of VI, so that, just as the last part of IV was amplified by V, VI is really closed by VII. These chapters consequently form a cleanly jointed mosaic.

VIII is very short and completely epic in character. It serves as an introduction to IX and describes merely the marching of the Polish bands. Naturally, the beginning again forms a contrast to the close of VII, while the conclusion prepares us for IX.

IX itself forms the first climax in the action. Bely has drawn attention to the magnificence of the description of the great festival[63] of the battle. The prose sometimes becomes metrical, without one seeing that hybrid which is, of all rhythmic prose, the least tolerable, namely the poem which just lacks the strength to raise itself from the ground. Gogol has here displayed a feeling for keeping within bounds, which at once marks him as being a master of style.

Rubí, kozák! gulyáy, kozák. Tesh molodétskoye sérdtse – "Hackaway, Cossack, make merry! Comfort your gallant heart."

After the four iambics three dactyls, and then prose resumes its rights.

The feast of the battle forms a strange parallel with the wedding feast in the first chapter. Danilo's attitude in the face of death is compared with that of a drunken man.

The Cossack slept, never to wake again . . . deeply has your lord been carousing; in drunken sleep he lies on the damp earth.

The chapter finishes with Katerina's funeral lament, the first words of which are:

Husband, is it you lying here with closed eyes? Rise up, my peerless falcon, stretch out your hand! Stand up!

The final words are:

Bury me, bury me with him! Throw earth upon my eyes! Press the maple boards upon my white bosom! My beauty is useless to me now!

Nothing more than a single sentence concludes the chapter:

Katerina grieved and wept; while the distant horizon was covered with dust: the old Esaul Gorobets was galloping to the rescue.

There then begins the tenth chapter with the powerful song of the Dnieper, the sublime calm of which has the effect of a majestic andante after an impassioned allegro. The passage is so famous, so many Russian school-children have learnt this page by heart, that people in Russia sometimes forget that Gogol wrote the whole of "A Terrible Revenge".[64] It is our purpose here to assess the function this too often isolated fragment fulfils in its surroundings. It will be found that, by doing this, we acquire a new insight into the short story.

[63]   The comparison also occurs in popular poetry, see Shenrok, *Mat.*, II, 62.
[64]   According to A. Bely, *op. cit.*, p. 47. Bely has made some particularly penetrating statements concerning rhythm and sound values in Gogol's prose, particularly on pages 71–76 and 218–27.

In this tremendous fragment of lyricism, in which the river appears as a primaeval force, the greatness of which cannot be measured by any human standard, nothing else happens except that, liberated, a melody forges ahead which has not only sounded continuously as an accompanying figure in all sorts of contrapuntal involvements, but which started clearly in the second chapter. There the boat of Katerina and Danilo, who are just about to look upon the dead, glides on the wonderful Dnieper. The whole episode takes place on the Dnieper. The name of the river is then repeatedly linked with the association of fate and death. I now give a selection of the most interesting passages.

Katerina says in III: "Dnieper, the cold Dnieper will be my grave". When, in IV, Danilo is on his way to the wizard's castle, everything is still.

All he could hear was from three sides the hollow murmur of the Dnieper down below and the resounding splash of the waves for a moment awakening one after the other. It was not in a turmoil; like an old man, it muttered and grumbled and found nothing to its taste. Everything has changed about it; it keeps up a feud with the mountains, woods and meadows on its banks and carries its complaints against them to the Black Sea.

In VI, the wizard, whose castle ("on the Dnieper") is burning, hears in his dungeon no sound that can offer him any hope. He looks out on a deserted road.

Beneath it rippled the Dnieper, it cared for no one; it murmured, and its monotonous splash sounded dreary to the captive.

"Where am I?" said Katerina, sitting up and looking round her. "The Dnieper is splashing before me, behind me are the mountains . . ."

These are her words at the beginning of the seventh chapter, at the end of which Danilo threatens to kill her by drowning in the Dnieper.

Apart from these passages, there are also several others in which the river is mentioned, in half a sentence, sometimes by a single word, but all these major and minor features contribute to form the impression that the river dominates the landscape. The character of this landscape is that of a wild borderland. Behind the Dnieper there begins a new hostile world, from which the wizard suddenly rises up and where no further Cossacks live and the true faith is not recognised.

If the Dnieper was in the previous chapters a *Leitmotiv,* the lyricism frees itself from the story in the tenth. *Chúden Dnépr pri tíkhoi pogóde,*[65] the song of the Dnieper sounds independently. This gives us,

[65] In common with most lyrics, this can also not be translated.

also in connection with what is to follow, the right to speak of more than a *Leitmotiv*. The Dnieper now becomes a symbol of the action on the first plane. It is therefore so important that everything should rise to cosmic dimensions: the woods are not reflected in its centre, seldom does a bird fly so far, only the sun and the blue sky look at it.

Lovely then, too, is the Dnieper, and no river is like it in the world!

In this tenth chapter, the action of the first plane, which is approaching its final stage, rises to a climax and at the same time touches that of the second plane, which has now definitely begun with the appearance of the avenger. It is perhaps strange to consider the Dnieper passage as a moment in the action. It undoubtedly is however. In the Dnieper, calm, mercurial or boiling in a mad frenzy but always noble, the world of the Cossack finds a symbol and a powerful summary.

This lyricism glides over almost imperceptibly into the last scene. The present tense used in the description is joined by the present historic in the story of how the wizard starts out into the stormy night, and this is quite naturally replaced a moment later by the preterite.

Strange and black are the burnt tree-stumps and stones on the jutting bank between the warring waves. And the landing boat is beaten against the bank, thrown upwards and flung back again. What Cossack dares row out in a boat now that old Dnieper is raging? Surely he knows not that the river swallows men like flies.

The boat reaches the bank, out of it stepped the wizard.

The end is abrupt and spasmodic.

The wizard turned white as a sheet; he shrieked in a wild unnatural voice and overturned the pot . . . All was over.

In the following four chapters the two levels alternate, while in the fifteenth the first rises to the height of the second.

"Take comfort, my dear sister", said the old Esaul Gorobets, "rarely do dreams come true!"

This opening once again forms a contrast, both to the end of X and the conclusion of this same eleventh chapter.[66] An irony appears in it, the light of which shines on all the assurances of Cossack fidelity and strength by which Katerina is set at ease. The evil power nevertheless forces its way in unhindered. There is no protection.

[66]   Naturally also with the beginning of IV, where Danilo says: "Yes, dreams contain much truth".

All surrounded the cradle and were numb with horror when they saw that the child in it was dead. None uttered a sound, not knowing what to think of this unheard-of crime.

Another theme is heard in XII, being completely new and not having any connection with the preceding chapter. The Carpathians loom up.

Far from Ukraine, beyond Poland and the populous town of Lemberg, run ranges of high mountains. Mountain after mountain, like chains of stone flung to right and to left over the land, they fetter it with layers of rock to keep out the resounding turbulent sea.

There is in the description of these mountains a curious analogy with the description of the Dnieper. Here, too, all stress is laid on the gigantic and superhuman element. The river is however seen in a movement, the smoothness of which would initially suggest a stagnation, but which is afterwards replaced by a wild, tumultuous torrent, while the Carpathians appear in a movement which has been brought to a standstill.

They are a wonderful sight. Was it some angry sea that broke away from its wide shores in a storm and threw its monstrous waves aloft and they turned to stone or remained motionless in the air? Or did heavy storm-clouds fall from heaven and cumber up the earth? For they have the same grey colour and their white crests flash and sparkle in the sun.

The figure of the avenger stiffens into the same immobility at the top of the Krivan.

There is no mountain in the Carpathians higher than this one; it towers like a monarch above the others. There the horse and his rider halted and sank into even deeper slumber and the lowering clouds hid them from view.

"Hush . . . don't knock like that, nurse: my child is asleep."

Katerina who has lost her reason prowls around mumbling, waiting for the opportunity to kill her father. In common with the eleventh chapter, this thirteenth also begins in the middle of a conversation, just as it ends with a murder and the powerlessness of the Cossacks.

The astounded Cossacks dashed at him, but the wizard had already leapt upon his horse and was gone.

The fourteenth chapter now begins: just as impassively as the twelfth.

An unheard-of marvel appeared beyond Kiev.

Since it is the Carpathians and the horseman which have become visible, a dim connection with the preceding chapter already begins to shine through. Appearances become certainty when the wizard feels himself overcome by horror at that sight and flees, pursued by the whole of nature.

The despairing wizard fled to the holy places in Kiev.

The two dramas then merge in XV. Once again, as if in foreshortened perspective, the same course is repeated, namely from calm to criminal action and despair and flight, but now at last, also to retribution. To this last chapter of the first part Gogol gives a close in which the drama – one now – is fixed for good in its cosmic dimensions. He relates how a whispering sound like that of a thousand mill-wheels in water has often echoed through the Carpathians. That is the gnawing of the dead in an infinitely deep abyss. And when the earth sometimes quakes from one end to the other, then learned men explain it as the effect of fire which has burst out from distant mountains.

But the old men who live in Hungary and Galicia know better, and say that it is the dead man who has grown so immense in the earth trying to rise that makes the earth quake.

Chapter XVI forms the second part of the short story. It is as if a completely new story were beginning, the distance between its first line and the close of XV is as great as possible.

A crowd had gathered round an old *bandura*-player in the town of Gluhov and had been listening for an hour to the blind man's playing.

A description of his person and playing is followed by the content of the song about Ivan and Petro. The tension rises in stages with each of the short fragments into which it is divided, and the song ends at the same point as the fifteenth chapter:

... the strange horseman still sits on his steed in the Carpathians and sees the dead men gnawing the corpse in the bottomless abyss and feels how the dead Petro grows larger underground, gnaws his bones in dreadful agony and sets the earth quaking fearfully.

This is not however the end. The mood of the last words of the *bandura*-player is fixed and expressed once again in the attitude of his listeners.

The blind man had finished his song; he began thrumming the strings again and singing amusing ballads about Homa and Yeryoma and Stklyar Stokoza ... But his listeners, old and young, could not rouse themselves from rêverie; they still stood with bowed heads, pondering on the terrible story of long ago.

We can now, after a short summary of the above, make an attempt to approach to a certain extent the meaning which results both from the form and content of this short story.

As regards their form, the first fifteen chapters of "A Terrible Revenge" are an extremely varied play of contrasts and parallels which proceeds in ever more violent rises and discharges of tension. The way in which the chapters are separated and connected is characteristic of this. The action is dominated by two symbols: the Dnieper and the Carpathians, each of which represents a world of its own. They are also the first and second plane respectively of the action.

The first half of the short story, apparently merely a mystery story, nevertheless borders on the anti-legend.[67] Since the use of this word perhaps requires to be justified and this also offers an opportunity to penetrate further into the short story, I shall now give a few arguments in favour of the choice of this designation.

There is no doubt in my mind that Gogol wanted to represent by the wizard the incarnation of evil and the counterpart of what is holy. This appears from the final chapter: Petro's last descendant had to be a sinner, the like of which the world had never seen. This also appears from the designation "antichrist".[68] There is however much more. Again and again a holy person or something holy functions as a counterpart to this sinner. His last crime, the murder of the hermit, is the climax in a struggle of evil with what is holy. Gogol calls the victim holy a few times in succession, the crime is committed at a holy place, the "holy book", the "holy letters" are indeed pregnant with holiness, they have a magic power.

Earlier indications acquire a special value in this context. Upon his first entry the wizard is unmasked by the power of the ikons which Gorobets has obtained from "a venerable hermit". Before his daughter he dares to allude to the great sinner who nevertheless became a saint, namely Paul. He himself wants to become a hermit. Yet, the criminal who speaks in this way is a prisoner – in the cell of a saint that is still so strongly filled with holiness that his own devilish strength is powerless to break the holy spell. For this, the help of Katerina, the innocent one, is necessary.

The personification of evil, the antichrist, the Judas (this is what the *bandura*-player calls his forefather) is Katerina's father, the only person who remains nameless in the story. Is he also guilty according to com-

---

[67]   See André Jolles, *Einfache Formen* (Halle/Saale 1930), p. 51 ff.
[68]   This word has in Russian not solely the meaning of a proper name, also being used as a term of contempt.

mon parlance? Andrey Bely, whose interpretation of "A Terrible Revenge" seems to me unacceptable as a whole, in spite of his many magnificent remarks about details, has to my mind very rightly answered this question in the negative.[69] The wizard is the bearer of Ivan's curse, bearer of the guilt of his family. He is more a sufferer than an offender, and becomes less and less active as his crimes accumulate. The point where the criminal becomes the pursued lies just after the first murder he commits, namely that of Danilo. (The murder of Katerina's mother is pointed out as previous history, but falls outside the action of the short story.) That is the meaning of the strange apparition at the end of the chapter which begins with the description of the Dnieper. It is in fact a turning-point in the action. Katerina's father had wanted Danilo's death, while he was forced to commit that of the child and Katerina herself. The murder of the child is the reflection of Petro's act towards Ivan's son. As a result of Katerina's death, her father becomes the last of his race.

There is in these crimes also externally a gradation. The murder of Danilo is seen to be committed as a deliberately intended act, that of the child is not shown, while by killing Katerina, her father is already defending his own life. There finally stands face to face with the hermit a madman who is dominated by an obsession. We obtain an indication of this in the second chapter in which Katerina informs Danilo how the wizard imagines that everyone is laughing at him. The madness of this is expressed in the laughing of a horse, in the seizing of all nature. Madness – at least if we have a right to speak for a moment in psychological categories, which is possible, as long as we restrict ourselves to the first plane. On the second plane it is not in the least madness that animals and trees should turn against one who has been rejected by the whole of creation.

Once again on the first plane, the wizard's atrocities are motivated by the incestuous desire for his daughter. Danilo has therefore to die, his son also, being the only one who still connected Katerina to her husband. There now however arises the question why incest, as the most terrible sin, is not committed. This question can be answered from the second plane only. In the wizard's struggle for Katerina, Petro's family shrivels up into itself. The sinful desire which leads to the lowest deeds without finding satisfaction is the gnawing at the tree of the family, begun before that tree had died. The "antichrist" does not get the "holy one" into his power.

[69]   A. Bely, *op. cit.*, p. 67.

There is a different question to be raised concerning this matter, and this has in fact been asked. It is the extent to which her father's incestuous tendency is pleasing to Katerina.[70] In my opinion, there is no possible doubt about Gogol's intention. At a time when people had no idea about psycho-analysis, he wrote down these words: "You don't even know a tenth of what your soul knows." Gogol could, in my opinion, not have indicated more clearly that he meant by the word "soul" the same as we mean by "the unconscious". He has, by comparing the objectification of Katerina's dream with the impression of that dream on her memory, once again clearly expressed the contrast between comprehending and unconsciously understanding. Katerina's objective soul, including the unconscious part, however adopts the same attitude of horror towards her father's desire as does Katerina's consciousness.

The opposite view is defended with much skill by A. L. Bem. He says amongst other things:

Gogol reproduces this [Katerina's subconscious desire] very expressively by means of the popular belief that the soul and body become separated during sleep. "Poor Katerina," says Katerina's soul, commiserating with Katerina as an independent living being, "she does not know much of what her soul knows."

It is clear [Bem continues soon after] that this also explains the suffering of Katerina herself, who in her unconscious surmises not only her father's tendency, but is also in herself not in a position to combat to the end the leaning towards him.[71]

On the contrary, all this would really be perfectly clear if Gogol had not rendered completely objective the extent to which Katerina's "soul" knows more than she herself and had not precisely represented this "soul" as being completely insensitive to her father's desires. Bely points out correctly that during the conjuring-up scene Katerina's eyes seek Danilo who is standing outside.[72] However obvious Bem's explanation may seem in our time, it is as if Gogol had had an idea of the possibility of this interpretation and had wanted to reject it with undeniable clearness. It may now appear difficult for a moment to find a motive for Katerina's liberation of her father. Yet, in reality, there is nothing simpler. She can do that precisely because she, the innocent

[70] I was unable to consult the article by V. Rozanov, "Magicheskaya strana u Gogolya" in Vesy, 1909. The question itself is, of course, not permitted according to Bely!

[71] A. L. Bem, "Dramatizatsiya breda", in O Dostoyevskom, I (Prague, 1929), p. 112.

[72] Op. cit., p. 60, 61.

one, is unable to comprehend her father. Her innocence is merely one more reason to see in her father an "antichrist".

One further important objection is to be made here. We can distinguish between what Gogol consciously wanted to say and what he expressed unconsciously. That is however something quite different from exposing the artistic motivation in the present work. In other words, the help of psycho-analysis is in this way involved a stage too early. "A Terrible Revenge" is, like any work of art, organised according to its own immanent set of rules, which is just as aesthetically determined as the construction of a symphony. In an aesthetic investigation we must try as long and earnestly as possible to discover this inner logic, just as we should have first exhausted all grammatical and lexicological aids before deciding on the emendation of a text.

If we try to visualise clearly the main outlines of Gogol's plan, then the design planned on two levels appears of decisive importance. The saga first gives the anti-legend sense. This saga is, in the final instance, the story of a judgment and one in which both brothers are condemned – Ivan to the eternal carrying out of his revenge, Petro to the suffering thereof. The end is stiffening, which the condemned persons can merely resist convulsively, a revenge in which the cosmos participates. Everything which appeared to be free movement in the landscape of the Dnieper, everything that resembled a play of human passion and faith and courage, is in the final analysis determined by a fate which leads to nothing but a bottomless abyss in a world of stone.

Thus, this cosmic short story of fate with its "Wendepunkt" (the first appearance of the avenger), its connecting symbols (Dnieper and Carpathians) and its two interdependent levels has become the embodiment of a philosophy of life. Of which?

When answering this question, we should bear in mind that nothing entitles us to consider "A Terrible Revenge" as a *complete* expression of Gogol's nature. Gogol has after all also been a humorist. If we accept, as Bely briefly states: "I refuse to have anything to do with Gogol's 'humour', to which Mandelshtam has devoted half his study, for something of that sort is unknown to me"[73] – then we simplify matters in an unpermitted manner. In this way, we violate Gogol's complicated personality and also fail to appreciate the special position which "A Terrible Revenge" occupies amongst Gogol's earlier work, even amongst all his work. He never again wrote anything of such

[73]   *Ibid.,* p. 70.

inexorable seriousness. It is most important to establish that we are here confronted with an element of Gogol's nature which we find in other works always to a greater or lesser extent combined with other elements, namely anxiety. We certainly find this in many of his other works. Anxiety undoubtedly lies at the very bottom of Gogol's soul, but what interests the literary man is precisely the multiplicity of forms in which anxiety is expressed and equally the host of other feelings with which it is connected.

When answering the question we are concerned with, Bely sought parallels in other works from this period. Shenrok had already preceded him on this path, but had drawn few conclusions.[74] Bely goes much further than he did. He was particularly struck by the points of resemblance with "St. John's Eve". In both short stories a Peter (Petro) occurs as a criminal, in both a child called Ivan is murdered, in both the perpetrator loses his reason. Petro in "St. John's Eve" also stands outside his family (he is even called *Bezrodny* – the kinless), just as the wizard, just as the other Petro, just as Gogol himself. This latter fact is then for Bely the hidden meaning, not only of "A Terrible Revenge", but of all the work dating from the first phase of Gogol's development.

... collectivity is shown by Gogol as by nobody else; he showed as nobody else the horrors which result from it, that a dead form of life and one not answering to reality maintains itself as the only permitted one.[75]

For this reason, the wizard is always denoted in the short story by negative descriptions. According to Bely, he is a "gap" in collectivity, a personality that is an unforgivable crime towards the race, the rigid race. Seen in this way, "A Terrible Revenge" has a clear social tendency, but it is at the same time the tragedy of Gogol himself, "a renegade from his race, his family, his class, the milieu which had produced him and unable to maintain himself in any other one".[76]

In my opinion, Bely sees the short story too much as a reflection of Gogol's inner life recognisable in detail and sees the drama of Gogol's life too exclusively as having been determined by social factors. As far as the first point is concerned Bely cannot, as I indicated above, do anything with Gogol's gaiety and he has to distort or ignore the light-hearted stories in order to make them fit into his

---

[74] Shenrok, *Mat.*, II, 54–69. He sees a relationship, in particular, in separate motives and compares "St. John's Eve", "Viy" and "Taras Bulba".
[75] *Op. cit.*, p. 47.
[76] *Ibid.*, p. 55.

scheme.[77] As far as the second point is concerned, Gogol had certainly become detached from his milieu, and this had painful consequences for him but, as far as I know, there is no proof that Gogol was at such an early stage conscious of having been uprooted in any way and that he would have felt it as an irrevocable fate. He certainly did not have any anxiety for revenge with regard to his social milieu. On the contrary.

The horror by which "A Terrible Revenge" is dominated certainly depends on a feeling of guilt, which was however so terrible, since it cannot have been conscious. This is why Gogol objectified his anxiety preferably in the form of a saga or folk-tale. If we now wish to try to find the basis of this anxiety, psychology should in fact be able to offer an illuminating word. If there is anything in the supposition we have expressed in the chapter on "Gogol and Anxiety", this would mean a clarification of the manner in which his anxiety has been expressed in this short story. The father-daughter relationship could then be a reversal of the son-mother relationship. This latter, a fixation in the Oedipal stage, may then have been the cause of a feeling of guilt without any recognisable reason, of an anxiety without a visible object. We remember here that the first person who had acquainted Gogol the child with the possibility of a terrible revenge was his mother.

The material of the short story now appears again in a different light. What was given to Katerina – to be innocent also in her un-conscious — remained withheld from Gogol. Katerina is however, if the above supposition be correct, also the representation of Gogol's mother, the object of his desire, an object which had at all costs to be innocent. The desire to which Gogol was doomed is objectified in the wizard. (Had Gogol himself not had the nickname of "the mysterious dwarf", amongst his companions, had he in his life and work not already adopted a number of guises, stranger than those in which the wizard appeared?) The guilt of Katerina's father is the result of a craving for which he bears no responsibility and also cannot bear any. His personality is already completely destroyed before his death. That craving cannot find any satisfaction. Gogol's consciousness obstinately rejects this possibility.

The desire is nevertheless punishable, even if the punishment is so cruel that God, the heavenly father, shudders at it. Gogol is not expelled and rejected by a dead collectivity which could not endure a personality, but is punished by himself, forced to his own expulsion and rejection

[77]   This he has to do e.g. with "A May Night".

because he, the guilty one, stood alone in his guilt. If this is correct, then we see in the creation of the wizard who becomes the victim and who is helpless with regard to an inexorable judgment, which crushes him while laughing, a desperate attempt to give form to his own tragedy.

All this is nothing but a provisional and incomplete indication. There is no question of this explaining the whole short story psycho-analytically. The connection between the first crime, that of Petro with regard to Ivan, and the wizard's guilt has remained completely outside this discussion. I shall have to content myself with a single remark. The first crime was purely aggressiveness, resulting from a feeling of envy, in other words of inferiority. In the case of the wizard, everything finally disappears behind aggressiveness, even the leaning towards incest. His hand is against everyone, and that of everyone against him, his deeds are no longer governed by his own will. It seems as if he is obeying a blind compulsion. Once again the feeling of inferiority is present, a complex is even unmistakable in the fear of laughing which threatens him from all sides.

Did Gogol also feel his own aggressiveness, which expressed itself – again an inversion – in his laughter, as hereditary guilt? We would assume that he did if we see how Petro's crime is a repetition of the first in the world, namely of Cain's murder of Abel. Can it be that this indicates the basis of all anxiety and guilt as being inherent in man, in the possibility of belonging to Cain's race? (The expression is Bely's.) I dare not decide. It is perhaps not superfluous to point out that for Gogol's great contemporary Kierkegaard, who was not a portrayer but a thinker, the concept of anxiety was bound up with that of original sin.

People have of course also asked themselves in connection with this short story where Gogol obtained his material from. In the first edition he himself called the story a *byl* (a true story) from olden times. Such a story is not however known in popular literature.

Parallels have been found amongst the German romantics. First of all there is "Petrus Apone" (also called "Pietro of Abano") by Tieck. A venerable old man, who appears to be a wizard, applies his arts in order to resurrect Crescentia, a dead girl, and to draw her to himself from the grave. The incantation scene shows an external similarity with that from "A Terrible Revenge", but is of course different in nature and purpose. This is the position with the whole short story – here and there a motif suggests Gogol, but the similarity does not extend further.[78] It is possible that Gogol knew this work by Tieck and that he borrowed a few features from it when creating "A Terrible Revenge", and that is all. The view held by Dauenhauer that there is a similarity in the whole composition of the two works is not tenable.[79] The writer cannot substantiate his conclusions except by diluting the real facts to very vaguely formulated abstractions and afterwards comparing them.

I shall choose only a few examples. Dauenhauer asserts: "Both short stories begin with a large popular assembly on the occasion of a family event in one of the best-known houses in the place where the action in each case takes place."[80]

This assertion would have conclusive force if there were not immediately added in brackets: "Wedding in the house of Gorobets, burial of the young Crescentia".[81] Many people will find the difference between a wedding and a burial more striking than the similarity.

Dauenhauer also points out that in both cases a female appears for a moment on the stage whom the reader cannot imagine to be the heroine of the short story. In fact, the position is such that Katerina is mentioned in passing and does not play any part at all in the first chapter of "A Terrible Revenge", while Crescentia occupies a central position with Tieck and is, moreover, a corpse.

If we are struck by such "similarities", if we moreover find some resemblance between the appearance of a respectable professor, whose boistrous students disturb a burial, but who comforts the family with a suitable word, and the unmasking of a monstrous wizard who disappears without a trace, then world literature probably offers a surfeit of similar compositions.

Once again, Gogol perhaps knew "Petrus Apone", a Russian translation having already appeared in 1828,[82] perhaps he also borrowed

[78]   See A. K. and Yu. F., " 'Strashnaya mest' Gogolya i povest Tika 'Petro Apone' " in *Russkaya Starina*, 1902, III, p. 641 ff.

[79]   See A. Dauenhauer, "Gogol's 'Schreckliche Rache' und 'Pietro von Abano' von L. Tieck" in *Zeitschrift für slavische Philologie*, 1936, p. 315 ff.

[80]   "Beide Novellen beginnen mit einer grossen Volksansammlung anlässlich eines Familienereignisses in einem der bekanntesten Häuser des jeweiligen Ortes der Handlung." See *ibidem*, p. 316.

[81]   "Hochzeit im Hause Horobec, Beerdigung der jungen Crescentia."

[82]   See A. Stender-Petersen, "Gogol und die deutsche Romantik" in *Euphorion*, 1923, p. 628 ff. M. Gorlin, *N. V. Gogol und E. Th. A. Hoffmann* (Leipzig, 1933), pp. 20, 21. Gorlin is certain that the motif of sinful love is not copied from "Ignaz Denner", but from "Petrus Apone". The distance is however fairly great between the love of an old man for a young girl and that of a father for his daughter. The current opinion makes a sharp difference, particularly as far as "sinfulness" is concerned.

the name Petro for his primaeval criminal from it, but neither this nor the construction of the short stories shows so much in common that one should think of a fruitful comparison.

The same applies to an even greater extent to "Ignaz Denner" by E. T. A. Hoffmann.[83] There is a slight resemblance between the wizard of this story and Katerina's father. The wizard in "Ignaz Denner" also kills his daughter's child. But again this is all. The function of the wizard-figure and the significance of the murder are in both short stories quite different.

I myself have not been successful in finding a source from which Gogol borrowed. I should like to draw attention to a curious parallel as regards a single motif only, namely the gnawing of the dead. In the 32nd and 33rd cantos of Dante's "Inferno" we find the vision of Ugolino who gnaws at Ruggieri's head. Both are riveted to the depths of the abyss of hell. Above all however: Ugolino in this way takes revenge on his murderer and that of his sons. It is, in my opinion, not impossible that Gogol knew this story, although we do not know when he first read Dante, for whom he had a great admiration in his later years.

2. *Ivan Fyodorovich Shponka and his Aunt*

"Ivan Fyodorovich Shponka and his Aunt" is the only story in the whole of this work in which neither peasants nor Cossacks occur, and it is just interesting enough to lament that it is not finished.

This judgment does not show much appreciation. It is the end of a criticism which displays little understanding, its author being Senkovsky.[84] It is, however, interesting because of its date, namely 1836, and because it establishes a fact which also struck later writers about the "Evenings". This short story differs from all the others in both collections through its material and form.

Gogol himself accentuated this difference by an introduction by Rudy Panko, in which he explains the vicissitudes of the text. He, Panko, heard the story from Stepan Ivanovich Kurochka who had even

---

[83] See Gorlin, *op. cit.,* p. 20. In a discussion of Gorlin's book Chizhevsky (D. Tschizewskij) rightly remarks that there are amongst the borrowed motifs many quite current ones which are not even restricted to romanticism (*Deutsche Lit. Zeitung,* 31st March 1935, pp. 555-57).

[84] *Biblioteka dlya chteniya,* 1836, quoted according to V. Zelinsky, *Russkaya kriticheskaya literatura o proizvedeniyakh N. V. Gogolya,* 3rd edition (Moscow, 1903), I, p. 143.

written it out for him, for Panko's memory was beginning to let him down more and more. Unfortunately the bee-keeper's wife, who could cook better than she could read, used a part of the manuscript to put her pies on. Panko had wanted to ask Stepan Ivanovich about the ending during a visit to his place of residence, but once again his memory played tricks on him – although he had placed a knot in his handkerchief and had blown his nose more than once, he was already quite a distance on his way back before he thought of the story. Now it has to make its way in the world without an ending. The reader can however easily call in on Stepan Ivanovich next time he goes to Gadyach.

We see that Gogol combines just as much as he separates by this introduction. It connects the story expressly to the others by means of the figure of Panko. It separates it from them by giving it not to the mouth but to the pen of another narrator.

It is necessary to draw attention to the connecting function of the introduction, for there are enough striking features in "Ivan Fyodorovich Shponka". It is possible in this story, which in fact appears to belong to quite a different sphere from the others, to see the beginning of a new line in Gogol's work and to catch sight for the first time in it of Gogol the realist. We can, without much trouble, discover in it analogies with later maturer work, with "Old-world Land-owners", with "Marriage" and even with "Dead Souls".

The introduction consequently confronts us with the following questions: Has the mention that the piece was written down for Rudy Panko a further meaning? If the content is realistic, why is it in the "Evenings"? Why was it not finished?

The answers must, in my opinion, be formulated briefly as follows: Shponka is in fact not "told" but "written"; it is a grotesque; it is finished.

We have only to pay attention to the title, the captions above the chapters and the constructional plan to realise that we are dealing with a new process.

The title does not point to a strange event, a curious place or mysterious time, as do those of the other stories in the collection, but simply mentions two persons. The first chapter is entitled "Ivan Fyodorovich Shponka". It contains nothing but a character sketch of the hero and two letters. In the first, his aunt requests him to leave military service and to come home, the second contains his affirmative answer.

The following chapter is called "The Journey" and describes little more than the meeting of Ivan Fyodorovich and Grigory Grigoryevich

Storchenko. This latter is characterised in detail. He turns out to be the owner of an estate which lies near to Shponka's properties.

No less detailed is the characterisation of Ivan Fyodorovich's aunt in the third chapter, which is called "Auntie". At the same time the reader learns here that this lady suspects Storchenko of having a document proving Shponka's rights to a certain pasture. She instructs Ivan Fyodorovich to go and demand this paper.

In the fourth chapter, "The Dinner", we see Shponka on a visit to Storchenko's, who has naturally never seen the document in question, but who does have two sisters, one of whom Shponka finds not unpleasant.

The last chapter contains "Auntie's New Plans". She obviously wants to achieve the status of grand-aunt in a hurry by a marriage of Storchenko's sister with Ivan Fyodorovich and visits Storchenko with her nephew for this purpose, for the moment without result.

That is all. No adventures, a very simple intrigue, which recedes before descriptions of persons and situations, in a language which avoids all extremes. The construction is very conveniently arranged, to the point of being schematic.

The story likewise does not start with lyrical or comic exclamations, any more than it places the reader suddenly in medias res, but it begins with a calm, carefully detailed description of its hero's youth. It creates the impression of objectivity, it never turns to listeners or readers, except in the very last sentence, and there only incidentally. It is "written", not "told".

Now a word or two about the characterisations themselves.

Although Ivan Fyodorovich is almost forty years old, his aunt often says in her thoughts: "He is still just a small child". He is fairly accurately typified by these words. We could merely add: "of predominantly female disposition". "Timid" is a word that Gogol likes to use for him. He is reserved and quiet, does not take part in the pranks of the other officers, does not drink any strong spirits, occupies his free time with the setting of mouse-traps or the polishing of the buttons on his uniform and requires nothing more than a letter from his aunt to say good-bye to the whole service and become a landowner.

Auntie is just as masculine as he is feminine. Having remained single, because no man ever found courage to ask her ("all men were sensible of a certain timidity in her presence"), she rules the country estate of Ivan Fyodorovich with an iron hand in the literal sense of the word.

She was of almost gigantic stature and her breadth and strength were fully in proportion. It seemed as though nature had made an unpardonable mistake in condemning her to wear a dark brown gown with little flounces on weekdays and a red cashmere shawl on Sunday and on her nameday, though a dragoon's moustaches and high topboots would have suited her better than anything.

The "child" Ivan Fyodorovich is of course like wax in her hands.

It is striking that Gogol continually places Ivan Fyodorovich face to face with figures who form just as complete a contrast to him. He contrasts in a similar way with Storchenko, his neighbour, also a giant of a chap, as smart, self-possessed and well-spoken as Shponka is credulous, wavering and untalkative. He is the third main character.

The position is however not different with the subsidiary characters. There is, right at the beginning, the inhumanly strict Latin master, who chastises him so unmercifully because he has for a moment succumbed to the temptation of a pancake. There is that whole wild regiment, in which Ivan Fyodorovich is as misplaced as an innocent girl in barracks can be. There is finally Ivan Ivanovich, a fellow-guest at Storchenko's, a man with an uncontrollable glibness of tongue, whose flow of words needs only one stammered remark by Shponka to break loose again at renewed speed.

The only person who is completely like him is his intended bride, being just as embarrassed and poor at speaking as her gawkish suitor.

Moreover, Ivan Fyodorovich acts with the mechanical docility of a puppet. He is a good pupil at school, does his military service with exemplary devotion to duty, immediately obeys the call from his aunt to leave the service, becomes an attentive landowner, does his difficult errand at Storchenko's properly because his aunt wants him to, and becomes upset only at the thought of marriage. His anxiety about it is symbolised in a dream, in which women oppress him on all sides. If the grotesque character of the story has not yet appeared from the above, then this dream, which forms its conclusion, is sufficient to prove this point.

First, he dreamed that everything was whirling with a noise around him, and he was running, as fast as his legs could carry him . . . Now he was at his last gasp . . . All at once someone caught him by the ear. "Aie! who is it?" "It is I, your wife!" a voice resounded loudly in his ear – and he woke up. Then he imagined he was married, that everything in their little house was so peculiar, so strange: a double-bed stood in his room instead of a single one; his wife was sitting on a chair. He felt queer: he did not know how to approach her, what to say to her, and then he noticed that she had the face of a goose. He happened to turn aside and saw another wife, also with the face of a goose. Turning in another direction, he saw yet a third wife; and behind him was still another. Then he was seized by panic: he dashed away into the garden: but there it was hot, he took off his hat, and – saw a wife sitting in his hat. Drops of sweat came out on his face. He put his hand in his pocket for his handkerchief and in his pocket too there was a wife; he took some cotton-wool out of his ear – and there too sat a wife ... Then he suddenly began hopping on one leg, and Auntie, looking at him, said with a dignified air: 'Yes, you must hop on one leg now, for you are a married man." He went towards her, but his aunt was no longer an aunt but a belfry, and he felt that someone was dragging him by a rope on the belfry. "Who is it pulling me?" Ivan Fyodorovich asked plaintively. "It is I, your wife. I am pulling you because you are a bell." "No, I am not a bell, I am Ivan Fyodorovich," he cried. "Yes, you are a bell," said the colonel of the P– infantry regiment, who happened to be passing.

Then he suddenly dreamed that his wife was not a human being at all but a sort of woollen material; that he went into a shop in Mogilyev. "What sort of stuff would you like?" asked the shopkeeper. "You had better take a wife, that is the most fashionable material! It wears well! Everyone is having coats made of it now." The shopkeeper measured and cut off his wife. Ivan Fyodorovich put her under his arm and went off to a Jewish tailor. "No," said the Jew, "that is poor material! No one has coats made of that now ..."

Ivan Fyodorovich woke up in terror, not knowing where he was; he was dripping with cold perspiration.

There are certain remarks to be made about this long quotation. As far as the content of the dream is concerned, the obsession with woman is reflected in a number of ideas of anxiety by the timid hero. The beginning reminds us of the scene from the beginning of the story in which Ivan Fyodorovich has his ear seized by his strict master, the only occasion on which he had forgotten his duty, this fact becoming decisive for his future life as Gogol mentions in passing. His aunt has now become physically so colossal as she already was for her nephew in the mental sense; it is his colonel (the third chief whom he had had in his life) who assures him en passant that he is a bell. Even the piece of wadding which hides a woman is a reference, namely to Storchenko, the brother of the bride to be, who always keeps something in his ear against cockroaches and has the habit of returning to this subject in every conversation.

The anxiety of being together with the woman is rather maidenly than male – opposite this is the male and, in particular, sober realisation that woman is something that one can be "taken in" by.

The formal importance of this dream will appear directly from what has been said. The preceding material is all recalled once again fleetingly in it, but now in a wild fantastic dance – the whole story is as a result transplanted to that plane from which one really has to view it. Here we find again, as is usual with Gogol, a *Sinndeutung* at the end, which in this case does not however refer to sense but to nonsense.

In a certain sense this grotesque is a "Wendepunkt" short story, but the romantic view is turned upside down. An existence that was even and flat is suddenly detached from its normal course by a trifle, but that trifle happens to be what in any case should be the great event, namely love.

From what has been said above, I think my view that the short story is finished, has also become clear. It is a, naturally again comical, example of the "open" form, for the conclusion reads:

Meanwhile a quite new design, of which you shall hear more in the following chapter, was being matured in Auntie's brain.

There we have for the first time a turning to the reader by a narrator who straightaway takes his leave with this promise.

Should one nevertheless require indirect proof for the supposition that this story is finished, then one should think of a continuation. A good analogous example is provided by "Marriage", which shows resemblances with "Shponka", and not only in situations. The hero is another Ivan Fyodorovich. The conclusion there is the escape of Padkolesin by the window just before the marriage is solemnised. Shponka would, however, figuratively speaking, always spring into his aunt's arms. A marriage of Shponka cannot be interesting at all; because he is nothing, he would remain the same.

Yermilov is certainly right when he remarks that it would be terrible to have to read a continuation of this story. The originality of the treatment of the subject lies, in his opinion, in the fact that the story is cut short.[85] As in all work by Gogol, Yermilov of course also sees in this grotesque a social satire. According to him, a novel could be written about every peasant of Sobakevich in "Dead Souls", but not about this contemptuous landowner.[86]

It seems to me that Gogol did not have any satirical intention with this story that he regarded as a joke without any consequences. In a joking letter to Danilevsky, who was in love, Gogol says that love prior

[85]   V. Yermilov, *Gogol* (Moscow, 1952), pp. 117, 118.
[86]   V. Yermilov, *op. cit.*, pp. 115–19.

to marriage is very much like Yazykov's poetry. It is fiery, but calculated for effect; after marriage it has to begin to resemble the deep,
grandiose poetry of Pushkin. Gogol then continues: "You have, I
think, already read 'Ivan Fyodorovich Shponka'. Prior to the wedding
he resembles the poems of Yazykov to a remarkable extent, while
after the wedding he becomes completely the poetry of Pushkin."

This work has however great importance amongst Gogol's output
for two reasons. Insofar as the story is idyllic, it forms a transition to
the "Old-world Land-owners" from "Mirgorod". Through the nature
of its humour it already suggests "Dead Souls". We have, on reading it,
continually the feeling that there is a small distance only between
"Ivan Fyodorovich Shponka" and Gogol's maturest work. It is however still the distance between play and seriousness. Here too, Gogol is
trying a form. Nothing suggests that he was conscious of already having
found a definitive form. The idyllic tone was to be used once again in
"Old-world Land-owners", the result being one of the most perfect
short stories in the whole of world literature. The other possibilities
implied in this proof were to remain unused for the time being. The
smile in this story is a smile with little tenderness, irony still has no
purpose.

In the second place, the story is psychologically interesting, also
because it is a play. Gogol has played here with his anxiety, something
which he was never to repeat again so jauntily. If we attempt in this
respect to see a further perspective, then the crazy dream of Ivan
Fyodorovich however acquires something oppressive.

Shenrok considers that there is in the embarrassed hero already a
foreshadowing of the poor Akaky Akakyevich in "The Overcoat".[87]
This is only partly correct. I should however like to point out that
here in the dream the woman is compared with a woollen material,
being something from which a coat could be made. We shall find in the
chapter on "The Overcoat" that this garment acquires the value of a
female being for the hero, and the drama he experiences with it that of
an erotic adventure.

The second part of the "Evenings" already points to the remotest climaxes in Gogol's work. With "A Terrible Revenge" such a climax has
in fact already been reached. "Viy" from "Mirgorod" will approach,
but not excel it. "Shponka" is, all things considered, the beginning of
Gogol's "realistic" work. It contains at once the warning that we must

[87]   Shenrok, *Mat.*, II, 288 ff.

be very circumspect with the word realism in Gogol's case. I am convinced that Gogol will indeed attack reality more seriously, but it never becomes his purpose to depict it simply.

It always remains the means to convince the reader that what appeared a familiar world is nothing but a puppet theatre, in which the puppets appear almost human, but are moved by demoniac forces.

CHAPTER III

MIRGOROD

Titles and title-pages are, in one cultural period, open and clear, in another humorous and playful. Sometimes they form a very concise table of contents, again they seem to be placed nonchalantly before a work and suggest something quite different from what really follows.

What would the associations of the average Russian have been with the name "Mirgorod"? Gogol gives an ironic answer to this question by placing two quotations below the title "Mirgorod, stories serving as a continuation of the Evenings in a Village near Dikanka."

Mirgorod is a particularly small town on the river Horol. It has one rope-work, one brickyard, four watermills and forty-five windmills. (From Zyablovsky's Geography)

Though in Mirgorod the bread-rings [*bubliki*] are made of black dough, they are rather nice. (From the Notes of a Traveller)

Readers of the "Evenings" could directly assume that this new book with a Ukrainian place-name as title would certainly contain something other than commentaries on a geography book or additions to the remarks of passing travellers; the provincial nest indicated in the mottos could not form the content of Gogol's stories. It does not either. Mirgorod is not even mentioned in three of the stories, in the fourth and last we do not hear anything about manufacturers or millers, any more than about bread-rings made from rye-flour.

Mirgorod ("Irenopolis" or "City of Peace" could be a translation of the name) is for Gogol the centre of that Ukrainian world which is the home of all his dreams, be they grandiose or tender, cruel or happy. He is well aware at the same time that this world is known differently in geography books and is invisible to hasty travellers. He is also aware of something else – this world no longer exists in reality for him either. This will however appear only from the further consideration of the book.

In spite of the subtitle, the stories from these two collections, which appeared in 1835, are not a simple continuation of the "Evenings". They are not placed within the framework of the meetings at the red-haired beekeeper's. The fiction of the narrators mentioned by name and nickname has also been omitted. In the first, "Old-world Land-owners", there is a completely new tone. This applies just as much to "Taras Bulba" which is really a small historical novel and cannot be discussed further here. Something else is however just as important. If we review the "Evenings", then only "A Terrible Revenge" stands out high above the rest. In "Mirgorod" the relationships are altered. "Taras Bulba" is in a later version only to expand completely to a large-scale Cossack epic, but two of the other stories have since their appearance been considered by connoisseurs as pinnacles of Russian literature. They are "Old-world Land-owners" and "The Tale of how Ivan Ivanovich quarrelled with Ivan Nikiforovich" ("The Two Ivans"). I hope to show that "Viy" is slightly less important.

Summarising then: the four stories which form "Mirgorod" show an increase in Gogol's mastery. They are as complete works independent of one another,[1] they show what Gogol was capable of as a short-story writer and already possess that inner equilibrium for which works of art are called classical.

1. *Old-world Land-owners*

As on an island of peace, the old couple Afanasy Ivanovich and Pulherya Ivanovna live on their little property in the midst of a patriarchal repose which is not even threatened by any ambitions. Their very simple existence is not disturbed by any material care, for liberal nature presents such rich harvests in that blessed land that the most unbusiness-like economy has no damaging consequences for people with such modest requirements. They live only for each other. Pulherya Ivanovna has no other care than the preparation of innumei-

---

[1] We can, with a certain amount of good will, see unity from the point of view of composition in "Mirgorod". The first short story ("Old-world Land-owners") and the last ("The Two Ivans") take place in a recent past, the author saying he has still known the main characters. In the first, this past is seen idyllically and, in the last, ironically. It is in both cases, however, seen with melancholy. "Taras Bulba" and "Viy", the second and third stories, take place in a historical past, both starting from the university in Kiev. "Taras Bulba" is however an epic, while "Viy" is a fantastic story in the sphere of the fairy-tale. The independence of the separate tales is however more striking than their mutual relationships which certainly also exist.

able fruit liqueurs and sorts of preserves, of endlessly varied pancakes and pies, and Afanasy Ivanovich no greater pleasure or more serious occupation than the tasting and enjoying thereof. They are completely happy only when they have a guest whom they can flood with delicacies and from whom Afanasy Ivanovich hears with childlike interest what is happening in the wide world.

An unexpected end comes to this idyllic existence when Pulherya Ivanovna feels herself summoned by death as the result of a seemingly unimportant event and yields without resistance to that summons. Afanasy Ivanovich remains behind like an orphan. Even years after, the slightest provocation is enough to cause him to burst into tears about his loss. He neglects himself and no longer pays the slightest attention to his property which visibly deteriorates as a result of shameless thefts by his subordinates. Finally, merciful death comes to him too. He dies, summoned by the voice of Pulherya Ivanovna.

A distant relative with "modern ideas", who claims the property as his inheritance, ruins it completely within six months.

This then is a description of the contents of a short story, in which what gives the story its charm has been omitted. The atmosphere in which everything is drenched is extremely important. We can merely try to approach this somewhat.

The beginning is particularly significant, from the first word, the personal pronoun of the first person: "I am very fond of . . ."

For the first time a subject which seems to show itself openly and wishes to express something intimate: its love. Then comes the object of that love:

I am very fond of the modest manner of life of those solitary owners of remote villages, who in Little Russia are commonly called "old-fashioned".

The adjectives "modest" and "solitary" recur in the following sentences; the predicate "quiet" is added with gentle emphasis. The whole of the introduction is a careful, very accurate fixing of the mood of the narrator and soon also that of the reader.

It is of great importance that the atmosphere which begins to surround them both should show itself continually as a contrast to another.

I like sometimes to enter for a moment into that extraordinarily secluded life in which not one desire flits beyond the palisade surrounding the little courtyard, beyond the hurdle of the orchard filled with plum- and apple-trees, beyond the village huts surrounding it, lying all aslant under the shade of willows, elders and pear-trees. The life of their modest owners is so quiet, so quiet, that for a moment one is lost in forgetfulness and imagines that those passions, desires and restless promptings of the evil spirit that trouble the world have no real existence, and that you have only beheld them in some lurid dazzling dream.

Is it solely the withdrawn nature and the quietness of rural life compared with the noise and panting unrest of the city? No, there are two elements which determine the mood even further. Gogol mentions them expressly. The last word he is to use to characterise this peaceful existence refers to an atmosphere beyond reality, it is the adjective "bucolic", the associations of which are further intensified by the picture which he connects firmly with the modest figures of his heroes, namely that of Philemon and Baucis.

The other element is the elegiac one:

They all have an inexpressible charm for me, perhaps because I no longer see them and because everything from which we are parted is dear to us. Be that as it may, at the very moment when my chaise [brichka] was driving up to the steps of that little house, my soul passed into a wonderfully sweet and serene mood.

Three things are notable in the last sentence. It is in the past tense and this is continued. Gogol distinguishes his feelings during writing from those while experiencing, and suggests that memory is more beautiful than reality was. And finally the expression "that little house". He has not yet spoken about his Philemon and Baucis and their dwelling. He is seemingly speaking about old-fashioned land-owners in general. His thoughts are in reality already with the story which is to follow. This is important, because the preceding passages acquire a different nuance as a result. When the writer says that he likes to lose himself in that atmosphere which has such an inexpressible charm for him, he is not thinking of a real visit he could pay to a couple of arbitrary land-owners of the old type, but means exclusively a yielding to a gently melancholy memory. He also finishes the introduction in its atmosphere: "It is sad! I am sad at the thought!"

It is as well to appreciate these simple facts, because they obviate a misunderstanding. There is, naturally, a sharp contrast, accentuated by Gogol himself, between this world and "the full life". As a result, we may be tempted to measure the bucolic world by the standards of the other one, and then come to the conclusion that the former is "empty". This conclusion involves a complete misunderstanding of Gogol's intention. The action takes place within the limits of those palisades beyond which no desire flits, in a closed region far from that full life that is propelled by an evil spirit, in time which stands still. If we wish to find a satirical tendency in this charming short story, then it is directed — not against the emptiness of a purposeless existence which was not great, not elevated, not even beautiful, but which knew love and charm – but rather against that "real life" which knows no peace and gentleness and has nothing to offer to replace the idyll than another emptiness which is ugly at that. The contrast with the "real life" which is rapid and passionate, also forms an essential constituent in the composition. Jokingly and in deep earnest, casually and with heavy emphasis, Gogol evokes that contrast at least twelve times in this story of about twenty pages. He does it in the first sentence when he compares the old-world land-owners with those old, tumbledown weather-beaten houses which contrast so favourably with the new ones which lack poetry; he does it again in the third sentence when he compares the quietness of their life with the demoniac drive of that of his own generation. A little further on, he compares their worthy obligingness with the insipid friendliness of the crawler from the fashionable world. Better however than increasing arbitrarily the number of examples, is to establish that there is a system in these comparisons. Gogol begins in the first sentence; seemingly unintentionally, he increases them on the first page to five or six. Thereafter, they recur sporadically only. For the most part they are facetious. Once Gogol has placed his readers in the bucolic world, he reminds them of the other only once or twice and with good-natured humour. Yet, towards the end, when tragedy has penetrated to Philemon and Baucis, we find the contrasts again, and now with great sharpness and worked out with serious fullness of detail.

After having reported the death of Pulherya Ivanovna, Gogol continues:

Five years have passed since then. What grief does not time bear away! What passion survives in the unequal combat with it?

There then follows, as an example, the story of a young man who had lost his beloved and, seized by an apparently incurable despair, twice tried to commit suicide. A year after his last act of despair he had nevertheless found consolation in a new alliance. Gogol then tells of the visit he paid to Afanasy Ivanovich after those five years. He meets him as a broken man, who bursts into helpless sobs upon trying to pronounce

Pulherya Ivanovna's name. Gogol once again draws a comparison. He asks:

What is stronger in us – passion or habit? Or are all the violent impulses, all the whirl of our desires and boiling passions only the consequence of our ardent age, and is it only through youth that they seem deep and shattering? Be that as it may, at that moment all our passions seemed to me like child's play beside this effect of long, slow, almost insensible habit.

And in the end, when also Afanasy Ivanovich has died, Gogol allows the final destruction of the beautiful world to take place through a figure from the other world. It does not matter in this aesthetic context that this person ruins the property through his reformations of an advanced nature. The final impression would scarcely be different if he had made a purposeful, business-like undertaking of it.

On what side is Gogol himself when he suggests this contrast? Ostensibly always on that of real life which is, after all, also his own. Only once, just before the end, do we find an identification of Gogol with his hero. It is the most mysterious part of the whole short story.

One day Afanasy Ivanovich ventured to go for a little walk in the garden. As he was pacing slowly along a path with his usual absent-mindedness, without a thought of any kind in his head, he had a strange adventure. He suddenly heard someone behind him pronounce in a fairly distinct voice: "Afanasy Ivanovich!" He turned round but there was absolutely nobody there; he looked in all directions, he peered into the bushes – no one anywhere. It was a still day, the sun was shining. He pondered for a minute; his face seemed to brighten and he brought out at last: "It's Pulherya Ivanovna calling me!" It has happened to you doubtless some time or other to hear a voice calling you by name, which simple people explain as a soul grieving for a human being and calling him, and after that, they say, death follows inevitably. I must own I was always frightened by that mysterious call. I remember that in childhood I often heard it. Sometimes suddenly someone behind me distinctly uttered my name. Usually on such occasions it was a very bright and sunny day; not one leaf in the garden was stirring; the stillness was deathlike; even the grasshopper left off churring for the moment, there was not a soul in the garden. But I confess that if the wildest and most tempestuous night had lashed me with all the fury of the elements, alone in the middle of an impenetrable forest, I should not have been so terrified as by that awful stillness in the midst of a cloudless day. I usually ran out of the garden in a great panic, hardly able to breathe, and was only reassured when I met some person, the sight of whom dispelled the terrible spiritual loneliness.

All humour has disappeared here; in other words nothing remains of that distance from persons and situations which Gogol otherwise continually preserves in the short story. Here he is one with Afanasy Ivanovich in his experience of the mysterious call from the world of the dead. In almost all Gogol's later short stories we can find a point where play ends, either for a moment or for good, and where the link between reality and dream or fantasy is at least indicated. What is more obvious than to choose that as the starting-point for penetrating into his intentions?

We could perhaps doubt for a moment the writer's seriousness when, turning to his readers, he assumes that they too know such a voice. That is, however, in no way the case. Belief in terror which overtakes man precisely at the still midday hour is old and widely spread.[2] I am convinced that Gogol himself knew such voices, not only because of the seriousness revealed by the quoted words, but because the phenomenon also appeared again with him, a few days before his death.[3] It is striking that he connects the memory of the call of death with his youth. We may, after all, assume that Gogol has painted Afanasy Ivanovich and his wife from types who still stood in his mind as images from his childhood days. They were probably his own grandparents.[4] It is known from Gogol's letters that anxiety about death was a constant companion of his youth and that it dominated the last part of his life. We also find it repeatedly in his work, precisely from this period, and here it is even described directly.

We know now what Gogol's children's paradise looked like: a place of complete quiet from which no movement emanates towards another world, but which cannot be cut off from the gentle, penetrating cries of anxiety and death.

It must certainly appear that too much stress is here being attached to a single passage. It does not however stand alone. We find its parallel at the turning-point in the story. Pulherya Ivanovna is also summoned

[2] See W. H. Roscher, *Ausführliches Lexicon der Griechischen und Römischen Mythologie*, Part II², column 2832 ff., under *Meridianus daemon*.
[3] See Kulish, *Zapiski*, II, p. 261, and Shenrok, *Mat.*, II, 849, 853. Gogol heard these voices at night.
[4] V. A. Chagovets, "Semeynaya khronika Gogoley" in *Pamyati Gogolya pod red. N. P. Dashkevicha* (Kiev, 1902), otd. III, pp. 3–71, has a few strong arguments. Apart from the facts already known from elsewhere, namely that Gogol's grandfather was called Afanasy Demyanovich and had also abducted his wife, he states having seen a book with recipes by A.D. in which there were all sorts of notes that were very similar to the wise words with which Pulherya Ivanovna sang the praises of her "decoctions". He also states that the neighbours of the Gogols are said to have been put out about the short story. He unfortunately does not indicate to what extent he himself checked the source of this story, which was apparently still being told in Vasilevka in about 1900.

by death. The immediate cause is of no significance. She had a cat to which she had become attached, without however cherishing special love for it. One day it disappears, it has yielded to the power of attraction of the wild tom-cats in the neighbouring wood. One midday Pulherya Ivanovna nevertheless finds it again in an emaciated state. She gives it food and puts out her hand to stroke it, but the animal again chooses freedom. That is for Pulherya Ivanovna the sign that she must die.[5]

There is of course no rational relationship between this story of the cat and Pulherya Ivanovna's certainty of her approaching end. Gogol stresses this by telling the story of the cat in a very amusing way. Pulherya Ivanovna is not however deceiving herself. After that day she languishes and soon dies. The fact seemed senseless as a symbol of death, but was not, really being its herald. This means merely that in this idyllic paradise and precisely here everything can be a symbol of death. Neither in the case of Pulherya Ivanovna nor of Afanasy Ivanovich is there however mention of fear of death. This exists for the writer alone. He experiences the mysteries of life and death in a way which is unknown to them, namely consciously and with reflection.

This same consciousness is in fact the basis of a characteristic of the short story which has so far not been considered, namely the humour we find there in all its nuances.

The way in which the old people express their love is humorous. Pulherya Ivanovna expresses hers in purely culinary language, and yet Gogol leaves no doubt as to the seriousness of her feeling. Just before her death, she does not prepare herself for it, she has only one care, namely how to ensure that Afanasy Ivanovich will miss her as little as possible. And her husband, seated at her deathbed, finds but one word: "Don't you want to eat something?" Yet, he mourns for her until she calls him.

On his side, love had expressed itself in still another way. He liked little bouts of teasing and used to frighten Pulherya Ivanovna with fantasies about a fire which could destroy their house or a war in which he would like to fight. When his wife, who no more believed in such possi-

---

[5] The material is borrowed from reality. Something similar had happened to the grandmother of Gogol's friend Shchepkin, who told it to Gogol. Communication by A. N. Afanasyev, quoted by V. Veresayev, *Gogol v zhizni* (Moscow-Leningrad, 1933), p. 147. — It is not inconceivable that this story also goes back to a youthful memory of Gogol, as told by Mrs. Smirnov (see above, p. 22, 23). The memory of "Old-world Land-owners" can however just as well have influenced Mrs. Smirnov.

bilities than he did, became a little bit anxious, he was satisfied. Here is humour in the fullest sense of the word. We smile because it is love which expresses itself in that senseless playing with childlike anxiety, but we feel a slight shiver when it soon appears that death announces itself in just as senseless a way.

Humorous also is the immediate cause of how the old woman met her death, namely the story of the cat which has run away and its love affairs with the wild tom-cats, which we must above all not confuse with the inhabitants of roofs in a city, but which are sombre and savage, devoid of nobler feelings and which miaow with an untrained voice. Here the contrast between "idyll" and "life in the world" is still casually set in a humorous light.

The humour becomes dry irony at the end when Gogol tells us about the reforms of the heir who still attends all fairs and always asks earnestly about the wholesale prices of agricultural products, but who never buys anything but flints and pipe cleaners.

Finally, humour is expressed most strongly in the apparent realism of detail with which the idyll is depicted. Gogol amuses himself with the thousands of trifles in which the dream is embodied, from the names and tastes of the innumerable dishes to the dirty fly-marks on the paintings on the wall which have become unrecognisable.

In order to give an example of this humour, I have deliberately chosen a quotation in which the gentle smile borders on gentle melancholy.

But the most remarkable thing in the house was the singing of the doors. As soon as morning came, the singing of the doors could be heard all over the house. I cannot say why it was they sang: whether the rusty hinges were to blame for it or whether the mechanic who made them had concealed some secret in them; but it was remarkable that each door had its own voice; the door leading to the bedroom sang in the thinnest falsetto and the door into the dining-room in a husky bass; but the one on the outer room gave out a strange cracked and at the same time moaning sound, so that as one listened to it one heard distinctly: "Holy Saints! I am freezing!" I know that many people very much dislike this sound; but I am very fond of it, and if here I sometimes happen to hear a door creak, it seems at once to bring me a whiff of the country: the low-pitched little room lighted by a candle in an old-fashioned candlestick; supper already on the table; a dark May night peeping in from the garden through the open window at the table laid with knives and forks; the nightingale flooding garden, house, and far-away river with its trilling song; the tremor and rustle of branches and, my God! what a long string of memories stretches before me then! . . .

The characterisation of the short story given here differs in all sorts of respects from both former and also present-day views. It is impossible to discuss them all in this study: I have chosen those which appeared to me to be the most important and those of which the treatment can contribute towards making clearer what I have said.

When in 1835 Belinsky wrote for the first time about "Old-world Land-owners", he was already full of admiration for Gogol's art. Yet, he needed Gogol's work for illustrating his own aesthetic theory,[6] which had been strongly influenced by Schelling. With the help of "Old-world Land-owners" Belinsky wanted to prove that it is completely immaterial what part of divine nature a true artist depicts. It suited Belinsky's argument to choose a borderline case. The less important the subject with which the artist achieved his magic effect, the clearer appeared the nature of art, the more powerful also was Belinsky's argumentation. The great critic was in "Old-World Land-Owners" confronted by two apparently conflicting facts: he had with his intellect to find that the heroes of the short story had not really led an existence worthy of human beings while, on the other hand, with his feeling he loved them. He was able to reconcile these facts by means of his theory.

... the nature of real[7] art consists precisely in drawing poetry from the prose of life and in moving the soul through a faithful representation of that life. And how strong and deep is Mr. Gogol's poetry with all its external simplicity and smallness! Take his "Old-world Land-owners": What do you find in it? Two parodies of mankind who, in the course of a few decades, drink and eat, eat and drink, and then die as is customary.

Where does the charm come from however? You see all the banality, all that is inferior in this animal, deformed and caricature-like life and, at the same time, you sympathise with the people in the story, you laugh at them, but without malice, and then you cry with Philemon about his Baucis, you share his deep, superhuman sorrow and you are angry at that good-for-nothing of an heir who squanders the possession of the two simple souls!

This comes, says Belinsky, because Gogol is true and simple in his presentation, because he has also discovered in the heroes of this "crazy comedy" a human feeling which causes them to live and act. This feeling is habit. Belinsky follows with a magnificent sally about this power in the life of every person, which we really must despise, but to which we pay all our debt. He ends thus:

[6] V. G. Belinsky, *Sobraniye sochineny,* pod red. Ivanova-Razumnika (St. Petersburg, 1911), I, column 147.
[7] Today one would say "objective art".

Mr. Gogol compares your deep human feeling, your high, fiery passion with the feeling caused by habit of a pathetic apology for a human being and he says that this feeling is stronger, deeper and more enduring than your passion, and you stand before him with lowered eyes and do not know what to answer, such as a pupil who, not knowing his lesson, stands before his teacher! ... Consequently the springs of our best deeds, our most beautiful feelings lie hidden there! Oh poor humanity, shabby life! And yet you feel sorry for Afanasy Ivanovich and Pulherya Ivanovna, you cry about them, about them who merely ate and drank and died thereafter! Oh, Mr. Gogol is a true wizard, and you cannot imagine how annoyed I am with him because he almost made me cry too about those who merely ate and drank and died thereafter.[8]

Belinsky himself apparently felt that he had violated the proportions of the short story for the sake of the construction of his argument. In an article dating from 1840, he speaks less haughtily and with warmer sympathy about the two old people and what he then recognises as their love.

He had in the meantime become a pupil of Hegel, even if he did understand this philosopher completely in his own way. He once again uses the short story as an illustration in an argument. Afanasy Ivanovich and Pulherya Ivanovna are very primitive phenomena of the mind and may consequently claim the predicate "real". The accent in their characterisation has been shifted quite a way.

Why do they attract you so much, these people who are good-natured but limited and who do not even imagine that there can be a higher sphere of life than that in which they live and which consists entirely in sleeping or eating and in giving to eat? Since these were people who, according to their disposition, were not capable of any evil, so good-natured that they were willing to entertain anyone until he could not take any more, people whose lives were so intertwined that the death of the one was the death of the other, a death a thousand times more terrible than a ceasing of existence, i.e. the basis of their relationship to one another was *love that became a habit which made their love more firm.*[9]

It is a pity that Belinsky, now that he saw one term of the contrast "habit-passion" so much more clearly, did not also throw a sharper light on the second. That is in fact much easier for us who are living later. We know that Pulherya Ivanovna occupies a completely unique place in Gogol's work. She is the only woman in it who is simply

[8] *Op. cit.*, I, col. 150, 151. – Chernyshevsky also has the deepest admiration for the passage about habit (N. G. Chernyshevsky, *Ocherki Gogolevskogo perioda*, St. Petersburg, 1893, p. 142).
[9] *Op. cit.*, I, col. 624. The italics are mine (F. D.).

lovable and nothing more, a creature with whom the concept of passion cannot be connected. Passion was however a feeling that Gogol
feared, because he knew that he "would burn to ashes" if that flame
were to take fire in him; a feeling that concerned the semi-super-
natural, semi-demoniac creature to whom he was never able to give a
figure of flesh and blood and which we can best get to know from the
unsuccessful fragment "Woman". Here imaginative power and rhetorical language overexert themselves to such an extent that the reader
no longer gains any single impression. He never depicted passion other
than as a "product of the evil spirit which moves the world".

It therefore follows that "habit", that faithfulness was to Gogol
an idealisation, belonging to the world of the dream. He himself did
not on the one hand feel secure from passion, but on the other, there
is nothing that this loneliest amongst men feared as much as a bond.
Even friendship in his life always came more or less from one side
and never completely from his.

Belinsky's words as quoted by me continue to haunt the literature
about Gogol, sometimes tampered with until they are unrecognisable.
Use is in most cases made solely of the negative aspect of his remarks;
with their help one can distort the tenor of the short story in whichever
way one wants to. People seek social criticism in Gogol's work and that
is found everywhere, including here.

Khrapchenko even exaggerates Belinsky's words. "The human
being is swallowed by the digestive process". The human features in the
two old people appear to be sketched in such a way "that the inanity of
their life is revealed even better."[10]

Stepanov considers that Gogol has depicted in a striking way the
fatal consequences of the system of serfdom.

At the same time, he shows in the figures of his heroes how even their
positive qualities of character acquire something monstrous in their expression and how they, to use Belinsky's words, degenerate to "parodies of
humanity".[11]

Yermilov goes even further. Belinsky had asked wherein lay the charm
of "Old-world Land-owners". "That secret lies precisely in the sad
thought that we have before us ... parodies of humanity." Gogol's
feeling is "melancholy at the vulgarisation (*oposhlenie*) of love", the

[10]   M. Khrapchenko, *N. V. Gogol* (Moscow, 1936), p. 61, 62.
[11]   N. L. Stepanov in his *Kritiko-biografichesky ocherk* for the edition of Gogol's
collected works. N. V. Gogol, *Sobraniye sochineny v shesti tomakh* (Moscow,
1950), I, XVIII.

whole short story is an "elegy, sadness about lost human dignity which is distorted to a caricature – not a malicious one, but nevertheless a caricature – of itself."[12]

It is likely that such remarks annoyed Chizhevsky, the learned literary historian and emigrant, so much that he forgot that Belinsky was not the culprit. At least, he begins by saying that Belinsky "has interpreted 'Old-world Land-owners' completely incorrectly, namely as a satire." Chizhevsky sees a didactic element in it:

This is in reality an ideological idyll; Gogol stresses the positive personal features of his old-world land-owners – their gentleness, cordiality towards friends, their hospitality – and above all their love, which is faithful until death. In the story that calm and unobtrusive love is contrasted with romantic love, this being passionate – and . . . fickle.[13]

It occurs to me that Belinsky said much the same more than a century ago.

Chizhevsky also considers he can find analogous contrasts in other works by Gogol, but this does not of course alter much in the interpretation of this short story.

For the rest, even in Russia itself, people sometimes seem to make a feeble attempt to break through the all too rigid schemes of interpretation. Pospelov, for example, who naturally repeats all the above-mentioned remarks about serfdom and the poor spiritual life of the old couple, ventures certain remarks which are worth mentioning. He finds that Gogol is seeking in the life of the Ukrainian nobility "certain positive moral principles and regretfully becomes aware that those principles used to be strong and firm, but are now rapidly beginning to disappear." Then that Gogol, who likes the patriarchal element, offers no criticism of the system of serfdom on which the whole of patriarchal society is based. Finally, he prints in italics that Gogol *"in creating a figure did not start from abstract moral standards, but from the typical peculiarities of the characters to be depicted."*[14]

The assertions themselves contain nothing unprecedented, but the fact that they were published in Russia in 1953 – even if buried amongst the customary clichés — can be taken as an encouraging sign.

The views of Eichenbaum and Gippius deserve more careful consideration. Eichenbaum was of opinion that we cannot take the initial words ("I am very fond of") or the whole story quite seriously, de-

[12] V. Yermilov, *Gogol* (Moscow, 1952), pp. 120–24.
[13] D. Chizhevsky, "Neizvestny Gogol" in *Novy Zhurnal*, 1951, p. 134.
[14] N. Pospelov, *Tvorchestvo N. V. Gogolya* (Moscow, 1953), pp. 94–98.

tached from the humour and even the irony which tinge Gogol's narrative tone so singularly.[15]

He refers to a letter from Gogol to Karamzin's old friend Dmitriyev, written in the summer of 1832, precisely at the time when Gogol was staying for the first time in years at his parent's house and collecting impressions for his new Ukrainian tales.

Gogol says in it that he is now living in the country, just as Karamzin has described it, and that Karamzin must certainly have been thinking of the Ukraine in his descriptions of nature. At the same time however (and that Eichenbaum considers most important), he finds that the people are poor in this exuberant nature, that the land-owners are beginning to understand that their salvation lies in industry, but that they cannot start anything because of lack of capital and are heading for ruin.

"These subjects and ideas are not expressed directly in this story, but undoubtedly form its basis", is Eichenbaum's opinion. He refers to the description of how the old-world land-owners are mercilessly robbed by the steward and the village sheriff, to the end, where the idyll is left for the realistic description of the ruin of the property, and he concludes that it is incorrect to see in the short story merely an idyll, just as it would also be incorrect to decide upon a predominantly "patriarchal manner of thinking" on Gogol's part from this short story. On the contrary: "In Gogol's development from the idyllic 'Evenings' to the critical realism of the comedies and the St. Petersburg stories, 'Old-World Land-owners' is tremendously important for overcoming the reactionary traditions of a sentimental idealisation of reality which predominated in Russian prose between 1820 and 1830." Eichenbaum also considers he has explained in this way the construction of the short story, namely that contrasting linking of idyllic style with comical situations and realistic details. The bucolic material of the idyll is rendered ironical in the story of the temptation of the cat by the wild tom-cats, the cat which complied with the romantic maxim: "Poverty with love is better than a palace."

Acute as Eichenbaum's explanation may be, his arguments nevertheless appear weak to me. In the first place, it strikes me that the quotation from the letter to Dmitriyev contains nothing new at all. Gogol's whole correspondence with his mother is one continuous testimony of the same view. From his school-years until his death, Gogol suffered

---

[15]   B. Eichenbaum in *Soch. A. N.*, II, 699, 700.

from a want of money, in the painful realisation that wealth lay at home for the taking, but could not be made productive. He continually tried to improve this, but in vain. It is consequently striking that the letter to Dmitriyev, after the general observations, as quoted by Eichenbaum, goes on:

I must say that it is hateful for me to watch the ruin of my mother's estates; if she had only a thousand roubles more, she could in three years realise six times as much as now.[16]

Economic advice to his mother, often childish, sometimes also very business-like, already dates from a long time before this.[17] A complaint, intended at the same time as a warning, about the lack of business acumen on the part of Ukrainian land-owners can be found in a letter dated 16th April 1831, i.e., a year before the visit in question and the letter to Dmitriyev.[18] It appears from this that Gogol, however much he may have idealised the Ukraine, never had any illusions in an economic sense about the excellence of patriarchal conditions. A new visit was certainly not in the least necessary for this. Does this theme in fact really form the invisible basis for the short story? I doubt it very much. In a somewhat different sense than Gogol intended it, one could say, to use his own words, that the old-world property in this

[16]   P., I, 219.
[17]   Thus the advice to use the clay that was found in Vasilevka for baking tiles (20th August 1826, P., I, 45). He likewise gives advice about the preparation of brandy (30th August 1827, P., I, 81) and the cultivation of potatoes (2nd April 1830, P., I, 151, 152, 160). Again and again his interest appears for everything which happens on the farm together with a very sober look at his mother's inefficiency.
[18]   "Be careful as far as possible about people who obtrude themselves in order to help you in the business, particularly if they have acquired a bad reputation through wrong actions, dissipation and complete ignorance of business notwithstanding their eternal bragging ... Our landowners are, for the most part, fired by a sort of Eastern love of ostentation: they keep a number of personnel, buy products which are quite easily replaced by those made at home and are surprised that their projects and new undertakings do not succeed, while they cannot keep any order in their home and farm as regards business and do not succeed in arranging matters so that expenses do not exceed receipts. It is exactly as if someone who had laid a foundation at random were to begin to build on it the huge walls of a building and then became angry if they shook. Oh, economy is a powerful thing: I should definitely like to send a whole lot of landowners to school in St. Petersburg. They would see how a huge household and business is administered by one person, and everything in the most perfect order; how prominent people know absolutely everything that takes place on their estates, pay out less than many who are not prominent and find much more satisfaction in the circle of their family than in clubs or at balls. No wonder that their fortune is growing constantly" (P., I, 175, 176).

story is surrounded by "palisades beyond which no desire flits." This settles the question. Such a secluded little kingdom was in reality scarcely conceivable. As soon as the slightest wish went outside its own field – to luxury, to machine-made utensils – then people were immediately confronted with the problem of converting the value of agricultural products into money. Gogol knew this since his school years: board, books, clothes, the money was always too late or too little for these, relatively small as the necessary amounts were. This childless pair wishes for nothing however, and the account of the thefts by the steward and his henchman, of the guests with their coachmen and lackeys, of the servants with their families concludes as follows:

Yet the blessed earth produced everything in such abundance, and Afanasy Ivanovich and Pulherya Ivanovna wanted so little, that all this terrible robbery made no perceptible impression on their prosperity.

That is not a veiled complaint against bad economy; it is the elimination of the whole concept. Within the circle of her daily field of vision, the motherly care of Pulherya Ivanovna in fact means very much: after her death the decline begins. Ruin nevertheless comes only when "reality" demands its rights and an "economist" appears on the scene, just as Gogol knew only too well, a man who makes demands on life and does not know how to put his affairs in order. He alone accomplishes in a moment what an army of thieves had not been able to achieve in years.

Dream, idealisation, this was the conclusion to which Gippius also came in his monograph on Gogol.[19] As proof of how remotely realistic the depiction of the details is, he cites with satisfaction Léger's remark that on the old people's property the elder blossoms, the cherries and plums ripen and the apples are dried apparently all at the same time. Gippius also quotes the letter to Dmitriyev, but in order to reach a different conclusion. "Through this reference to Karamzin, Gogol exposes the historical-psychological basis of his waverings, namely those between the individualistic rebellion of romanticism and the idyllic resignation of sentimentalism." He considers that there appears from the short story Gogol's consciousness of the contrast between his individualistic gushes and the attraction of the nirvana of the old-world land-owners and he compares Gogol's flight to the "chemical laboratory" of Pulherya Ivanovna with that of Pushkin's Aleko to the

[19]   V. Gippius, *Gogol* (Leningrad, 1924), p. 84 ff.

gypsies. Pushkin had come to the conclusion "Fatal passions are everywhere, and no defence is possible against fate."

"And Gogol," says Gippius, "answers the same, but replaces the passions by the habit which he could also have called love (. . .), and the second answer – against fate no defence is possible – he repeats simply by the fatalistic dénouement of the story."

In my opinion Gippius here goes much too far in his comparison. With Pushkin, fate is bound to passion; there is therefore no place where the Alekos can escape from it. They cannot, after all, eradicate their passions.

With Gogol, paradise must be devoid of passion in order to be able to exist, and it is indeed completely so and thus it remains up to the end. It is not however unassailable by death, which destroys it, in fact as a senseless fate which comes from the outside. The position is, in my opinion, that Gogol does not in "Old-world Land-owners" waver between two attitudes. The world of the idyll is cut off for good, and only by dreaming can one still lose oneself in it.

2. *Viy*

Amongst the baffling complex of Gogol's works, "Viy" is one of the most fascinating. Upon each new reading we suspect more strongly that there must be method in this madness and that it is the method by which Gogol's tormented soul is revealed in an extremely distorted way. The mystery continues to tempt us, but there is always the danger of losing our way. It is as if Gogol has wanted to destroy the traces which could lead to a discovery of himself, the danger he feared so violently. For what other purpose serve the few words which he gave to accompany the story: four sentences which scarcely have a purpose other than to repudiate "Viy" as the child of his mind?[20] Yet more powerful than the anxiety to expose himself must have been Gogol's urge for expression and he obeyed that urge, furtively, yet undeniably.

This work must then be understood as a veiled and distorted expression, as the product of conflicting forces, and it will be clear by now that an attempt to penetrate to its core must bear the character of a struggle with its creator. This has been tried several times already and

[20] "'Viy' is a colossal creation of popular imagination. Amongst the Ukrainians this name is used to indicate the head of the gnomes whose eyelids hang right down to the ground. This whole story is a popular tradition. I did not want to change it in any respect and I am telling it almost as simply as I have heard it." *Soch.*, I, 367.

now that it is to be endeavoured once more, grateful use will be made of the experience of predecessors.

Anachronisms in Gogol's terminology can only cause the very expert reader to doubt the period in which the story is intended to take place.[21] Its atmosphere clearly suggests the 17th or 18th century – a past, far enough away to serve as the background for a wild and fantastic action.

The world into which we are led is that of the Kiev Academy, whose students are, by origin, Cossacks, by training, theologians and, by nature, free-booters. Gogol sketches their life in a somewhat waggishly humorous tone, of which the following is an example.

They laid in no stores of any sort, but ate on the spot anything they came across; they smelt of pipes and vodka to such a distance that a passing workman would sometimes stop a long way off and sniff the air like a setter dog.

From this activity of learning, flogging, fighting and stealing, there broke away at Easter a group which made its way homewards singing and begging. Three of these holiday-makers, a philosopher, a rhetorician and a theologian, lose their way as night falls, but find shelter at a small lonely homestead in the middle of the steppe. The old woman who has taken in the wanderers has separated them from one another and housed them in different places, Homa Brut, the philosopher being in the sheep's pen. He wants to go to sleep, after having allayed his hunger with a stolen piece of dry fish, when the pen-door opens and the bent figure of the old woman steals up to him. In spite of Homa's attempts to avoid her, she springs onto his back; he feels himself powerless to resist her and runs outside with her. His speed increases steadily, his running becomes floating and beneath him he sees the steppe as a sea, from which a voluptuous figure of a nymph[22] rises up towards him. Slowly coming to his senses, the philosopher begins to mutter like a madman all the prayers he knows. That helps. His feet touch the ground again, he throws off the witch, now springs onto her back, she flies away with him, he succeeds in picking up a piece of wood from the ground and beats her until she falls down out of breath. In front of

---

[21]   There is repeated mention of the Kiev *Seminary* and its pupils. This was however not founded until 1817. Gogol probably had the Kiev *Academy* in mind. The name "grammatici" also points in this direction, being a class of pupils which was unknown at the seminary. The *bursa* likewise belongs in the Academy. See *Soch. A. N.*, II, 746, 747.

[22]   A *rusalka*, see p. 86.

him lies a girl of rare beauty who looks at him with tear-stained eyes. Homa flees, back to Kiev. There he finds neither colleagues nor victuals in the school-buildings, but he manages and finds company and a princely meal with a young widow in whose arms he forgets his whole adventure. Thus ends the first part of the short story.

A day later Homa Brut is fetched in order to come and sing the vigils by the daughter of a Cossack chief who is on the point of death and has mentioned his name. Nolens volens, oppressed by a vague feeling of anxiety, he goes. He is in fact the prisoner of the Cossacks who accompany him. The whole company gets drunk at an inn, the Cossacks become sentimental and Homa Brut would have made his escape if one of his guides had not obstinately wanted to speak to him about theology. After all, he himself is also more than a little tipsy.

During the night on which he arrives, the daughter of the Cossack dies, and the following day he recognises in her the witch who had ridden him. Her beauty is both enchanting and oppressive. During the night he is to read prayers by her in the church. At supper he hears all sorts of stories about the deeds of the deceased girl from the male and female servants. She has amongst other things drunk the blood of a child. She has also ridden on a male servant who was afterwards burnt to ashes.

In the evening Homa is locked up in the church. He lights all the candles. The silence is complete and he begins to read, louder and louder, while anxiety comes over him. He keeps looking at the coffin which finally opens, the dead girl standing up and feeling for him. In his mortal fear he draws a circle around himself and murmurs prayers. She lies down in the coffin again and it begins to float, but cannot approach Homa inside his magic circle. Suddenly the cock crows, and everything is normal again.

The following day Homa immediately drinks himself drunk. After the midday-meal he is in fact in an excellent humour and makes a nuisance of himself amongst the girls of the village. His fear nevertheless returns in the evening. The night is even more terrifying than the first. With her dead mouth the dead girl who has risen again utters frightful exorcisms, a draught blows through the church, he hears the rustle of mysterious wings, the scratching of claws along the iron windows of the church. It seems as if a countless multitude of monsters is storming the door. At last, the cock crows in the distance.

When he is released by the verger and comes outside, the villagers see that he has turned grey during the night. He tries in vain to mollify the girl's father who does not wish to discharge him from the duty of watching by the witch for the third night as well. An attempt to escape which he tries at midday is almost successful, but is thwarted at the last moment by the old Cossack Yavtuh. In his despair Homa gets drunk again and breaks like one possessed into a wild dance, but when he is alone in the church the blessed intoxication very soon leaves him.

Once again the witch rises up, for the moment the philosopher is safe with his senseless murmurings within his circle, although many evil spirits now support her in her search. There then resounds the call of the dead girl: "Bring Viy". It becomes quiet in the church, a giant, thick-set human figure is led in. His face is of iron, his eyelids hang down to the ground, he is completely covered with soil. He is led to just opposite Homa Brut. "Lift up my eyelids: I do not see", the Viy says with a subterranean voice and is obeyed by the spirits. Although an inner voice warns him not to look up, the philosopher cannot control himself and looks. "There he is!" cries the Viy and directs his iron finger at Homa. All the evil spirits pounce on him and he falls to the ground and dies.

Then the cock crows, already for the second time, for the first time the gnomes did not hear him. They can no longer leave the church and remain hanging rigidly in the windows.

Since then people avoid the building and no-one can now find the way to it.

Gogol himself explained in a note to "Viy" that the story is based on a popular tradition which he has reproduced as faithfully as possible. Nothing is then more natural than that an attempt should have been made to find out what his source can have been. Various investigators[23] have devoted their attention to this question and have in fact found parallels in Ukrainian and Russian folklore. None of them has however dared go so far as to indicate a specific version of a given fairy-tale as the prototype for Gogol's "Viy". The last who once again reviewed all the material and who achieved new results was V. P. Petrov in his commentary on "Viy" for the large Gogol edition of the U.S.S.R. Academy of Sciences.[24]

[23]   N. F. Sumtsov, "Paralleli k povesti N. V. Gogolya 'Viy' " in *Kiyevskaya Starina*, 1892. – Shenrok, *Mat.*, II, 69–78, 381, 382; see also the previously (note 49 to chapter II, p. 83) quoted studies of K. Nevirova and G. Chudakov. I was unable to consult the article by V. Miloradovich, "K voprosu ob istochnikakh Viya" in *Kiyevskaya Starina*, 1896.
[24]   *Soch. A. N.*, II, 732–748.

Petrov begins by reproaching all his predecessors with the same basic fault in method, namely that they regarded the whole material as being similar, while it is possible, according to him, to distinguish three different types amongst the various fairy-tales which come under consideration for comparison and of which there is a list in Bolte-Polivka.[25]

Petrov then paraphrases the contents of these types schematically and comes to the conclusion that Gogol very probably used a fairy-tale of the first type.

The folklore material is very extensive and it was not all available to me, so that it was impossible to verify Petrov's analysis in all its details. From the variants known to me it nevertheless unfortunately becomes obvious that the facts do not fit in with his schemes. A beginning which is, according to Petrov, essential for his second type occurs connected to an ending which would be possible only with the first. And with this, in my opinion, Petrov's conclusions no longer hold good.[26]

Another reproach which Petrov casts at the feet of two of his predecessors[27] is that they declared that all the relevant fairy-tales end well for the hero. Opposite these, Petrov places one variant in which the hero has to pay for his adventure with death, just as Homa Brut in Gogol's work.[28] Unfortunately, he does not paraphrase this variant and quotes only the last sentence: "When Spiridon had suffered the

---

[25]   J. Bolte and G. Polivka, *Anmerkungen zu den Kinder- und Hausmärchen der Brüder Grimm* (Leipzig, 1913–32), II, pp. 531–37.

[26]   According to Petrov, I always begins with a scorned love, the hero is from the same village or town as the witch, he causes her death and her burial forms the conclusion. In II, on the other hand, the hero has to come from foreign parts, the witch is already dead, during the third night he watches with her she is released from an enchantment, becomes a young girl and marries the hero (*Soch. A.N.*, II, 736, 737). Nevertheless, the beginning of variant b of "Rasskazy o vedmakh" in A. N. Afanasyev, *Narodnye russkiye skazki* (Moscow, 1897), II, p. 326 does not fit in with any of Petrov's types. Here, a priest's son sees how a queen takes her head from her shoulders. For the rest, the queen is, according to Petrov, typical of II, the fact that she and the priest's son are from the same town however belongs to I, that the boy is not the cause of her death belongs to II, and the further course of the story is characteristic of I. In variant c (*op. cit.*, 326–28), the hero comes from foreign parts (II), is in fact the cause of the witch's death (I), but does not disdain her love as would be the case with I. The rest of the story takes place again according to I.

[27]   Petrov reproaches Miloradovich and Nevirova with this, *Soch. A. N.*, II, 740.

[28]   Petrov (*op. cit.*, p. 736), it is true, speaks of "certain variants", but on p. 740 states: "only in one of the fairy-tales from the Sumy district does the young man perish."

torment, he went outside and died immediately." This gives us food for thought. One exception is enough to render the rule invalid, but if Petrov finds this exception so important, why does he not then identify the fairy-tale in question[29] with Gogol's model? Most probably because it differs in other details from "Viy".

For the rest, it should be borne in mind that the similarity with "Viy" of this conclusion is less great then perhaps appears at first sight. Spiridon dies after his adventure and does not fall into the hands of demoniac powers. This discovery does not consequently deal a very heavy blow to the general view that the fairy-tales to be compared have, in most cases, a happy ending and even have a comic character.

It certainly appears from the above that little of a methodic nature can, in my opinion, be achieved with abstract schemes. In order to give the reader an idea of how closely "Viy" is related to the popular tales, I can do no better than to paraphrase three of them.

1) A young farmer loses his way in the steppe, finds accommodation with an old woman who lets him sleep in the stall. At night she comes to him, springs on his back and rides on him. Then he throws her off and hurries off on her back until she falls down dead.[30]

2) A youth breaks off his engagement to a girl with whom he was at first in love. She visits him at night in the form of a cat, he rides on her and kills her. Then he is condemned to keep watch by her for three nights in the church. His mother advises him not to look up and not to give any answer. At midnight, the girl rises up out of her coffin. The young man pays no attention to her questions and when the cock crows she creeps back again into her coffin. The second night the same performance is repeated. During the third night the girl invokes the help of other corpses. A newly born child is then fetched at her request and finally a tarred stick. All these means are of no avail, the cock crows and the following day the body of the witch is burnt.[31]

3) Having returned to Kiev after fifteen years' war service, a soldier sees a girl in the market-place. Laughingly he calls to her: "You are a comely girl, but not broken in." She answers that the question is who is to ride on whom. His grandfather to whom he relates this, warns

---

[29]   B. Grinchenko, *Etnologicheskiye Materialy*, I, p. 71. This edition was not available to me; it dates from 1897. It is not out of the question that this fairy-tale was influenced by "Viy".
[30]   P. Ivanov, *Sbornik Kharkovskogo ist.-fil. obshchestva*, 1891, III, p. 202 ff.
[31]   A. Dyminsky, *Kazky ta opovidannya z Podillya v zapysakh 1850–1860 rokiv* (1928), pp. 55–56. (Quoted according to Petrov in *Soch. A. N.*, II, 737, 738).

him. She is to come to him at night, for she is a witch. He must however call out "Tprru – whoa, nag!" before she can say anything. This is done, she becomes a mare, he springs onto her back and beats her to death with a piece of wood. The following day the girl's father invites him to read the psalter by her body. His grandfather advises him to go, but to creep onto the stove when the walking of ghosts begins. This he does. At midnight the wind rises, the coffin begins to move, the lid flies off, and the soldier climbs onto the stove and mutters prayers. Devils help the dead girl in her search, but just when they are at the stove, the cock crows. In the morning the soldier receives fifty roubles from the father who requests him to come and read again that evening. Again on the advice of his grandfather, he hides himself on the stove on the second night and gets a hundred roubles in the morning. On the third night, even the "oldest devil" joins in the search, sees him sitting on a post, but poorly protected by a casserole bought specially for the purpose. The devils light a fire in order to get him down, but the cock crows just in time. He now receives a hundred and fifty roubles.[32] The conclusion of the story, in which the perilous journey of the soldier to the cemetery with the coffin is related, is of no importance for us.

If we restrict ourselves for a moment, bearing in mind these facts, to a broad comparison, then there is one thing that deserves attention above all others. "Viy" which has borrowed so many motifs from certain fairy-tales, even important features of its construction, nevertheless in no way gives the impression of being a fairy-tale, or even of being a free adaptation thereof. There are various reasons for this which can all be summarised into a single formula. In "Viy", Gogol has, in spite of his solemn assurance to the opposite, not retold a folk-tale more or less faithfully. He has, on the contrary, used material from a fairy-tale for writing a short story. That means that two genres have crossed here which, however often they may in 18th and 19th century literature be inextricably intertwined, form the opposite of one another.

Just as precarious as the definition of the "art" form of the short story is that of the "natural" form of the fairy-tale. It is however easy to examine in what respects they form one another's counterpart and this procedure gives precisely the results we are interested in here.

---

[32] A. Afanasyev, *Narodnye russkiye skazki*, 3rd edition (Moscow), II, 326–29. The fairy-tale comes from the district of Kiev.

André Jolles has studied this question in a series of original investigations and his results will be recalled in brief here.[33]

The first characteristic difference to be mentioned is that the short story has a well-defined event as its centre, while the fairy-tale, springing from one event to the other, portrays a whole course,[34] the second being that the short story endeavours to represent this event as possible in reality, while the fairy-tale continually moves in the sphere of the miraculous.

The third great difference consists in that in the short story a part of the world acquires form and that it now also represents or "presents" this piece of world independently, while in the fairy-tale the world is transformed, according to a principle which is specific to this and this form alone. This principle is that of the naïve moral – in the fairy-tale things happen as they ought to in the world; this does not mean that it is specially virtue which is always rewarded and evil that is punished, but it is the injured person who scores off the privileged, the weak one who gets the better of the strong one, the despised man who marries the king's daughter. In contrast to the short story, reality is consequently destroyed in the fairy-tale, and it further follows from this that the miracle is in this form of literature not marvellous, but obvious and necessary.[35]

Finally, the short story as an "art" form is once and for all fixed by an artist, while the fairy-tale as a "simple form" can be repeated again and again by another "in his own words".

If we now compare "Viy" from these points of view with the fairy-tales quoted, we are confronted by a number of differences. It is particularly instructive to make immediately a comparison between the beginning of "Viy" and that of the fairy-tales.

"A man loses his way in the steppe and finds accommodation with an old woman", "a lover makes an end to a love affair", "a soldier

[33] André Jolles, *Bezieling en Vorm* (Haarlem, 1923), pp. 40–115; „Het sprookje" in *Handelingen van de Maatschappij der Nederlandsche Letterkunde,* 1923–24, pp. 18–42, *Einfache Formen* (Halle/Saale, 1929), pp. 218–46.
[34] This contrast is somewhat too sharp. Jolles is thinking in the first place of the Tuscan short story, particularly of the Decamerone. The point is, for the rest, of very little importance, and I have mentioned it merely for the sake of completeness.
[35] Concerning the concept „naïve moral" see *Handelingen van de Mij. der Ned. Lett.,* 1923–24, pp. 26–29. Jolles is generalising here, with the reservation, however, of "a small minority of exceptions" for Western European fairy-tales. Whether the rule also continues to serve, need not be discussed; it does certainly for the fairy-tales under discussion.

returns from war" – in this way we can summarise in one sentence
the beginning of each of the three fairy-tales. The three situations
indicated in this way are in reality quite conceivable, and the beginning
of "Viy" which can be paraphrased by the same words as the beginning
of the first fairy-tale, does not deviate in any respect therefrom. This
nevertheless applies only as long as we regard matters schematically.
Things become quite different as soon as we relate the beginning to what
follows, in other words, when we begin to pay attention to its function.

The fairy-tales apparently start in everyday reality; in the third this
is even localised very exactly for a fairy-tale, not "somewhere", not
"in a distant land", but "in Kiev". Yet, as soon as the action has
started, this reality no longer matters. The real Kiev no longer has
any further importance in the fairy-tale. Not only do we meet a witch
in the market-place in broad daylight, but when she is dead, no priest
and no church from the holy city interferes, her father turning to
a dismissed soldier – who later also takes care of the burial on his
own at midnight. In a word, reality has been deformed completely
according to the rules of the fairy-tale. We can also formulate it as
follows: the reality in which the fairy-tale seems to begin and the
struggle with the demons which form its main content, the grandfather
and the witch, the casserole and the oldest devil, all belong to the same
world. It lies in one plane and has nothing in common with what in
everyday life we are accustomed to call "reality".

Coupled with this is the slight importance which should be attached to the individualisation of the persons and the localisation of the
place. We can replace Kiev by Poltava, the soldier by a priest's son or
a pedlar, the grandfather by a grandmother, without thereby changing
anything of the nature of the fairy-tale. This mobility is a regular feature of the "simple form". It is what Jolles calls its "Jedesmaligkeit"
(general applicability).

Can we in the beginning of "Viy" notice anything of an attempt at
least to approach this form? There is little evidence of this.

"There was once a soldier who had served God and the great Tsar
for fifteen years..." thus begins Afanasyev's fairy-tale, our third
example. – "As soon as the rather musical seminary bell which hung
at the gate of the Bratsky Monastery rang out every morning in
Kiev..." That is the beginning of "Viy".

Compared with the general formula, there is a stylistic swing which
is conventional enough, but as such is typical of a literary beginning.
It is the customary trick by which the reader is brought in medias res.

What follows confirms this first impression. The third sentence is so excessively long (61 words) that we cannot imagine it being spoken. The fourth contains, in its comparison of the scratches and bruises on the faces of the rhetoricians with rhetorical tropes, an imagery which would never come into the mind of a popular narrator. The construction of the last part of the sixth sentence is scarcely conceivable in spoken language.[36] The whole is a piece of pure artistic prose of such a personal style that we can with unfailing certainty recognise the capricious author in it.

We do not however need to stop at this stylistic observation. If we read further on, we gain more and more strongly the feeling of being confronted with a historical short story. The milieu in which the students of the Kiev Academy live, the way in which they amuse themselves and provide themselves with the necessities of life, is all depicted, with broad strokes it is true, but as if it were a question of reality. It is in fact that for Gogol. He has, with material borrowed chiefly from Narezhny's "Bursak", that is to say literary material, given a definite picture of the historical past which is to a large extent his own, in spite of the borrowings.[37] He has, in other words, suggested a strong illusion of reality.

When the real intrigue begins and he starts to use fairy-tale material, no essential change is made. The miraculous element does not enter into the world of the philosopher in the attitude of a fairy-tale, as if it were completely at home there. On the contrary, it begins by adapting itself as far as possible to the customary idea of reality. In what form do people experience miracles daily and do they also grant them a certain recognition? Only in one, namely in that of the dream. The miracle in "Viy" does not however simply appear in the form of a dream. What was just as much in Gogol's mind, was a representation of that demoniacally miraculous element as a reality. He does not consequently represent the first adventure with the witch as a dream, but merely gives the reader suggestions in that direction. The more trained the reader is, the more certain he is to become the victim of it.

The latter, on finding himself alone, instantly devoured the carp, examined the hurdle-walls of the pen, kicked an inquisitive pig that woke up and

---

[36] ". . . ot nikh slyshalas trubka i gorelka, inogda tak daleko, chto prokhodivshy mimo remeslennik dolgo yeshche, ostanovivshis, nyukhal, kak gonchaya sobaka, vozdukh."

[37] Published anew by V. Pereverzev: V. T. Narezhny, *Izbrannye romany* (Moscow-Leningrad 1933), pp. 235–657.

thrust its snout in from the next pen, and turned over on his right side to fall into a sound sleep.

Each part of this sentence describes a piece of tangible reality which can be fixed exactly. The last section has however not been translated literally: *"chtoby zasnut mertvetski"* is the Russian. *Mertvetski* is derived from the word *mertvets* meaning "corpse". It is quite usual for indicating a sound sleep, complete drunkenness, and yet, we regret here the lack of a pure equivalent, in which there should also be expressed the basic meaning "like a dead person". The other difficult word *chtoby* is precisely rendered by "in order to". It leaves a slight doubt: is Homa really falling asleep?

All at once the low door opened, and the old woman bending down stepped into the pen.

"What is it, granny, what do you want?" said the philosopher.

But the old woman came towards him with outstretched arms.

"Aha, ha!" thought the philosopher. "No, my dear, you are too old!"

He turned a little away, but the old woman unceremoniously approached him again.

"Listen, granny!" said the philosopher. "It's a fast time now; and I am a man who wouldn't sin in a fast for a thousand golden pieces."

But the old woman opened her arms and tried to catch him without saying a word.

The philosopher was frightened, especially when he noticed a strange glitter in her eyes. "Granny, what is it? Go – go away – God bless you!" he cried.

The old woman said not a word, but tried to clutch him in her arms.

He leapt on to his feet, intending to escape; but the old woman stood in the doorway, fixed her glittering eyes on him and again began approaching him.

The philosopher tried to push her back with his hands, but to his surprise found that his arms would not rise, his legs would not move, and he perceived with horror that even his voice would not obey him; words hovered on his lips without a sound. He heard nothing but the beating of his heart. He saw the old woman approach him. She folded his arms, bent his head down, leapt with the swiftness of a cat upon his back.

That creature which approaches silently, which is avoided in vain, that anxiety, that sudden powerlessness to use limbs and tongue – these are indications of a nightmare. And the philosopher's words, "Aha! she's a witch!", are not such as to help the reader change his mind.

The uncertainty is expressed in the description of the floating and the vision of the *rusalka*, in which the words occur: "Did he see this or did he not? Was he awake or dreaming?"

Only when Homa is standing on the ground again and the witch is lying in front of him does the reader know: it was . . . well, in any case not a dream. Homa might however in the meantime lose something of his reality, get on the way to becoming the hero of a fairy-tale. Gogol prevents that at the same moment.

He stood up and looked into her face (there was the glow of sunrise, and the golden domes of the Kiev churches were gleaming in the distance): before him lay . . ., etc.

There emerges as a matter of course in the section in brackets the demand to see what has happened as being real. It is as if Homa not only comes back to earth, but that he is caught up in reality.

He flees back to the real Kiev and finds with a carnal young widow, who sells ribbons and is wearing a yellow jacket consolation for what could look like a dream, but which had been another reality.

We can however replace the awkward indications "normal" and "other" reality by two words which have a special usefulness because of their associations, namely "day" and "night". They are in this story symbols of the two worlds. "At night everything becomes different from during the day", that is, expressed as vaguely as possible, Homa's experience. Not only the appearance and course of worldly things change at night, but he himself also becomes a different being.

We can consequently paraphrase the first part of the short story as follows: it was day, it became night and thereafter day once again. Is the second day the same as the first? Has something changed in Homa?

That same evening the philosopher was seen in a tavern: he was lying on the bench, smoking a pipe as his habit was, and in the sight of all he flung the Jew who kept the house a gold coin. A mug stood before him. He looked at all that came in and went out with eyes full of cool satisfaction, and thought no more of his extraordinary adventure.

These words form the end of the first part.

The division into two parts will no doubt have been borrowed from the fairy-tales. The same also applies to the subdivision of what follows. The three nights and their gradation of terrors are also a feature of the fairy-tales. Yet there is a great difference. In the fairy-tales day has but one significance: it brings counsel. This does not happen in "Viy". Homa misses nothing as much as an advisor.[38] The day is certainly

---

[38]   This has already been noted before, e.g. by Nevirova.

described, and something takes place which is missing in the fairy-tales: night slowly penetrates the world of day and takes possession of it. For it is merely an illusion that Homa Brut has again become his former self. During that first terrible night he became acquainted with something that penetrated his being and which is to demolish it completely, namely anxiety. The black shadow continually grows larger and larger – at the end of the story the world of day has been done away with.

There is certainly no lack of detail in the description of the first two days from the second part, which merge into one another, being scarcely separated by a night of unconscious drunkenness.

Homa's conversation with the Cossacks, the scene in the inn, the description of the Cossack village – everything is done fully and realistically. The scenes are steeped in a bright and shining light.

There are however dark patches. There is the mysterious premonition of Homa who really does not want to go. There is a first unreasoned attempt to escape. During the night of his arrival something happens, without his knowledge, something decisive: the girl dies. And although he does not know why, Homa wants to escape in the morning. He is however stopped by the old Cossack Yavtuh. Then there comes the recognition of the witch in the dead girl and there finally follow the conversations in the kitchen during which the philosopher can compare his experiences with those of others.

We must follow everything carefully to see how gradually the rise is brought about. Each effect is immediately subdued again. That of Homa's refusal and being carried off as a prisoner through the humorous scene in the inn, the failure of his first attempt at escape through the comic description of his own drunkenness.

It is doubtful, however, whether the escape could have taken place, for when the philosopher tried to get up from the table his legs seemed to have become wooden, and he began to perceive such a number of doors in the room that he could hardly discover the real one.

The last and most powerful penetration of the nocturnal elements, before night really falls, are the conversations in the kitchen from which Homa learns exactly about the person with whom he has to deal and also hears the stories about the dog-boy Mikita who was burnt to ashes and the woman who with her child became the victim of the witch. These stories are however introduced in a comic fashion, are interrupted by comic intermezzi and concluded with a few sentences

which render the seriousness of what has gone before even more
doubtful.

The subject of the witch seemed inexhaustible. Each in turn hastened to
tell some tale of her. One had seen the witch in the form of a haystack
come right up to the door of his cottage; another had had his cap or his
pipe stolen by her; many of the girls in the village had had their hair cut
off by her; others had lost several quarts of blood sucked by her.

Certainty comes during the night. Its slow approach and the gradual
creeping up of Homa's anxiety are described with perfect mastery.
There is first the mystery of the dim church and Homa's resistance to
the feelings aroused thereby.

"Well," he said, "what is there to be afraid of here? No living man can
come in here, and to guard me from the dead and ghosts from the other
world I have prayers that I have but to read aloud to keep them from
laying a finger on me."

He tries to cling to day as long as possible. He lights all the candles he
finds on the lectern:

I must light up the whole church so that it may be as bright as by daylight. Oh, it is a pity that one must not smoke a pipe in the temple of God!"

The night has been repelled somewhat, but . . .

Only overhead the darkness seemed more profound, and the gloomy ikons
looked even more sullenly out of their carved frames.

The dead girl is standing in the full light and looking at him with
closed eyes. He begins to read aloud with a voice that finds no echo in
the deathly silence.

"What is there to be afraid of?" he was saying meanwhile to himself. "She
won't rise up out of her coffin, for she will fear the word of God. Let her
lie there! And a fine Cossack I am, if I should be scared. Well, I've drunk
a drop too much — that's why it seems dreadful. I'll have a pinch of snuff.
Fine snuff, good snuff!"
  Raising his voice, he began singing in various keys, trying to drown the
fears that still lurked in him, but every minute he turned his eyes to the
coffin, as though asking, in spite of himself: "What if she does sit up, if
she gets up?" But the coffin did not stir. If there had but been some sound!
some living creature! There was not so much as a cricket churring in the
corner! There was nothing but the faint splutter of a far-away candle, the
light tap of a drop of wax falling on the floor.
  "What if she were to get up . . . ?"
  She was raising her head . . .

The distance which lies between this beginning and the end of the night is expressed in a symbol. Before he begins his prayers Homa has once again looked at the girl who lies there in perfect beauty. Death has not imprinted any stamp on her features. She who is standing before him has the blue cadaverous colour of one who has already been dead for days. A world has indeed passed away.

Is the certainty now complete? The philosopher throws himself dead-tired onto his bed and sleeps until it is time to eat. "When he woke up, all the events of the night seemed to him to have happened in a dream." The day resumes its full rights. The philosopher drinks brandy like water, devours almost alone quite a large sucking-pig and afterwards gets into a tender pleasant mood . . . "Lying down with his pipe in his teeth he watched them all with a honied look in his eyes and kept spitting to one side." He does not speak about his adventure. " 'Yes, all sorts of strange things happened,' " is his only reply to the inquisitive people. Only after eating does his mood become really good. He goes out into the village and plays Adonis so palpably that he is thrown out of the door at two places, a young woman having to take a spade to prevent him from a further examination of the material of her jacket.

Yet, the nearer evening comes the more silent Homa Brut becomes. Before the evening meal, the Cossacks are amusing themselves with a sort of game of skittles. The winner has the right to ride about on the back of the loser. Does this arouse associations for the philosopher? "Homa tried in vain to give himself up to this game; some gloomy thought stuck in his head like a nail." After supper, his anxiety increases with the darkness which extends over the sky.

The same old Cossack Yavtuh who had prevented him from escaping accompanies him to the church. Things now happen differently there. There is no question of slowing down and gradually raising the tension. Night already has Homa in her power. This appears from the way in which he inspires himself with courage.

"Well," he said to himself, "now there's nothing marvellous to me in this marvel. It was only alarming the first time. Yes, it was only rather alarming the first time, and even then it wasn't so alarming; now it's not alarming at all."

He goes to the lectern, draws a circle around himself and reads for an hour without looking up. Then he wants to take a pinch of snuff, but first looks cautiously in the direction of the coffin. "His heart turned cold; the corpse was already standing before him on the very edge of the circle."

Then the tension proceeds very quickly. Her exorcisms begin to sound against his own, a hoarse murmur of words "like the bubbling of boiling pitch". And at these words a wind passed through the church "and there was a sound as of a multitude of flying wings." The monsters clatter in vain with their wings against the windows, force themselves in vain against the door, but when dawn comes, a man is found in the church on the point of death.

He was leaning with his back against the wall, while with his eyes almost starting out of his head, he stared at the Cossacks as they came in.

There now follows the last day, which is nothing but a last resistance against the grip of night. It is violent and protracted and is described with tormenting precision. The result is certain before it has even begun. Homa Brut already bears a permanent mark of the night: half his hair has suddenly turned grey. This extremely conventional way of indicating the intensity of anxiety which has been experienced ac-quires a very singular stress. The fact is found – not by the Cossacks who fetch him from the church, not by the frightened group which has formed around him when he stammers out his terror in a few words, but by a vain and seductive female who comes along by chance and whose image Gogol has set down in a long sentence. Homa Brut verifies it in front of a triangular fragment of a fly-blown mirror hanging in the kitchen and concerning which the reader is requested to note carefully the forget-me-nots stuck in front of it and the marigolds around it – in a word reality.

Homa tries to escape his fate in a quite natural way by talking over the Cossack chief. This dialogue is reproduced completely and not without comic force. All the dialogues in "Viy" are comical. They accordingly have their place in the day. In common with the others, this one also has a macabre undertone.

When this attempt has failed, Homa decides to flee at any cost. There is also a gradation in his attempts to escape. The first remained but a desire, the second stopped just as it was to be put into operation, while this last attempt seems to be going to succeed. Homa Brut is, he thinks, already a long way into the steppe when he hears the voice of Yavtuh near him. He has described a wide arc and is almost back at his starting-point. He is himself caught within a circle!

Then comes the extreme, convulsive defence.

"Though, after all, what am I thinking about? What am I afraid of? Am I not a Cossack?"

The whole Cossack wants to show himself once again. He drinks with his friend Dorosh almost a half pailful

so that the philosopher, getting on to his feet, shouted: "Musicians! I must have musicians!" and without waiting for the latter fell to dancing a *tropak*[39] in a clear space in the middle of the yard. He danced till it was time for the afternoon snack, and the servants who stood round him in a circle, as is the custom on such occasions, at last spat on the ground and walked away, saying: "Good gracious, what a time the fellow keeps it up!" At last the philosopher lay down to sleep on the spot, and good sousing of cold water was needed to wake him up for supper. At supper he talked of what it meant to be a Cossack, and how he should not be afraid of anything in the world.

"Time is up," said Yavtuh, "let us go."
[The Cossacks walk to the church through a hellishly dark night and the victory of night takes place inside.]
"I won't be afraid; by God, I will not!"

Yet the words he reads are quite different from those in the holy texts.
"All of a sudden . . . in the midst of the stillness . . . the iron lid of the coffin burst with a crash and the corpse rose up." A whirlwind swept through the church, "the ikons fell to the ground, broken glass came flying down from the windows. The doors were burst from their hinges and a countless multitude of monstrous beings trooped into the church of God." The wall of the sacred is stormed and taken, only the last, the narrowest circle around the philosopher still stands firm. It too is finally broken through from the inside, anxiety forcing Homa to look Viy in the eyes.

The last picture of the struggle is the fatal embracing of day and night, a nightmare in stone: the gnomes and monsters stuck firmly for ever in the doors and windows of the sanctuary – this being desecrated and enfeebled, they being fixed eternally in the victory of death.

It is not without significance to know that this picture was originally intended as the conclusion to the short story.

Only by chance was Gogol compelled to make an addition for those "who after the last word still want to hear a very last one". Mirgorod had already been printed. Then it appeared that the first pages of the next story, that of the two Ivans had to be dropped,[40] resulting in a space of two pages and there arose the opportunity and even the need

---

[39] *Tropak* (there is another form of the word: *trepak*) – a popular dance.
[40] See the following part of this chapter about "The Two Ivans".

to provide "Viy" with an epilogue. Gogol reacted to this possibility with the infallibility of his genius. It was a hundred years before these facts were discovered, and a critic has never noticed that the conclusion of "Viy" did not form part of the original conception.[41] This epilogue is not superfluous, the last thing had remained unsaid.

When the rumours of this reached Kiev, and the theologian, Halyava, heard at last of the fate of the philosopher Homa, he spent a whole hour plunged in thought.

A fixing of the place and a return to the starting-point. Not only Kiev but also Homa's friends rise up into our consciousness again. In a few words we are once more moved to their peculiar company. Tibery Gorobets still exists, he has now become a philosopher. And the theologian's nose is always broken, for in his present capacity as bell-ringer he has to cope with the rickety steps to the tower.

In the inn, they together recall Homa Brut, and the new philosopher appears to be a wise man.

"I know why he came to grief: it was because he was afraid; if he had not been afraid, the witch could not have done anything to him. You have only to cross yourself and spit just on her tail, and nothing will happen. I know all about it. Why, all the old women who sit in our market in Kiev are all witches." To this the bell-ringer bowed his head in token of agreement. But, observing that his tongue was incapable of uttering a single word, he cautiously got up from the table, and, lurching to the right and to left, went to hide in a remote spot in the rough grass; from force of habit, however, he did not forget to carry off the sole of an old boot that was lying about on the bench.

The expression "fixing of the place" which I have just used may be applied to this whole conclusion. Literally: we are again in that old world, within the boundaries of which Homa once lived and was safe. Figuratively, Homa's nature is defined in one formula: he is a Cossack who could be afraid. Finally, and this is the most important thing, Gogol here jokingly defines his own position.

The demoniac element exists for everyone who fears it and it is present everywhere. For the unimaginative it is quite simple to settle accounts with it. Tibery Goborets will never need to apply his arts

---

[41] Such a thought could not have occurred to Louis Léger who understood so little of the composition of "Viy" that he could write: "Thus finishes this nightmare of three nights which could have been prolonged for 998 further nights if it had pleased the poet to give free reign to his fantasy." *Nicolas Gogol* (Paris, 1913), p. 85.

of exorcism. The theologian is sleeping off his drunkenness in the steppe and will be sober again tomorrow. No-one any longer knows the way to the old church. Night nevertheless borders on day. This manner of fixing the place, the playful or serious confrontation of the two realities is a formal feature of all of Gogol's fantastic short stories. In order to realise that this final word still has a further function, we must think again of the original state. The last sentence was initially:

And so the church was left for ever, with monsters stuck in the doors and windows, was overgrown with forest trees, roots, rough grass and wild thorns, and no-one can now find the way to it.

This sentence would even be conceivable as the close to a fairy-tale. We hear the tranquillity of the end resounding in it. The sphere is nevertheless scarcely changed. And this is what happens in the final version, the ultimate effect again being subdued.

One could object that this can scarcely have been Gogol's intention if he wanted to bring out the fantastic atmosphere as strongly as possible. It was, however, in this story not Gogol's sole intention to show the power of the demoniac, but also its reality. This ending could serve this purpose. The more impassive the world of day appears, the deeper anxiety becomes.

Now that we have indicated the main outlines of the construction in this way, we must devote some attention to the finer lines which spread their arches like a network over the whole.

Walzel was, I think, the first to use the term *Leitmotiv* in writings on literature, and it is very useful here for naming the small, recurring motifs which are connected with a definite mood, a definite figure or with a major motif. I shall mention a few here, in increasing degree of importance.

When the students have become lost in the steppe, Homa cries out, but in vain, his voice dies away without finding an echo. "All they heard was, a little afterwards, a faint moaning like the howl of a wolf." The theologian nevertheless wanted to spend the night under the open sky, but Homa was not in favour, for he was famished. "Besides, in spite of his cheerful temper, the philosopher was rather afraid of wolves."

I should not dare to endorse the words of Osipov[42] that this is in fact

---

[42]   N. Osipov, "Strashnoye u Gogolya i Dostoyevskogo" in *Zhizn i Smert* (Prague, 1935), p. 10 ff.

the first appearance of Viy. It certainly is that of anxiety however. We should note how this happens: in a small absurd sentence, an alogism in fact. There also begins here for the first time the hovering between reality and the fantastic, although nobody can notice that at the first reading.

Was it the howling of wolves?

When Homa is on his way for the last time to the place of terror with Yavtuh and Dorosh, the night is just as dark as on that first occasion. Different perhaps. "Hellish" Gogol says, and that is not completely figurative.

A whole pack of wolves was howling in the distance, and even the barking of the dogs had a dreadful sound. "I fancy something else is howling; that's not a wolf," said Dorosh. Yavtuh was silent. The philosopher could find nothing to say.

Finally the howling of the wolves sounds really as the Leitmotiv of Viy. The dead girl has summoned him.

And suddenly a stillness fell upon the church; the wolves' howling was heard in the distance, and soon there was the thud of heavy footsteps resounding through the church.

It remains uncertain whether the howling came from wolves. The vagueness heightens the ghostly element. The binding character of the *Leitmotiv* is nevertheless expressed very clearly in these passages.

This applies even more strongly to the use Gogol makes of the "evil eye", the demoniac look. This motif is also repeated far more often.

When the witch visits Homa in the stall, the first thing that alarms him is that "he noticed a strange glitter in her eyes". The eyes of the *rusalka* whom he sees when hovering above the earth are "clear, sparkling, keen". The eyes of the witch transformed into the beautiful girl are full of tears, those of the dead girl are of course closed, but it seems to Homa as if she is nevertheless looking at him, and from under one of her eyelids there appears a tear which is a drop of blood. The dead eyes open when she has risen up out of the coffin. They become more and more terrible. The second night they are green, yet they see nothing. Homa's fear is nevertheless to the greatest extent a fear of being seen, a fear of eyes. That is also the significance of the strange, formless creature which stands before him on the last night, before Viy appears, and of which he distinguishes only the terrible eyes through the confused net of hair. Yet, not only this monster stares at him. "They were all looking at him, seeking him, but could not see him, surrounded by his mysterious circle." Then Viy is fetched, and the meeting with his gaze is death.

The countermotif to the demoniac power is formed by the effigies of the saints which are mentioned anew every night and finally fall to the ground, a symbol of the fact that God has deserted the philosopher.[43]

His desertion by everything and everyone, and by himself in the end, also has its symbols, and they too form connecting lines over the whole work.

In what has been said above the field of the purely formal has repeatedly been left, but here, when we are about to approach the basic thought of the work, we must, with the form, also necessarily discuss the content and even the "material". While the motifs we have just mentioned could not be found in the fairy-tales, this basic motif of Homa's loneliness forms a conscious deviation from the fairy-tales, not just a modification, but a radical change in their character.

In the fairy-tales the hero always has an assistant, a grandfather, a wise old woman, who knows how one must defend oneself against fiendish powers. In "Viy", the old adviser is replaced by the old Cossack Yavtuh, who always leads Homa back to his fate. Homa stands alone in his struggle, and that is indeed necessary. The heroes of the fairy-tales belong and continue to belong to one world with which they never completely lose contact. With the coming of dawn, they triumphantly shake off the drops of the waters of death and are the same people as before. Homa has however been drawn into another sphere; at a certain moment he feels for his heart and seems to have lost it. The demoniac element has found a point of attack right inside him; what external means would be of use against it?

We mentioned Homa Brut's loneliness. When, at the beginning of the short story the three adventurers are introduced to the reader, this takes place very conventionally and officially. They are introduced one by one, with a brief indication of their appearance and character. Homa is mentioned as the middle one, between the theologian and rhetorician. There is nothing in the way that Gogol typifies him to suggest the main character in a tragedy. On the contrary.

The philosopher, Homa Brut, was of cheerful temper,[44] he was fond of

---

[43] V. Gippius, *op. cit.*, p. 50, sees the siege and fall of the church as the main content of "Viy".

[44] This is repeated in the alogism already quoted.

lying on his back, smoking a pipe; when he was drinking he always[45] engaged musicians and danced the trepak. He often had a taste of the "peck of peas"[46] but took it with perfect philosophical indifference, saying that there is no escaping what has to be.

Is this not the hero of comedy, a type which always saves himself, and through this proves his superiority to the fluctuations of fate that he always remains himself? It is however Gogol's will actually to cause the unexpected to happen, to create the situation in which Homa loses the balance, in which his nature denies itself completely.

For this, just as the small group has freed itself from the mass and has become lost in solitude, Homa has again to be disengaged from that group of three in whose midst he was so safely placed and begin his great adventure in the solitary state. He then discovers, trembling, half-conscious, that there is another, unknown world, but moreover that he can be another person than himself. This discovery, this disengagement occurs during the night and is on each occasion renewed at night. It takes place extremely gradually. From the conversation of the three friends in the steppe Homa slowly comes forth as the main person. He insists on seeking lodgings, and when they are finally found and he is in the sheep's pen, he is alone. It stands in a completely innocent context. "The latter, on finding himself alone, instantly devoured the carp . . ." etc. But the adventure has begun. At the beginning of the description of each of the three terrible nights, we find the laconic statement: "The philosopher was alone"; three times a door is closed after him.

To be alone is his fate, and Gogol stresses that he had been alone since his birth.

"Who was your father?"
   "I don't know, honoured sir."
   "Your mother?"
   "I don't know my mother either. It is reasonable to suppose, of course, that I had a mother, but who she was and where she came from, and when she lived – upon my soul, good sir, I don't know."

Taken from the context of the conversation between the Cossack chief and the philosopher, the words sound more tragic than in their surroundings. Gogol avoided tragedy in the world of day. The words have their comic parallel in the scene at the inn.

---

[45] In Russian *nepremenno*, the word that Homa also uses at the end: "Muzykantov, nepremenno muzykantov!"
[46] A schoolboy expression for "whipping".

One Cossack with grey moustaches, a little older than the rest, propped his cheek on his hand and began sobbing bitterly at the thought that he had no father nor mother and was all alone in the world.

Yet, it is by no means chance that this very figure is the same as old Yavtuh who always prevents Homa from fleeing, who calls him every evening to his difficult task – of being alone.

Gogol has made a further use of the first characterisation of Homa Brut. When he accepts the inevitable and gets into the cart that is to take him to the Cossack village, he mutters "What is to be must be!" The ample proportions of the cart cause him to remark: "We need only hire some musicians and we might dance here." And he cries "Musicians!" when the old Homa asserts himself for the last time and dances the trepak before the night in which he is destroyed.[47]

In this way we have arrived via our consideration of the *Leitmotive* at the discussion of a question which is directly related to the choice of material and the significance of the content. There is a second point to be compared with what has just been treated, because Gogol has here too deviated from the fairy-tales and here too this deviation has a clear purpose. I mean the episode of the hovering with the witch and particularly the vision of the *rusalka*. This is not merely a literary processing of material which appeared soberly and concretely in the fairy-tales. It is also more than an enrichment thereof by an emotional content, as Petrov seems to think.[48] Through the element of erotic desire introduced here, something completely new has arisen. Eroticism and even obscenity are not of course lacking in the fairy-tales.[49] Yet, we never find at the same time desire and obsession, and even less, of course, their identification. Here is an extensive quotation.

The witch is sitting on Homa's back. He is her hovering horse without a will of his own.

He was aware of an exhausting, unpleasant, and at the same time, voluptuous sensation assailing his heart. He bent his head and saw that the grass which had been almost under his feet seemed growing at a depth far away, and that above it there lay water, transparent as a mountain stream, and the grass seemed to be at the bottom of a clear sea, limpid to its very

[47] Gogol also still uses the characterisation of Homa's friends. The urge to steal on the part of the theologian is shown as soon he enters the old woman's dwelling and it forms the material for the last section of the last sentence of the short story. And when Tibery Gorobets has become a philosopher, he also spreads that powerful aroma of brandy and tobacco which we already know about from the beginning of the short story.

[48] *Soch. A. N.,* II, 739.

[49] See the third example quoted above, p. 138.

depths; anyway he saw clearly in it his own reflection with the old woman sitting on his back. He saw shining there a sun instead of a moon; he heard the bluebells ringing as they bent their little heads; he saw a water-nymph float out from behind the reeds, there was the gleam of her leg and back, rounded and supple, all brightness and shimmering. She turned towards him and now her face came nearer, with eyes clear, sparkling, keen, with singing that pierced to the heart; now it was on the surface, and shaking with sparkling laughter it moved away; and now she turned on her back, and her cloud-like breasts, dead-white like unglazed china, gleamed in the sun at the edges of their white, soft and supple roundness. Little bubbles of water like beads bedewed them. She was all quivering and laughing in the water . . . Did he see this or did he not? Was he awake or dreaming? But what was that? The wind or music? It is ringing and ringing and eddying and coming closer and piercing to his heart with an insufferable thrill . . .

"What does it mean?" the philosopher wondered, looking down as he flew along, full speed. The sweat was streaming from him. He was aware of a fiendishly voluptuous feeling, he felt a stabbing, exhaustingly terrible delight. It often seemed to him as though his heart had melted away, and with terror he clutched at it.

Just as there is at the beginning the transition from galloping to hovering, we feel the descent approaching at the end. Yet who has, in spite of the mention of her image, not for a moment forgotten the figure of the witch? Even Homa Brut has done so, one might say. Is it possible in this vision, where the moon becomes a sun, shining in the sea below Homa's feet, to distinguish between "below" and "above"? Is the *rusalka* anything but the witch, desire anything but terror of death? All contrasts merge into one another here. Homa's feeling is terrible and sweet, horrible and voluptuous, language is strained to the utmost, even over-strained, in order to join these contrasts in one word.

The philosopher feels for his heart. Is it still there? The resolution of his being has begun, a resolution in the double sense, for ecstasy and destruction go together in this combination of demonism and eroticism, of obsession and temptation, of bliss and terror of death.

It is really superfluous to state once again that Gogol is here infinitely far from the atmosphere of the fairy-tale, and also that every trace of healthy sensuality is lacking. Thus we come automatically to the question of the significance of the figure of this feminine beauty.

It is demonism which is embodied in the witch – terrible old woman and perfect youthful beauty during the first phase – beauty and corpse during the second. The phases correspond chiastically.

Striking is the transition into one another of these three manifestations.

The old woman is replaced by the *rusalka* during the hovering, but finally changes into the young girl who lies low touchingly and defenseless, and thus her image is as it were fixed.

... before him lay a lovely creature with luxuriant tresses all in disorder and eyelashes as long as arrows. Senseless she tossed her bare white arms and moaned, looking upwards with eyes full of tears.

When Homa flees, he cannot give any account "of the strange new feeling that had taken possession of him".

The witch is later again recognised in this fixation, Homa is standing by the girl's death-bed.

A shudder ran through his veins: before him lay a beauty whose like had surely never been seen on earth before. Never, it seemed, could features have been formed in such striking yet harmonious beauty. She lay as though living: the lovely forehead, fair as snow, as silver, looked deep in thought; the even brows – dark as night in the midst of sunshine – rose proudly above the closed eyes; the eyelashes, that fell like arrows on the cheeks, glowed with the warmth of secret desires; the lips were rubies, ready to break into the laugh of bliss, the flood of joy.

He however recognises in her the witch for these features have something "terribly penetrating"; a smarting pain forms in his soul "because the rubies of her lips looked like blood surging up from her heart."

In the church, on the first night, he is also overcome by a similar feeling:

The striking beauty of the dead maiden certainly seemed terrible. Possibly, indeed, she would not have overwhelmed him with such panic fear if she had been a little less lovely. But there was in her features nothing faded, tarnished, dead; her face was living, and it seemed to the philosopher that she was looking at him with closed eyes.

A few moments later, the dead maiden rises up from her coffin.

... She turned livid all over like one who has been dead for several days. Homa had not the courage to look at her; she was terrifying. She ground her teeth and opened her dead eyes; but, seeing nothing, turned with fury – that was apparent in her quivering face – in another direction ...

From this point on, Gogol keeps referring to her as "the corpse". He has by this metamorphosis at the same time depicted an identity. The terror of the perfect beauty is in nature nothing else than that of the deformed corpse and the "nature" is the demoniac. It has disguised itself inscrutably quickly from the old woman into the *rusalka*, there-

after into the beautiful young woman, in whom it has remained fixed as
death and beauty in one, and it rises up again as a terrible image of
death itself. In all this (as we have already noted above in another
context), it is principally the eyes which acquire relief.

Homa's attitude towards the demoniac is initially passive. It takes
possession of him, the witch springs onto his back, the *rusalka* rises up
towards him, he submits helplessly to her "unbearable" charm. Then,
however, he becomes active in the killing of the witch who is transformed by his blows into dying beauty and through her death acquires
a hold on him which is never again released. The dead maiden has a
right to him, and this is the root of his anxiety.

Yet, before we pass on to consider Homa Brut, it is possible to
identify the witch more closely. Every reader of Gogol already knows
her features. They are nothing but a concentration of the beauty of all
beautiful girls in Gogol's Ukrainian tales. We find them in Pidorka and
Hanna, in Oksana and the fatal Polish girl in "Taras Bulba", scarcely
"grecified" in the first sketch which Gogol sent into the world with
his signature, namely "Woman".[50]

We saw in a previous chapter that Gogol depicted there his ideal of
beauty. It has the same "marble forehead" on which "the proud
movements of her divine soul" can be traced, the "marble arm"
shines in "a naked blinding splendour", the "translucent clouds of the
breasts", "the locks, which are black as the night", the "flashing
eyes" – none of these attributes is missing. It does not matter very
much whether we find the portrayal of Alcinoë's figure horrible. It is
important for us that we find all these features again in the witch in
"Viy". It follows from this that in her Gogol exposes his feminine
ideal of beauty as demoniac.[51] Another identity is also proved by this:
Homa Brut's anxiety is that of Gogol.

How must we view the figure of the philosopher? Belinsky, who
objected somewhat to certain aspects of the fantastic in "Viy"[52] was
thoroughly enchanted by Homa Brut.

Oh, unforgettable Dominus Homa! how great you are in your stoic indifference towards all that is earthly, apart from brandy! You have endured
terrible grief and anxieties, you have almost fallen into the devil's clutches,

---

[50] It was already noted by V. Gippius that Alcinoë has the same aesthetic power
as the witch in "Viy", *op. cit.,* p. 50.
[51] Seen genetically, this is in my opinion the image of Gogol's mother. See
above, p. 36.
[52] Belinsky objected particularly to the description of the monsters in the church.
Gogol cut this passage down in a later edition, see p. 162.

but you forget everything when you have a deep and wide mug, on the bottom of which your wisdom and philosophy are lying hidden. When they ask you about the horrors you have seen, you make a gesture with your hand and say: "You come into contact with all sorts of rubbish in the world": one half of your hair has turned grey in one night, but you dance a trepak such that the people who look at you spit on the ground and exclaim: "How terribly long that fellow dances!"[53]

Merezhkovsky, who apparently shares Belinsky's enthusiasm, goes a questionable step further and identifies Homa Brut with the "earthly" part of Gogol's personality. For this, he quotes a charming passage from a letter by Gogol to Maksimovich, his Ukrainian friend, who was apparently passing through a period of depression and lack of zest for work. Gogol asks him whether he never dances a trepak in his shirt in the morning through his room and advises him to drink a good bottle of wine, so that the next day he will be able to set to work with an iron will. Merezhkovsky then begins to philosophise too deeply. That iron will is ῥώμη, Rome, and in that he sees again a connection with the pagan element in Gogol's soul, on which his love for Italy was said to depend. What Homa Brut views in his vision of the *rusalka*, the translucent, shining female body, that is "the mystically real, animated flesh", that is heathen and Greek and by which Gogol himself is also fascinated. "The power which kept Gogol away from woman, was not a shortage but, on the contrary, a special, orgiastic excess of sensuality' '.[54] Thus Merezhkovsky forces matters ad absurdum.

Yet it is true that Gogol called himself a light-hearted Cossack. The Cossack is, in the "Evenings" and in "Taras Bulba" always drawn with great predilection, however traditional the type of the brave, unworried son of the steppe may be. Did he really feel himself so closely related to it?

As soon as we read the passage quoted by Merezhkovsky and other similar ones in their context, i.e also in connection with other letters dating from the same period, the delusion disappears. The letter to Maksimovich was written by a man who was himself suffering from or considered he was suffering from poor health, who was in the process of failing as a professor, who invoked continually and in vain his own "iron will" for scientific work which was never completed, and scarcely even begun.

The passage begins as follows:

[53]   Belinsky, *op. cit.*, I, col. 163.
[54]   D. S. Merezhkovsky, *Gogol* (St. Petersburg, 1909), p. 96.

"Truly, we have moved terribly far from elementary life [literally: from our primordial elements]. We (and particularly you) shall never get used to viewing life as a good joke, as the Cossack always did."[55]

We can of course with Merezhkovsky lay stress on the word "elementary". In my view, just as much attention should however be paid to the idea of removal. When, in December of that same year, he wrote to Pogodin: "All that damned nonsense with the university is over,[56] I shall within a month once again be a light-hearted Cossack", then the word "again" may strike us as being strange. Had he ever been? In Nezhin, at the grammar school, or in the first years in St. Petersburg thereafter? No, there does not speak from all these words – any more than from the literary texts – a heathen who perceives pagan Rome through the "bodiless visions of Christianity" with its "heaven which is earthly and its human being who is God".[57] Languishing in a barren reality, Gogol dreams of a source which flows positively, but not for him. The Cossack in his freedom, his naturalness and manliness which are not slowed down by any reflection, embodies precisely what Gogol has never been able to be and which he therefore admired.

What has been said here however concerns the Cossack type in general, but Homa Brut is more than that. Belinsky overlooked something very essential when he described Homa Brut as the type of robust, insensitive athlete.

What distinguishes Homa from "the" Cossack is his ability to feel anxiety. It is the weak point in the armour of his stoic Cossack philosophy. Gogol took care to make that harness appear as strong as possible, and he had his reason therefor. Not only does the terrible aspect of his destruction acquire more relief as a result, but it appears also from it that no-one is safe from the demons. If he had understood, Homa would have laughed at the assurance that in that night of his hovering eroticism and flesh had been revealed to him, mystically or otherwise. He had already known that for a long time. He even has recourse to that when he forgets his terrors in the arms of the beautiful young widow. Two kinds of sexual desire are distinguished in "Viy" and kept quite separate – one which is purely animal and the satisfaction of which is placed on a par with that of hunger, and another, demoniac, which is rooted in the mysterious depths of human personality. The

[55] *P.,* I, p. 340, letter of 22nd March, 1835. I do not know of any good equivalent for the Russian expression *tryn-trava.*
[56] *P.,* I., 357. "Ya rasplevalsya s universitetom".
[57] See Merezhkovsky, *op. cit.,* 92.

total reversal which has already been mentioned, of "above" and "below", of bliss and destruction, really has something of a perversion about it.

It is anxiety about this which connects Gogol with Homa Brut. People have repeatedly placed together the famous words from the letter to Danilevsky,[58] in which Gogol says that love "would have burned him to ashes" if he had succumbed to it, and the passage from "Viy" in which Mikita the dog-boy really succumbs to this fate because he has allowed himself to be ridden by the witch. Petro in "St. John's Eve" also burns to ashes. Perhaps more can be mentioned in this context. It is customary to ascribe Gogol's "flight" from St. Petersburg in 1829 to everything apart from the reason which he himself mentioned as the primary one, namely his hopeless love for a woman who was unattainable. There are reasons for this: his friends knew nothing about the case, he himself never speaks about it afterwards and also later gives all sorts of other reasons for his departure. Yet, from the rhetorical words in this letter to his mother, one thing appears, I think, more than clearly.[59] It is not that Gogol had in fact met a woman, from whom he had to flee, although I do not consider that impossible, but that he should have felt the meeting with such a woman as the complete ravaging of his soul, to which, according to him, a flight would have been the only reaction.

Gerhard Gesemann has shown[60] that Gogol's work continually shows traces of sexual aversion, this being coupled with an "Entwertung" (devaluation) of woman. "Viy" undoubtedly offers an example of this.

We have finally arrived at the question in which this whole investigation must result. What is the significance of the figure whose name stands at the head of the short story? No investigator has yet found an adequate explanation for the origin of Viy. He does not occur in the fairy-tales and hardly, if at all, in popular belief. We do not in fact know to what extent the scanty material produced by folklore has been influenced by Gogol's story. Gnomes, whose king he is supposed to be, according to Gogol's note, are completely unknown in Ukrainian popular literature. Be this as it may, whether this figure is Gogol's own

[58] See *P.*, I, 211; above p. 37.
[59] *P.*, I, 124–29. See above p. 29 ff. There is in the description of the fateful woman much that is reminiscent of "Viy".
[60] G. Gesemann, "Der Träumer und der Andere" in *Dostojevskij-Studien*, published by D. Chizhevsky (Reichenberg, 1931), pp. 7–18.

creation, or whether there was a model for him, he is completely unknown in a role such as he plays in this short story. How important his
position is there, is proved by the title. The whole fatal development
leads up to his appearance. This forms a last and very essential difference to the fairy- tales.

Has one a better insight into his function within the story? Scarcely,
and that is very easy to understand. After all, the figure does not arise
from a logical development. The third night in the fairy-tales brings a
climax in horror, and when it is reached, the cock crows and the story
is finished. The last thing happens in Gogol's case just when the cock
crows. The fairy-tale offered no model for that, since there the logic of
the fairy-tale is broken through. The form of the fairy-tale also suffers
a last violation here. Viy cannot be compared with "the oldest devil",
he belongs to a different genus. He is the king of the gnomes, not in
folklore but in the short story, yet of gnomes such as do not occur in
any single popular literature. Gogol has in his first conception and also
in the first edition of "Viy" ventured the impossible, and wanted to
give form to formless terror. In the last version of "Viy" the demons
announce themselves during the second night merely through their
ominous sounds, in the earlier one we find a scene such as no artist
would ever put on a canvas. The imaginative faculty of every reader
fails at the description of these creatures covered with slime and scales,
whose forms lack any relationship to those which are living and earthly:

something white, wide, with sort of white bags hanging down to the ground
instead of paws; instead of hands, ears and eyes there adhered the same
white bags.
   One consisted solely of heads, another of a frightful wing which flew
about with an unbearable whistling sound.[61]

And when there is a deliberate comparison with existing forms, then
these are excessively magnified to such an extent that the effect is more
grotesque than terrifying. Belinsky's and Shevyryov's criticisms have
had a result: Gogol omitted this whole passage in the new edition; he
also removed one monstrous figure from the portrayal of the third
night, including the very significant one which consisted "only of
eyes with eyelids". This gave fantasy a wider field. It is the same
artifice which Poe used in "The Pit and the Pendulum" in which he
avoids the extreme horror of describing the look into the pit. The
hideousness is now concentrated all the more strongly in the anxiety of
being found, touched and seen.

[61]   *Soch. A. N.*, II, 576, 577.

Viy is certainly "King of Terror". This old name for death is particularly appropriate here, for Viy himself is not shapeless.

And suddenly a stillness fell upon the church; the wolves' howling was heard in the distance, and soon there was the thud of heavy footsteps resounding through the church. With a sidelong glance he saw they were bringing a squat, thick-set, bandy-legged figure. He was covered all over with black earth. His arms and legs grew out like strong sinewy roots. He trod heavily, stumbling at every step. His long eyelids hung down to the very ground. Homa saw with horror that his face was of iron. He was supported under the arms and led straight to the spot where Homa was standing.

"Lift up my eyelids. I do not see!" said Viy in a voice that seemed to come from underground – and all the company flew to raise his eyelids.

"Do not look!" an inner voice whispered to the philosopher. He could not restrain himself and he looked.

"There he is!" shouted Viy, and thrust an iron finger at him. And all pounced upon the philosopher together.

Here too it should be mentioned that Gogol achieved an intensified effect by shortening. The last of the cited sentences was in the manuscript: "He could not restrain himself and looked: two black balls looked right at him, the iron hand of Viy rose and pointed a finger at him." In the first edition this remained almost literally and was extended only by the following sentence: " 'There he is', said Viy, and all together, all the odious monsters, pounced on him." The moment of the crossing of the looks was omitted in the last version, or rather, it was compressed to a minimum of time and summarised into two words *Vot on!,* by Viy, the replacement of the original *von* by *vot*[62] resulting in an unmistakable gain in the sound effect.

This scene suggests very much a court. Was it influenced by the thought of the last judgment? It is certain, as we have already noted, that a picture representing this caused one of Gogol's strongest youthful impressions and that it was his mother who explained it to him, the only person to whom he was not indifferent in those years.

The question arises: not of what, but why is Homa afraid? His anxiety of being seen points to a common reason – "compulsory publicity" to use Kierkegaard's terms, that is to say guilt. Did he have that, and towards whom or what? According to the judgment of the world of day, towards nobody or nothing, but he has been in contact with night, he has known a blissful voluptuousness and destroyed it – but not completely. It has maintained its grip on him. If he had suc-

---

[62]   *Vot on, Von on* – "There he is."

cumbed will-lessly – he would have been burnt to ashes; now he has resisted, but in vain, and he is just as much lost.

And the parallel with Gogol? We could say: He, who feared every bond with people, not only in love but also in friendship, as an exposure of himself, as an attack on his personality, has, at the same time, when threatened by demoniac powers outside and inside himself, felt lonely and weak, he has thought with terror of the moment at which he would be "seen" as he was.

All this still does not explain Viy, and so we shall never solve the riddle as to why he – a man covered with earth who cannot see, but who sees when one answers his look – has to be the executor.

It now seems to be unavoidable to leave the path of aesthetic consideration. To me at least, there is no further means available that would bring us a step further. The figure of Viy cannot be explained by the usual means because the appearance of this figure represents a sharp break in composition; in other words, because in my opinion we are here concerned with that part of the short story which is not formed from immanently aesthetic necessity. Another sort of necessity may lie in an urge within the soul of the writer to give a symbolic form to unconscious feelings. If we assume this and call in the help of psycho-analysis, then we must be aware of working with an auxiliary construction, because our own method has left us in the lurch. The basis must then be: the identification of Gogol with Homa Brut. Not with the fearless "dominus" – Gogol would have wished that, but he was never his double. Certainly with the man frightened to death who watches in a church with a dead girl who wants to seize him, and who is afraid of being seen. If we think for a moment that we are concerned with an anxiety dream of Gogol himself and that it is he who stands there in God's sanctuary and no longer finds any protection in Christian magic, what is then pressing on his soul?

There is an old woman who is at the same time a young girl – her love has made him anxious, but he has nevertheless answered it with a feeling of bliss and terror. Externally, she represents his ideal of beauty. We are confronted by an unmistakable repetition of the Oedipus situation.

The dreamer has killed the witch and has fled from his feeling. She has however risen up and tries to seize him. What has been repressed from consciousness, does not die and maintains grip – as anxiety.

There is a man who is covered with earth – let us assume that he comes out of the grave. He cannot see, his eyelids hang down to the ground – I think because he has died so long ago. When he sees, recognises and is recognised, he kills. Viy with his iron face is the image of an inexorable father who comes to avenge his son's incest.

The dreamer is afraid of seeing. His anxiety concerns becoming conscious of unconscious aspirations and unconscious guilt. He is to discover his father, covered with earth. The symbol is doubly fixed, the earth is also the indication of what is earthly and sinful. What is sinful is connected with the father. It is possible to think here of the satisfaction of the forbidden desire via the father himself. We should then have encountered latent homosexuality.

One being is missing in the church, namely God. Now that the judgment of the earthly father has come about, heavenly protection has disappeared. The magic symbols of his protection are powerless.

The story "Viy" is once again one of "terrible revenge" for unconscious guilt. Just as in the short story of that name, all the incarnations of anxiety pounce upon the guilty one. Here too, the end is stiffening and death.

It is certainly possible to develop this explanation further. This does not appear to me necessary here. My only purpose was to give an attempt at the solution of the riddle of Viy. If this attempt is still defective, if not only an extension, but also a modification turn out to be necessary, it is my firm conviction that only a search in the direction indicated here can prove successful.

3. *The Two Ivans*

It seems as if it is going to be a very funny story, "The Tale of how Ivan Ivanovich quarrelled with Ivan Nikiforovich". Ivan Ivanovich is a fine chap and Ivan Nikiforovich is an excellent person. They are bosom friends, models of mutual devotion, even if they are contrasts in many ways. Ivan Ivanovich is thin, Ivan Nikiforovich fat. Ivan Ivanovich has the gift of the gab and likes to pay compliments, while Ivan Nikiforovich is silent with a slight tendency to be coarse. One of them shaves twice a week, the other once, and so on, but all that does not prevent them visiting one another daily and going together to church on Sundays. Their inseparability is proverbial, their warm friendship a model in Mirgorod.

Until one day Ivan Ivanovich wants an old gun from his friend which the latter never uses, but does not want to give up, not even for a brown sow and two sacks of oats, and Ivan Nikiforovich utters that one rude word in the heat of the negotiation, namely "gander". It is a mortal insult to Ivan Ivanovich, it is fatal for the friendship, it has immeasurable consequences. Immediately there is that goose-stall, built in one night by Ivan Nikiforovich, just at the place where his lean friend could previously step over the fence separating their farms. And the subsequent violence of Ivan Ivanovich who at the midnight hour saws through the poles on which this infamous structure rests, this act of desperation making him so afraid of revenge that he fears an attack on his life and resorts to a legal action, something to which he is just ahead of his former friend. And the action itself, which does not follow. at least not yet directly, but in which so many people are involved before it begins: Agafya Fedosyevna, the fat concubine of Ivan Nikiforovich, who adds fuel to the fire; the brown pig of Ivan Ivanovich, that snatches away from the table in the court-room his adversary's indictment; the mayor, who wants to arrest the pig and bring the friends together; the judicature, which tries to stop the suit by calmly forgetting the files . . . it is impossible to say in a single sentence how widespread the complications are.

Yet everything could still have ended well. At a larger dinner given by the mayor, the two friends have been brought together through a trick. They are almost driven into one another's arms by force, and it seems that they will let bygones be bygones. Ivan Nikiforovich then however commits the unpardonable indiscretion at this important moment and in the presence of ladies of mentioning the cause of the argument and again saying that fatal word, namely "gander". Everyone feels that this is the end.

The suit continues, not in Mirgorod, but in Poltava. When the writer visits Mirgorod after twelve years, he meets there two wrecks of men, grey, emaciated and ruined, who both expect a judgment in their favour the following day, just as they have been doing for years. And it does seem as if he suddenly no longer finds everything so funny, for the story of this visit is in a minor key and its last sentence is: "It is a dreary world, friends!"[63] This sentence has become classic and has been quoted innumerable times. People usually see in these words the sum-

---

[63]   "Skuchno na etom svete, gospoda!" *Skuchno* means in most cases "boring, dull", then acquiring the secondary meaning of "onerous, dreary". Sometimes it means exclusively the latter, as here. We could also translate the sentence as follows: "There is a miserable mess in this world, gentlemen!" See note 64.

mary of Gogol's philosophy of life at that point in his development. It is however not so simple to give an answer to the question as to the origin of that sadness.

The first who did that was Belinsky.[64] In an essay on Griboyedov's famous comedy he makes quite a long digression about Gogol's short stories and he ends his observations about the story of the Ivans with the words:

Yes, it is sad that man, that noblest organ of the mind, can live and die as a phantom amongst phantoms, without even realising the possibility of a real life! And how many such people are there in the world, how many Ivan Ivanoviches and Ivan Nikiforoviches there are in the world! . . .

In order to understand this sentence properly, we must bear in mind that Belinsky in 1840 regarded life as "real" only if it were pervaded by the mind which comes to self-realisation in it; everything falling outside being chance, senseless, an empty form, a "phantom".[65]

Gogol was consequently considered to find the world of the Ivans dreary because they had missed grasping the chance also offered to them to ennoble their senseless existence and to occupy a place in "the long chain of phenomena of the mind", thanks to their "education, brutish laziness, emptiness and lack of development".[66]

Although it is of course possible to draw this conclusion from the short story and although it is not incorrect, I do not think that this thought will come to the mind of any reader while reading it. It is a result of reflection from a certain point of view, but it is not the point of view that the writer wishes to force upon his readers here. There is no trace of annoyance with Gogol, either about the laziness or lack of culture of his heroes. Apparently Belinsky realised that very well. He at least prefaced his views with the remark that objectivity in depiction excludes any moral judgment and that a writer must love his creations, even if they are moral monsters.[67] This argument would serve completely if the depiction of the Ivans were in fact objective. There is on the contrary a continuous interference by the author (even if initially

---

[64] Belinsky, op. cit., I, col. 618 links up directly with the words discussed in the previous note, but for "dreary" he uses the unambiguous grustno.
[65] I am deliberately not considering Belinsky's terminology further here. It shows unmistakably the traces of his veneration for Hegel. The word I have translated as "phantom" is the Russian prizrak, the abstract noun from it prizrachnost has practically the value of "appearance" as opposed to "reality" in the Hegelian sense.
[66] Op. cit., I, col. 617.
[67] Op. cit., I, col. 615.

in disguise) who tries to influence the reader's mood. That influencing does not go in the direction of Belinsky's conclusion. When the reader laughs, it is without sadness or annoyance and when he shares Gogol's sadness at the end, it is not because of the souls which have been lost in the Ivans.

It occurs to me that Belinsky was so full of his own view of reality in general and of Russian reality in particular that he considered he found it in Gogol. This is the beginning of the misunderstanding between the two great Russian writers which was to assume such a catastrophic form at the end of both their lives.

Many a contemporary literary investigator is preoccupied in a somewhat different way. As an example I choose N. Stepanov, who succeeds in offering an extraordinarily interesting argument[68] for his view that the story has a satirical, polemic, social tendency, "after the manner of Shchedrin".

One copy of Mirgorod has in fact been known for a short time in which the story of the Ivans has a preface reading as follows:

I consider it as my duty to state at the beginning that the event described in this story takes place in a very distant past. Moreover, it is completely fantasy. Mirgorod is now quite different. The buildings are different, the puddle in the centre of the city has long since dried up and all the officials: the judge, the clerk and the mayor are reputable and well-meaning persons.

Thanks to Stepanov's investigations, we now know why this preface is missing from all the other copies of the first edition of Mirgorod. Gogol had had difficulties with the censor. Before giving his permission for the printing of the short story in Smirdin's almanach "Novoselye", the censor Nikitenko had cut a few passages, which Gogol resented. Just at the time when "Mirgorod" was in the press, Nikitenko was put in prison because of a censoring matter in which he had been too lenient. Gogol now made use of his absence to prepare this preface. But when "Mirgorod" had just been printed, Nikitenko returned, and the preface was removed from all copies, either at his insistence or in order to avoid difficulties.[69]

Does it now appear from all this that the story was intended as a social satire and had as such suffered seriously? I cannot see it. Everyone who knows how sensitive censorship was under Nicholas I and

---

[68] See *N. V. Gogol*, Materialy i issledovaniya pod red. V. Gippiusa (Moscow-Leningrad, 1936), I, p. 5 and 22–24. Likewise *Soch. A. N.*, II, 750–53.
[69] In order not to make the publisher print the last pages again, Gogol added a conclusion to "Viy", so that the numbering of the pages could remain the same.

particularly, in what strange places its sensibilities lurked, will admit the possibility that, for reasons we cannot trace, certain comic lines have been suppressed. As long as no manuscript of the short story is known, from which it appears what these contained, we must restrict ourselves to the known text for conclusions about the tendency of the story. In my opinion it shows extremely little that points to social satire and, as such, fits in completely with the rest of the Ukrainian collections.

It is my view that the words "It is a dreary world" become more intelligible if we give our attention to the place where they stand. They form not only the last sentence of the short story, but this is also the last story of the last collection Gogol was to dedicate to the Ukraine. They bear the character of a farewell and that is the character of the whole of "Mirgorod". Whether Gogol sees the world described therein idyllically as in "Old-world Land-owners" or heroically as in "Taras Bulba", or comically as in the short story of the two Ivans, it continues to show one feature: it is a past world and therefore what remains, i.e. the present world, "reality", is a dreary mess.

That is of course also a judgment on the world of the Ivans, not on the lazing friends in their magnificent *bekesha*[70] or their sybaritic nakedness, not on foolish Mirgorod with its disorderly streets and its huge puddle in front of the building of the bungling court, a world which basks in the rays of a beneficial sun, but on the mopish provincial nest in the rain with two emaciated old men, deadly enemies because of a trifle, who slave away to destroy one another; a world, in a word, which has lost the glow of a fool's paradise and bears the grey tint of a sad triviality.

This conclusion shows not only a curious similarity with that of the first story of the "Evenings", namely the "Fair at Sorochintsy", but also with the introduction to the first story from "Mirgorod", namely "Old-world Land-owners". Gogol in fact says there that it is difficult for him to tell the story because he becomes "sad beforehand".[71] Thus the conclusion also has a function in the composition of "Mirgorod". For really the same world is described twice in the first and last short story, only in the first it is seen as idyllic and in the latter as comical. Yet comical like a *vertep,* not as despicable reality.

How strongly Gogol himself originally imagined the story as being in the sphere of Dikanka, appears from two things in the first

[70]   *Bekesha* – a sort of fur coat.
[71]   Here Gogol uses the word *grustno.*

edition.[72] There it was provided with the date 1831, of which Tikhon-ravov has already shown the improbability,[73] and furthermore with the subtitle: "One of the unpublished true stories of the beekeeper Rudy Panko". We may only guess why Gogol omitted this subtitle when "Mirgorod" was published. Was he afraid of destroying the unity of "Mirgorod" by mentioning the beekeeper? Did he find the conclusion, which could scarcely have been by Rudy Panko, too much in contra-diction with the subtitle?

The two suppositions do not cancel one another out. We now how-ever have a name for the first narrator of the short story; the fact that there are two appears in my opinion from what has been said above.

Ivan Ivanovich has a splendid bekesh! Superb! And what astrakhan! Phew, damn it all, what astrakhan! Purplish-grey with a frost on it! I'll bet any-thing you please that nobody can be found with one like it! Now do just look at it – particularly when he is standing talking to somebody – look from the side: isn't it delicious? There is no finding words for it. Velvet! Silver! Fire! Merciful Lord! Nikolay the Wonder-worker, Holy Saint! Why have not I a bekesh like that! He had it made before Agafya Fedosyevna went to Kiev. You know Agafya Fedosyevna? Who bit off the tax-assessor's ear.

That is a voice we know. It is the sound of the old gossip, frère et compagnon of his heroes. The stylistic means are also once again comic hyperboles, and in what follows also puppet-like sketches ("Ivan Iva-novich's head is like a radish, tail downwards; Ivan Nikiforovich's head is like a radish, tail upwards") and alogisms in symmetrical form ("Ivan Ivanovich is rather of a timorous character. Ivan Nikiforovich, on the other hand, wears trousers with such ample folds that if they were blown out you could put the whole courtyard with the barns and barn-buildings into them").

The description of Ivan Ivanovich has literally and figuratively started on the outside. It is begun again and again in the same way and keeps on running into external features.

An excellent man is Ivan Ivanovich! What a house he has in Mirgorod!

There follows a description of that house and garden.

An excellent man is Ivan Ivanovich! He is very fond of a melon.

And the reader learns how he is in the habit of savouring it under his verandah, after which he collects the seeds in little bags on which there is written the date they were consumed.

[72] In "Novoselye", 1834.
[73] See *Soch.*, I, 703. Likewise Stepanov in *Soch. A. N.*, II, 751.

An excellent man is Ivan Ivanovich! The Poltava Commissar knows him too.

And then we are treated to all sorts of interesting comments concerning persons from Ivan's surroundings.

"And what a devout man Ivan Ivanovich is!" We now hear how he goes faithfully to church and, after the service is over, has a chat with every beggar. The small scene, which is given as an example of such a conversation and from which it appears how he first arouses in the beggars the hope of a gift and then lets them go without alms, would give a miserable impression of his character, if the reader did not already have the feeling that Ivan Ivanovich has no soul at all and that the narrator is not portraying a person but a comic figure from a puppet play. This small scene is in fact borrowed from the *vertep*.[74]

The *vertep*-like character is also present in the style. The narrator is sitting behind his puppets, speaks their language, thinks and feels as they do, finds no words to praise them, and only the all too great stress with which this happens betrays the joke. He ends his characterisation with a long series of contrasts, the schematic and materialistic element of which is unmistakable. I quote merely the conclusion thereof.

Ivan Ivanovich has big expressive snuff-coloured eyes and a mouth rather like the letter V; Ivan Nikiforovich has little yellowish eyes completely lost between his thick eyebrows and chubby cheeks, and a nose that looks like a ripe plum. If Ivan Ivanovich offers you snuff, he always first licks the lid of the snuff-box, then taps on it with his finger, and, offering it to you, says, if you are someone he knows: "May I make so bold as to ask you to help yourself, sir?" or if you are someone he does not know: "May I make so bold as to ask you to help yourself, sir, though I have not the honour of knowing your name and your father's and your rank in the service?" Ivan Nikiforovich puts his horn of snuff straight into your hands and merely adds: "Help yourself." Both Ivan Ivanovich and Ivan Nikiforovich greatly dislike fleas, and so neither Ivan Ivanovich nor Ivan Nikiforovich ever let a Jew dealer pass without buying from him various little bottles of an elixir protecting them from those insects, though they abuse him soundly for professing the Jewish faith. In spite of some dissimilarities, however, both Ivan Ivanovich and Ivan Nikiforovich are excellent persons.

This first chapter seems simply and tightly composed. Since it is the sketch of a few portraits, there is nothing surprising in the fact that it is written in the present, at least as long as one does not try to think of the narrator as a real person. If we do this, then we become aware that he

---

[74] See *Soch. A. N.*, II, 757–58.

must after all know that friendship no longer exists between the two Ivans and also that all sorts of details of his description are no longer accurate. It seems easy to solve this small difficulty. The narrator imagines the scene so clearly before his eyes and experiences it so strongly that for a moment it again becomes the present for him, a case that occurs innumerable times in literature throughout the world. We could be satisfied with this explanation – if that present and the mental attitude suited to it were preserved quite consistently. Something is however missing from it here and there.[75]

Rudy Panko interrupts his loud glorification of Ivan Ivanovich unexpectedly with the words:

Goodness, how time flies! He had been a widower ten years even then.[76]

"Then"! Suddenly the reader discovers that he has been set back in the past. The narrator however glides back unnoticed in the present again.

He had no children. Gapka has children and they often run about the yard, etc.

A little later he tells in the present how Ivan Ivanovich puts on his fur coat every Sunday and sings bass in the church-choir.

When the service is over, Ivan Ivanovich cannot bear to go away without making the round of the beggars.

There now follows a gradual transition to the preterite.

He would, perhaps, not care to go through this tedious task if he were not impelled to it by his innate kindliness. "Good morrow, poor woman", he commonly said.

The whole scene with the female beggar follows in the preterite. At the end there is an unexpected return to the present.

"Well, go along and God be with you," said Ivan Ivanovich "What are you staying for? I am not beating you, am I?" And after addressing similar enquiries to a second and a third, he at last returns home or goes to drink a glass of vodka with his neighbour, Ivan Nikiforovich, or to see the judge or the police-captain.

---

[75] In Russian the question of the use of tenses is very complicated because of the Russian system of aspects. As a result, the deviations in the original are far less conspicuous than in the translation. There are, for example, no separate forms for the pluperfect.

[76] In this sentence the word "then" is the only indication of time.

In place of "goes" one would expect "went", and moreover if Ivan Ivanovich's showing of kind-heartedness belongs to the past, then also surely his friendship with his neighbour.

Shortly thereafter it is said that the two Ivans *are* such extraordinary friends, but then follows half a page further the communication that they *did* not resemble one another in everything, and there even comes in the middle of the comparisons which follow, which are all in the present, the sentence:

In earlier times he [Ivan Nikiforovich] *went* sometimes to Ivan Ivanovich.

On the last page of the chapter we no longer find any deviations in the use of tenses, and the final sentence is:

However, both Ivan Ivanovich and Ivan Nikiforovich *are* excellent persons.

We cannot derive very much from these stylistic peculiarities alone. We could think of carelessness on the part of the writer, we could assume that we were here observing a silent battle between Gogol, who is continually thinking of the further course of the story, and the beekeeper, for whom the border between past and present has fallen away for a moment. Yet, upon looking carefully, there seems not only to be something lacking in the present form, but also in what I should like to call the present attitude of the narrator.

The first paragraph of the short story as quoted above ends with the sentence:

You know Agafya Fedosyevna? Who bit off the tax-assessor's ear.

If we read this for the first time, then we think: "There he is again, the old tattler, who forgets that not everyone is conversant with the internal history of Mirgorod." Yet, upon subsequent reading, it is certainly possible to answer this quasi-silly question. Agafya Fedosyevna is, after all, the woman who first properly started off the quarrel between the two Ivans. She visits Ivan Nikiforovich on the evening after his famous indiscretion.

As soon as she arrived, everything was turned upside down. "Don't be reconciled with him, Ivan Nikiforovich, and don't you beg his pardon; he wants to be your ruin; he's just that sort of man! You don't know him." The damned woman went on whispering and whispering, till she brought Ivan Nikiforovich to such a state that he would not hear Ivan Ivanovich's name.

Consequently, directly with the first presentation of the first of the two heroes, there is also the first reminiscence of the quarrel, which is however unintelligible to the unsuspecting reader.

The paragraph after the mention of Ivan Ivanovich's love for melons begins thus:

The late Mirgorod judge always looked at Ivan Ivanovich's house with admiration.

The late judge is the man who tries to stop the suit and who requests the mayor to make an effort at reconciliation.[77]

And just in the curious sentence after the story of the beggar woman with its unexpected transition from preterite to present, we have all three together, the figures with whom Ivan Ivanovich cannot be combined without thinking of the quarrel, namely Ivan Nikiforovich, the judge and the mayor.

Finally, the first time the friendship between the Ivans is mentioned, it is in these words:

They are such good friends as the world has never seen. Anton Prokofye-vich Golopuz, who goes about to this day in his cinnamon-coloured coat with light blue sleeves (. . .), *used* frequently *to say* that the devil himself *had* tied Ivan Nikiforovich and Ivan Ivanovich together with a string; where the one went the other would turn up also.

Here we have both phenomena again, a deviation from the present form and from the present attitude together. Anton Prokofyevich is the man who drags Ivan Nikiforovich to the mayor's dinner perjuring solemnly that he shall not see Ivan Ivanovich there – in the hope that reconciliation will come about through the meeting of the two parties. He is the last to play a part in the previous history of the suit.

No doubt is, in my opinion, possible. All these deviations are deliberate artifices. No narrator is conceivable who would make so many "mistakes" in tenses, who would "by chance" enumerate all the important people in the story of the quarrel and who would at the same time experience his story as being in the present.[78]

The chapter which seems so innocent is one continuous ambiguity.

The seemingly good-natured twaddle of Rudy Panko contains in his incidental citing of all sorts of unknown persons just as many pointers to the further course of the story. This introduction is misleading

[77] The fact that it is he and not any arbitrary judge, appears from the conclusion of the story where his death is reported. See p. 176.
[78] Deviations in the use of tenses do not occur any more. The first sentence of the second chapter is in the preterite which is then maintained up to the end.

only on a first or superficial reading. Given greater attention, it appears really as an overture, in which all the themes of the piece that follows are indicated, even in the correct order. In other words: we have from the first page on nothing more to do with Rudy Panko, but with Gogol in a disguise of which he again and again deliberately draws back the folds.

Does he also appear in the short story himself? Certainly, and in those parts where the "narration" passes into "high literature".[79] There the style acquires an elevation, too heavy with irony to be able to pass still for the silly ecstasy of a simple soul.

As an example, I have chosen the description of the close of the first quarrel.

The whole group presented a striking picture: Ivan Nikiforovich, standing in the middle of the room in full beauty completely unadorned! The serving-woman, with her mouth wide open and an utterly senseless terror-stricken expression on her face! Ivan Ivanovich, as the Roman tribunes are depicted, with one arm raised! It was an extraordinary moment, a magnificent spectacle! And meanwhile there was but one spectator: that was the boy in an enormous overcoat, who stood very tranquilly picking his nose.

These sentences are no longer naïve, not even in appearance. Here direct irony has taken the place of indirect irony. And this is presumably also the true reason why Gogol, when the story appeared for the second time, freed it from the figure of Rudy Panko. Upon re-reading it must appear how little it still really has to do with the beekeeper.[80]

The last pages of the short story show to some extent the opposite: we hear there the voice of someone other than the beekeeper, only here and there do we hear echoes of the old accent.

Five years ago I was passing through the town of Mirgorod. It was a bad time for travelling. Autumn had set in with its gloomy, damp weather, mud and fog. A sort of unnatural greenness – the work of the tedious, incessant rains – lay in a thin network over the meadows and cornfields, on which it seemed no more becoming than mischievous tricks in an old man, or roses on an old woman. In those days weather had a great effect on me: I was depressed when it was dreary.

Is that Rudy Panko who depicts the mood of an autumn landscape in this way, who is so nervously sensitive of the influence of the at-

[79] This phenomenon occurs on a few further occasions. Consider the description of the nocturnal attack on the goose-stall.
[80] I should like to point out expressly that this does not imply anything about the origin of the short story. It is conceivable that matters are, seen genetically, precisely the other way about and that the "overture" was the first to be written.

mosphere? Of course not. This is Gogol without his mask. Yet, we could feel a slight hesitation if we read further:

But in spite of that I felt my heart beating eagerly as I drove into Mirgorod. Goodness, how many memories! It was twelve years since I had seen Mirgorod. Here, in those days, lived in touching friendship two unique men, two unique friends. And how many distinguished persons had died! The judge, Demyan Demyanovich, was dead by then, Ivan Ivanovich, the one who squinted, had taken leave of life, too. I drove into the principal street: posts were standing everywhere with whisps of straw tied to their tops: they were altering the streets! Several huts had been removed. Remnants of hurdles and fences remained standing disconsolately.

It seemed for a moment as if Gogol wanted to fall back into the tone of the beekeeper when he began to speak of the great men of Mirgorod and wanted to continue that when he provided the sentence about rendering the city more beautiful with an exclamation mark. The end of the passage however once again has the tone of the beginning; what looked like a joke, appears after all to be irony with a sad tinge. Mirgorod is not completely as it was of old.

If, with this thought in mind, we read the omitted preface once again, then it acquires a new meaning. It is not only an expression of annoyance towards the censor. The Mirgorod in which the great puddle had dried up and in which the court consists of such upright people, is no longer the place where such magnificent fools could find their paradise.

After the writer has related how he has with difficulty recognised Ivan Nikiforovich as a faded old man in the church where the candles spread in the "sickly" daylight a "strangely unpleasant" glow, and how he informed him that he hopes to win his case tomorrow, he describes his meeting with Ivan Ivanovich.

Then I caught sight of a thin, wasted figure. Was that Ivan Ivanovich? The face was covered with wrinkles, the hair was completely white. But the bekesh was still the same. After the first greetings, Ivan Ivanovich, addressing me with the good-humoured smile which so well suited his funnel-shaped face, said: "Shall I tell you my agreeable news?"

"What news?" I asked.

"Tomorrow my case will positively be settled; the court has told me so for certain."

I sighed still more heavily, and made haste to say good-bye – because I was travelling on very important business – and got into my chaise.

The lean horses, known in Mirgorod by the name of the post-express horses, set off, making an unpleasant sound as their hoofs sank into the grey mass of mud. The rain poured in streams on to the Jew who sat on the box covered with a sack. The damp pierced me through and through. The gloomy gate with the sentry-box, in which a veteran was cleaning his grey accoutrements, slowly passed by. Again the same fields, in places black and furrowed and in places covered with green, the drenched crows and jackdaws, the monotonous rain, the tearful sky without one gleam of light in it. – It is a dreary world, friends!

This "friends" contains a weak reference back to the beginning. The last sentences could not have been uttered by the old beekeeper, but these last words prove that the narration is still going on and that the narrator is making a call on his audience. They remove from the final sentence the absolute certainty of a general statement, they sound mitigating and leave room for a smile, even if it is not joyous. They are an indication of the subjective sphere which fits in so well with the "art form of the short story".

If we wish to investigate the construction of this short story and consequently form a clear idea of what lies between that curious first chapter and these strange pages at the end, then comparative material offers itself as if automatically. We cannot in fact doubt that Gogol wrote his story of the two Ivans under the unfluence of a work by Narezhny, namely "The two Ivans or the Passion for going to Law".[81]

Narezhny's novel is also set in the Ukraine, the action likewise begins in Mirgorod and finishes in Poltava, and there are many details which we also notice in Gogol's Ukrainian stories.[82] Then there are two Ivans who, just as in Gogol's story, continue court actions for ten years, not however against one another, but against a common enemy, *pan* Khariton Zanoza, a neighbour with whom they have lived for a long time on friendly terms. They are much more active than Gogol's Ivans. Whereas Ivan Ivanovich hardly dares to saw through the legs of his friend's goose-stall, the two Ivans of Narezhny have destroyed a whole flock of geese, massacred a whole group of pigeons and killed a quantity of large and small cattle. If an attempt at arson by Ivan Nikiforovich exists only in the imagination of his adversary, in Narezhny's story possessions of the litigating parties repeatedly go up in flames, on one occasion they even come to blows.

[81]   Published anew by V. F. Pereverzev. "Dva Ivana ili strast k tyazhbam" in V. T. Narezhny, *Izbrannye romany* (Moscow-Leningrad, 1933), pp. 661–886.
[82]   For example, culinary terms such as *varenukha*, the term *zhid* in place of *evrey*. There is mention of *vechera* ("evenings" in the sense that we also come across it in Gogol), there is even a sacristan who is called Foma. Examples of words which are less familiar to the Russian reader and which are used by both writers include: *hashtan, khutor* (in the meaning "hamlet"), *chub, peysiki*. Narezhny goes less far in the use of Ukrainian words than Gogol.

The course of the action is very different in both works. The story by Narezhny is not such a very long, but highly complicated novel of adventure, full of quid pro quo's and mysterious strangers. It has the clear tendency of constituting a warning against the consequences of a passion to which the Ukrainian landed gentry seems to have yielded more than once. Those who combat vice are of course not lacking. Both Ivans each have a son and *pan* Zanoza has two daughters. Soon we have two married couples whose secret weddings are about to be blessed with an offspring when the fathers are still lying in wait for one another's ruin. The most powerful partisan of virtue is *pan* Artamon, the uncle of the two Ivans who, without them suspecting it, helps to steer their fate, who lets them ruin themselves, just as their adversary, in order to return to them generously what they lost after a complicated story of conversion and reconciliation. Such an ideal figure is seldom missing in Narezhny's works. It after all belongs in the whole atmosphere of the optimistic, moralising Russian novel of the period.

It will be apparent from the little that could be said here about the content of the book which served Gogol as a model, how far he deviated from it. The similarities and differences have been studied more than once, but not much has been achieved except placing the facts side by side.[83] It is however interesting to investigate in what respects both works differ as regards composition. This will be attempted here, the aim naturally being to render clearer the construction of Gogol's work, while that of Narezhny's novel will serve merely for purposes of comparison.

Only the basic constructions can be compared, for in both writers the "fable" has been developed in a very different way. If we reduce this to its simplest form, then it can be paraphrased as follows: Two friendly neighbours quarrel about a trifle, this leads to a suit which destroys both parties. This common feature has been shaped in a completely different way by both writers to give their "sujet".[84]

With Narezhny the quarrel is already in full swing when the reader

---

[83]   There is much information about style and tendency in Pereverzev's introduction to the above-mentioned collection of Narezhny's novels. There are very sound remarks in Stepanov, *Soch.*, II, 754 ff, where the older literature is also listed.
[84]   By "fable" I mean here, in accordance with the Russian theoreticians of the formalistic school: the actual data in their causal-temporal context, while I mean by "sujet": the same data as they are artistically formed and placed in the work of art. It is obvious that a causal-temporal order is not binding for the "sujet' and that the same "fable" can be formed into various "sujets". See B. Tomashevsky, *Teoriya literatury,* 6th edition (Moscow-Leningrad, 1931), p. 134 ff.

makes the acquaintance of the heroes, its origin is later introduced as previous history, but its course is the main thing that is described. The extent of the enmity and the dimensions of the hostilities increase steadily and lead to a catastrophe. This is followed by an unexpected deliverance, which finally ends in a reconciliation.

With Gogol, on the other hand, we are shown at the beginning the friendship of the future enemies. After this only, comes the origin of the quarrel on which full attention is directed, this, after all, forming the turning-point in the story. What then follows is a number of accelerations and retardations which do not lead to a catastrophe, not even to a suit. On the contrary, they lead to nothing but a repetition of the first turn.

Once again, the fateful word is uttered, now however not as the culmination in a slowly rising quarrel, but as the end of an almost successful reconciliation. At this moment the suit begins, yet the short story breaks off. Nothing is mentioned of the ten years that the suit lasts. There is no question of a deliverance, the short story ends with an "apparent conclusion", about which we shall have something to say in a moment. The comic element in Gogol's construction lies in that the real short story is little more than the story of a number of complications activating or slowing down the action between two identical turning-points.

Summarising, this means that Narezhny's novel is principally dynamic, while Gogol's short story is static; Gogol deals with a phase of the quarrel which is hardly discussed in Narezhny's work, and breaks off where his predecessor begins. The rise, following on the fall and the final state of peace are lacking completely in Gogol, while in Narezhny everything is directed towards it. Narezhny the optimist addresses reality in moralising tones, while Gogol the pessimist withdraws in aesthetic disgust.

There is much less sense in seeking parallels between the various ways in which the two writers have "thematically filled in" their construction. That is however necessary and instructive as regards one point. The most striking similarity between both works is that of their titles and the same name of the main characters appearing in them. An uninitiated person could assume that "The two Ivans or the Passion for going to Law" was the shortened title of "The tale of how Ivan Ivanovich quarrelled with Ivan Nikiforovich". Yet what a difference is concealed under that superficial appearance.

With Narezhny, the Ivans stand side by side, not opposite one another, and they are so slightly differentiated that one can hardly distinguish them from one another; none of the two figures has sharp outlines. The same applies to their sons and the daughters of *pan* Khariton. We gain the impression that they are nothing but one another's doubles and that they exist in duplicate only because otherwise the stage would be too empty. The Ivans accordingly always act simultaneously and in the same sense, just as the other doubles. Compared with this, there all at once appears Gogol's genial touch and the consciousness with which he does not leave his model, but reverses it. His Ivans are in nature so completely similar to one another as the one void to the other, but they have acquired a personality, the characteristic of which consists almost exclusively of external features, while the differences in character never reach to the centre of a human soul, for the souls of the Ivans have none. Finally, the masterful pages in which he introduces his heroes to the readers are built up from such contrasts that the similarity is more striking to those readers than all the differences, care at the same time however being taken to accentuate these futile contrasts in character only through which the possibility of a conflict is created. The Ivans of Narezhny are intended as human beings, but their creator lacked the ability to give them form. Gogol's heroes are devoid of everything which makes a human being a human being, but these dead souls have received a very tangible bodily life.

What has been said here may be enough to show that Gogol's imitation of Narezhny is a struggle with his model, not merely as regards the tendency (which Stepanov has already noted), but also as regards the whole composition.

This short story has justifiably been regarded for a long time as one of Gogol's best works. It is this also from the point of view of the form which is truly one with the content. As has already been said, the "sujet" moves between two climaxes which are the same in nature. For what lies in between is – seen objectively – a number of scenes in which time is marked; seen however through the eye of the "naïve" narrator, it is there that a whole dramatic intrigue takes place. The smile about this identity of movement and stagnation is humorous. It is also reflected in the language. It is obvious that a dénouement is impossible, for the story of the two Ivans has for Gogol only really begun. He finds that perhaps movement can be observed in the stagnation, but then slowly backwards, towards a miserable reality. The word is therefore finally taken from the naïve narrator and the author gives the concluding observation which is only in appearance a conclusion.

There is reason to think of Gogol's further development at these last words. Not Mirgorod, but the whole world is dreary.

It is nevertheless necessary to make a reservation here. Humour results from the linking of contrasting elements. If these are weighed against one another, sorrow will always appear heavier than joy. We take sorrow more seriously than happiness. In Gogol's case, this preponderance will easily occur, his sadness is always an undercurrent and at the end of his life and also at the end of his happiest works often becomes uppermost. Yet, we must avoid the danger of forgetting that he was a humorist, i.e. that his manner of reacting to "the dreary world" is a resistance through smiling. Gogol lost this struggle in the end, but this knowledge should not confuse our vision of his youthful work.

CHAPTER IV

THE OVERCOAT

Although "The Overcoat" is amongst Gogol's best-known stories, a somewhat thorough analysis is not possible without a short summary of the course of the story, with at the same time a rough indication of its construction.

In a certain department a certain oldish, bald-headed, pock-marked little official used to sit, with a "haemorrhoidal" complexion, eternally bearing the rank of titular councillor and the name *Bashmach-kin*.[1] His christian name, Akaky Akakyevich, is just as ridiculous, and Gogol relates in detail how the poor devil got it. How and when he appeared in the department no-one knows any more. He is known there solely as a copyist. Since he is weak and defenceless, he is constantly exposed to being teased by his colleagues. He does not however let this disturb his work, namely copying, which dominates all his thoughts.

It was only when the joke got too unbearable, when somebody jogged his arm and so interfered with his work, that he would say, "Leave me alone, gentlemen. Why do you pester me?" There was a strange note in the words and the voice in which they were uttered: there was something in it that touched one's heart with pity. Indeed, one young man who had only recently been appointed to the department and who, following the example of the others, tried to have some fun at his expense, stopped abruptly at Akaky's mild expostulation, as though stabbed through the heart; and since then everything seemed to have changed in him and he saw everything in a different light. A kind of unseen power made him keep away from his colleagues whom at first he had taken for decent, well-bred men. And for a long time afterwards, in his happiest moments, he would see the shortish Civil Servant with the bald patch on his head, uttering those pathetic words, "Leave me alone! Why do you pester me?" And in those

---

[1] The name cannot be translated. "Shoeman" more or less indicates the meaning. *Bashmak* means "shoe".

pathetic words he seemed to hear others: "I am your brother." And the poor young man used to bury his face in his hands, and many a time in his life he would shudder when he perceived how much inhumanity there was in man, how much savage brutality there lurked beneath the most refined, cultured manners, and, dear Lord, even in the man the world regarded as upright and honourable . . .

This serious intermezzo from the otherwise comic beginning has been quoted here in full, because it has acquired much notoriety and is usually indicated in Russia as the "humane passage".

After this passage there is a depiction of the happiness Akaky Akakyevich finds in writing. He takes documents home for sheer pleasure and knows no other amusement than copying.

He should consequently have been able to live from his salary of four hundred roubles, if he had not had an enemy, namely the St. Petersburg cold. This forces Akaky Akakyevich, who has never paid any attention to his external appearance, to the discovery that his coat is half worn away on the shoulders and in the back.

A visit to his tailor Petrovich is of no avail for the moment, for Petrovich refuses to mend the overcoat and says that only a new one would be any good. This means an enormous expense, eighty roubles to be sure.

By imposing on himself the greatest privations, drinking no more tea, walking on his toes to save his soles, yes even writing as little as possible at home (for that uses up candles), he succeeds in several months in scraping the money together. During that time something changes in him, his life acquires a purpose, namely the new overcoat. When the dream has finally been realised and the overcoat is ready and Akaky Akakyevich comes to the department unrecognisable, he is once again teased. His colleagues consider that he now has to treat them. A higher official saves him. He is giving a party that evening and invites the whole company. Akaky Akakyevich enjoys the evening only moderately. He leaves before the end and at a lonely spot he is robbed of his new treasure.

Attempts to trace it through the police lead to nothing, a charitable collection amongst his colleagues provides little, the only hopeful possibility is to turn to a certain "important personality". He has only recently been important, is still practising his worthy role and considers he cuts a better figure the more he snaps at lower-placed persons. Akaky Akakyevich, who has not applied to him by the hierarchical path, gets the full brunt of him and when he stutters something in reply, the great man becomes so furious that Akaky Akakyevich totters out of the room horrified.

In the street he catches cold, and dies shortly after from pneumonia.

"And St. Petersburg carried on without Akaky Akakyevich." These words form the introduction to a second humane passage, which – although quoted less often than the first – is no less important.

The story is not yet finished however. Soon there are rumours about a corpse that haunts St. Petersburg at night and robs people of their overcoats without regard to person and even to rank. Finally the "important personality" also falls victim to such a robbery. He clearly recognises Akaky Akakyevich in his attacker. Since then he speaks more gently to his inferiors. After this last robbery, the ghost is no longer seen.

We have to thank Gogol's friend Annenkov for the information as to how Gogol arrived at this material. He heard at a party the story of a poor official, an ardent Sunday-hunter, who had put all his savings into a valuable rifle. The first time he went hunting with it, in a boat, he dozed off and the rifle slipped from the bows into the water without him noticing it. The unlucky hunter was so upset by this that he went to bed ill with misery and caught a heavy fever which would have resulted in his death if his colleagues had not had a collection and got him a new rifle. He could never bring himself to speak about this terrible adventure thereafter without becoming deathly pale from emotion. Annenkov finishes his recollection thus:

Everybody laughed at the anecdote, which was based on a true happening, apart from Gogol, who listened thoughtfully and let his head sink onto his chest. This anecdote was the first thought for his magnificent story "The Overcoat" and it did not leave him after that evening.[2]

The similarity between the short story and the anecdote is obvious. At the same time, it is easy to note that Gogol changed significant points: the overcoat has taken the place of the rifle, and the conclusion has become tragic, for the colleagues of the victim do not save him.

Shenrok is very probably correct in relating the replacement of the rifle by the coat to an experience from Gogol's own life. In a letter dated 2nd April 1830 to his mother, the poor official Gogol complains that lack of funds compels him "not only not to have a dress-coat, but

[2] P. V. Annenkov, *Vospominaniya i kriticheskiye ocherki*, I (St. Petersburg, 1877,) pp. 188–89, quoted in *Soch.* II, 610–611.

not even a warm coat" made, this being essential for the winter. "It is fortunate," he continues, "that I have become somewhat used to the cold and have managed the whole of the winter with my summer-coat."[3] There is one further detail to be added to these facts which apparently escaped Shenrok. Eighty roubles was the price of the over-coat of Akaky Akakyevich and eighty roubles was what it cost Gogol to have that summer-coat altered. We are in this case consequently in the happy position of knowing the origin of Gogol's subject. We also know that he had himself experienced the suffering of the minor official.

The way in which this material is developed has given rise to very varied contemplation. In the following account I shall try to reach a satisfactory view, naturally making use of the work of the most important investigators who have studied "The Overcoat". Special attention will be given here to the structure of the short story. It does not do to quote everyone who has written something about "The Overcoat". There is of course scarcely an article about Gogol in a history of literature or an encyclopaedia in which this short story is not mentioned. I shall discuss only a number of studies in which an essentially new point of view is expressed. I am not therefore considering Soviet literature after Eichenbaum. It is at present again customary in Russia to see Gogol as a realist and social critic and that means here a return to the "classical" view, being the first to be discussed.

"We have all emerged from under Gogol's 'Overcoat' ". These words are ascribed to Dostoyevsky and, authentic or not,[4] they may serve very well as a succinct formulation of a view which had become classical during the 19th century.

This sees in Gogol's short story the starting-point of the literature which is dominated by social pity and which demands attention for the humiliated and insulted. From this point of view, all light falls on the

[3] P., I, 148 and Mat., III, 20, 423.

[4] It goes back to a remark by de Vogüé in Le roman russe. He says: "Plus je lis les Russes, plus j'aperçois la verité du propos que me tenait l'un d'eux très mêlé à l'histoire littéraire des quarante dernières années: 'Nous sommes tous sortis du Manteau de Gogol'. On verra plus loin combien la filiation est évidente chez Dostoïevskij; le terrible romancier est tout entier dans son premier livre, les Pauvres Gens, et les Pauvres Gens sont en germe dans le Manteau". E. M. de Vogüé, Le roman russe, 20th edition, p. 96, 97. It seems to me from the context fairly clear that Dostoyevsky was not de Vogüé's informant. The words spoken by de Vogüé at the remembrance ceremony in Moscow in 1909 seem no clearer. He speaks there again of Gogol's spiritual heirs and goes on: "but all this power-ful progeny has issued from Gogol's Overcoat", without even mentioning that these are the words of a Russian literary man. Gogolevskiye dni v Moskve, (M., 1909), p. 142, 143.

first part of the short story and particularly on the humane passages, only the first of which is almost always quoted, it being considered as the revelation of Gogol's deepest intention.[5]

People are then rather at a loss what to do with the fantastic element and particularly with the ending.

I shall choose two examples from writings by well-known experts on Gogol's work. Speaking about Akaky Akakyevich, Ovsyaniko-Kulikovsky says:

> Only the great artist had pity for him, showing that the name of such unfortunate persons is Legio and objectifying that legion in Akaky Akakyevich; he dedicated the magnificent story "The Overcoat" to the depiction of his soul, his sad life and fate and that was the noble and generous beginning of that humane preaching for the defence of the "humiliated and insulted" which was later to form one of the most beautiful pages in the history of Russian literature. The direct continuer of Gogol's good work was Dostoyevsky, in the early period of his "cruel" works, which were at the time not yet so much cruel as sentimental. There is in Gogol no trace of cruelty or sentimentality, but a deep human feeling of pity and mercy with which the whole story is permeated and which is expressed with particular force in the following simple and moving words (there follows the humane passage).[6]

Kotlyarevsky says virtually the same:

> This story has a very special significance in the history of our literature. It is chronologically the first and, at the same time, one of the most perfect examples of this sort of work which later becomes very general and had a great social importance. It is a page from the history of the humiliated and insulted, of the same whom Dostoyevsky immediately after Gogol took under his protection. This protection of weaker brothers began in writing and deeds in the West at about the same time, with the growth and rapid extension of socialistic ideas.

The humane passages serve well to point out this tendency to the reader.

The conclusion, which Kotlyarevsky considers to have been "added arbitrarily" has, according to him, perhaps also a purpose.

Perhaps a strange, fantastic conclusion has been attached to this realistic story to satisfy moral feeling.

[5] Belinsky had taken the lead here. In his discussion of Dostoyevsky's "Poor Folk", in which for the rest he vindicates his originality, there occurs the statement: "...yet Gogol remains so to speak for ever his father in the artistic field." And further on: "Gogol remains for ever the Columbus of this immeasurable and inexhaustible field of activity in which Dostoyevsky has to move." (Belinsky, *Soch.*, III, col. 543)

[6] D. Ovsyaniko-Kulikovsky, *Gogol v ego proizvedeniyakh* (Moscow, 1909), p. 70.

But Kotlyarevsky does his best to prove that the fantastic element here is not romantic.

Gogol uses the miraculous only for the sake of the small genre pieces, with which he concludes the story.[7]

This manner of consideration has been preserved down to our own day. In the book by M. and R. Hofmann, which appeared in 1946, we can find the same view, formulated even more sharply. The writers object to everything described after the theft. The "important personality" is, according to them, superfluous for motivating the death of Akaky Akakyevich and they refer to the conclusion as a failure.[8]

The great interest of "The Overcoat" is not in its subject, nor in its development, but in a new theme which glides in there quite timidly, a theme which was to inspire novellists of the second half of the 19th century to compose their vast symphonies.[9]

The first humane passage is once again used to prove this thesis.

Summarising, we may formulate the classical view as follows: "The Overcoat" is a realistic, tragic story, with a humane tendency. It certainly contains fantastic elements, but these are scarcely of importance for its correct understanding.

If one takes the 19th century view of Gogol, then the "classical" interpretation of "The Overcoat" is practically inevitable. If Gogol has in fact developed, as everyone then considered, from a writer of regional ghost stories and grotesques to the father of Russian realism, who in his mature, serious work strove for a painfully accurate depiction of Russian reality, then we cannot deny that "The Overcoat" belongs to that maturest work. It is then obvious to stress the depiction of milieu and to ascribe a humane intention to the writter of "Dead Souls."

If we identify ourselves with the classical point of view, then it is impossible to regard the fantastic element as an integrating part of the "The Overcoat". We can more or less gloss over it, but we violate the

---

[7] N. Kotlyarevsky, *Gogol,* 4th edition (Petrograd, 1915), pp. 371–75.

[8] "La conclusion du récit, quand le spectre de Bachmatchkine vole le manteau du principal responsable de sa mort, nous paraît encore plus déplacée, car elle détruit l'impression d'ensemble et transforme cette nouvelle *réaliste* et *tragique* en un conte fantastique d'une veine fort discutable." M. and R. Hofmann, *Gogol* (Paris, 1946), pp. 161, 162.

[9] "Le grand intérêt du Manteau n'est pas dans son sujet, ni dans le développement, mais dans un thème nouveau, qui s'y glisse encore assez timidement, un thème dont les romanciers de la seconde moitié du dix-neuvième siècle s'inspireront pour composer leur vastes symphonies." *Op. cit.,* 162.

short story to the same extent. If we word matters strongly, then we easily come to the conclusion which M. and R. Hofmann drew, namely that the story is really unsuccessful, being spoilt by the fantastic element. In other words: from this point of view the short story cannot be seen as a unity. We must of course not exclude a priori the possibility that Gogol should have worked for many years[10] on an unsuccessful story, but it is highly improbable that he would have attached the fantastic conclusion onto a realistic short story without any intention. It is also difficult to accept that these two heterogeneous parts were not closely connected in Gogol's mind and formed a significant unity. We should be able to investigate to what extent he has expressed that unity.

There was already in the 19th century a literary man who defended a radically different view and who denied not the fantastic element, but the realism in "The Overcoat".

Rozanov, who had already defended the view that later Russian literature had been not a continuation of, but rather a defence against Gogol, who had characterised the healthy, normal Pushkin as the "counterpart of Gogol", the hater of nature and love, the destroyer of his own talent,[11] devoted his attention particularly to the origin of the main figure in the short story.[12] He also took into consideration for his arguments earlier versions of the story which have in part been preserved.[13] His conclusions may be summarised as follows:

The man in the anecdote is living, has a primitive love of nature, the action of his colleagues is human. The figure of Gogol's hero is however, as it were, built up around one thematic feature. Everything that is added to it serves solely to strengthen that feature, everything that does not harmonise with it is carefully eliminated. We see merely one thing excessively sharply and nothing in the natural, melting light of day. In his first sketch, Gogol still seems to have wanted to include as many objects as possible, while in the second version all the light falls on Akaky Akakyevich. Yet a sentence such as: "At heart, he was a good-natured fellow", was omitted. Akaky Akakyevich is without life. Gogol did not depict reality, he enlarged or diminished it infinitely. His

---

[10]   The first idea of "The Overcoat" must have arisen in 1834; the story is first printed in 1842 in the edition of Gogol's collected works which appeared in that year.
[11]   V. Rozanov, *Legenda o velikom inkvizitore*, 3rd edition (St. Petersburg, 1906), pp. 15–23, 253–65.
[12]   *Op. cit.*, pp. 266–80: "Kak proizoshel tip Akakya Akakyevicha".
[13]   They can be found in the 10th edition of Gogol's collected works by Tikhonravov, II, pp. 171–97 and 611–35.

lyricism is nothing but an expression of sadness about his own creations. This applies certainly also to the "humane passage". It is, therefore, strange that Gogol never becomes lyrical when he is depicting
types which are not negative, such as in the "Evenings" and
"Mirgorod".

If we leave this last assertion, which is definitely incorrect, on one
side, there remains a penetrating and suggestive argumentation which
cannot easily be refuted and the merits of which have in fact lasting
importance, even if its conclusions go too far. Rozanov was the first
to point out the hyperbolic element in "realistic" Gogol, for which
people had had no eye in his later work. Certain of his ideas are found
developed in the famous speech by Bryusov[14] and they have been accepted as obvious by many later investigators.

We also find great affinity with Rozanov's ideas in the studies which
A. Bem devoted to the relationship between Dostoyevsky's first work
"Poor Folk"[15] and "The Overcoat". There is really no wonder, since
Rozanov had after all likewise come to his view through studying
Dostoyevsky. There is every reason for a detailed comparison between
"The Overcoat" and "Poor Folk", for Dostoyevsky's novel is a clear
reaction to Gogol's short story. 'A continuation and deepening", people
had long said, "an answer and a denial", in Bem's opinion.

According to him, there is here no question of imitation but of repul-
sion. When Makar Devushkin, Dostoyevsky's hero, feels himself personally touched upon reading "The Overcoat", then there is expressed
in this annoyance something of Dostoyevsky's own feeling.

What strikes him [Devushkin] painfully is not the realism in the description,
he had after all shed tears at Pushkin's "Station Master", but precisely that
unmotivated unveiling of life, the cruel revelation *not of the justice, but of
the injustice of life.*[16]

That is Dostoyevsky's protest against the lack of soul of Gogol's world.
There was to him something insulting in granting to an overcoat such
an important role in the life of a human being. Bem also shares this
opinion.

---

[14] V. Bryusov, Speech given on 27th April 1909 at a festive meeting of the
"Obshchestvo lyubiteley rossiysskoy slovesnosti" in Moscow. See: *Gogolevskiye
dni v Moskve* (Moscow, 1909), pp. 157–81.
[15] A. Bem, "Il superamento di Gogol", in *Cultura*, 1931, pp. 157–70. "Pervye
shagi Dostoyevskogo", in *Slavia*, 1933, pp. 134–61. In particular " 'Shinel' i 'Bed-
nye Lyudi' " in *O Dostoyevskom*, III (Prague, 1936), pp. 127–138.
[16] A. Bem, *O Dostoyevskom*, III, p. 137.

Gogol does not raise his humiliated hero when he brings about his rebirth for a moment through the overcoat, but he humiliates him even more, he tramples on him. There is something cruel in Gogol's conception itself.[17]

The place of the overcoat, the dead object, is taken in "Poor Folk" by a living being, the beloved girl.

Gogol possessed the peculiar gift of "killing the personality, of killing life itself, if you like". In his works we find

everything reproduced down to the slightest details, apart from the living soul, apart from life. The world of Gogol is a puppet theatre, a brilliant masquerade which makes us laugh or cry, but evokes no sympathy with his heroes. In order to give his works an ethical-aesthetic appearance, he has to resort to general maxims such as the famous humane passage in "The Overcoat".[18]

In Dostoyevsky's case, however, the living soul is, according to Bem, preserved, strange as its expressions may appear.

If we wish to venture criticism of the conclusions of these two investigators, then we shall have to start from a seemingly slightly modified, but essentially completely different view of Gogol's main figure. This is, in my opinion, possible and necessary. Recognising that Gogol did not copy reality, in spite of the microscopic accuracy of his drawing, assenting that his heroes usually make a static impression and seem to be reduced to a few dominating features, even sharing the conviction that in Gogol death predominates over life, we may nevertheless doubt whether that domination is complete and ask ourselves whether Akaky Akakyevich is not, certainly to a minimum extent, after all a human being. The answer to this question must, in my opinion, without hesitation be in the affirmative, although he lacks almost everything which makes a person a human being and although the human element in him has been reduced to virtually nothing.

He nevertheless has one thing, even at the very beginning, namely a love. I do not mean that for the overcoat, but that for writing. As a result of this, he is vulnerable. The teasings of his colleagues are so cruel because they strike a living being in his purpose in life, in what gives him a right to recognition. It may be noted that this right likewise applies to an animal, and that we also call a child cruel if it disturbs an insect building its home. Yet Gogol says expressly that his hero is not only diligent, but works with love and forgets himself

[17]   *Op. cit.*, p. 135.
[18]   *Ibid.*, p. 132.

completely in the process, to such an extent that he has no thought for his external appearance, his food, his relaxation.

Is such a self-forgetfulness conceivable while being directed to such a trifling purpose? Of course it is in the case of a man who has been baptised Akaky Akakyevich, who has the family name Bashmachkin and is predestined to be a titular councillor, who feels his own personality as being so inferior that it is not worthy of the slightest attention, in whom natural love of self has to seek an object and can find it outside its own "ego", yet so closely connected with it that it enjoys its full satisfaction therein. The still infantile copyist finds himself in his writing and without being in the least aware of it, he retires into himself while writing and is at the same time "not himself".[19]

Now the great shocks come in separate phases. Through the cold he is forced to devote attention to his old overcoat. The tailor Petrovich forces him to start thinking of a new one, this need in turn brings him to the discovery of himself. Gogol is very careful in depicting this development. When Petrovich speaks for the first time about a new overcoat, Akaky Akakyevich feels himself "as in a dream" (the expression is repeated), upon hearing the price he utters a cry, "probably for the first time in his life". Dreaming and muttering to himself he roams through the city. Then he recovers and there now begins a new monologue, but this time "not in broken sentences, but frankly and soberly, as though talking to a wise friend". Once he is familiar with the thought of the overcoat, he changes in character, becomes more lively, surer, the undecided element even disappears from his facial expression. He has an aim. This is all the result of the overcoat, his second love. He did not mind suffering from hunger,

for spiritually he was nourished well enough, since his thoughts were full of the great idea of his future overcoat. His whole existence indeed seemed now somehow to have become fuller, as though he had got married, as though there were someone at his side, as though he was never alone, but some agreeable helpmate had consented to share the joys and sorrows of his life.[20]

Upon the approach of the fulfilment, "his heart, which was in general extremely calm, began to beat"[21] and, how could it be otherwise, he

[19]   *Soch.*, II, 88. In the second-last version which is known, we still find: "There, in that copying, was for him a safe separate world" (*Soch.*, II, 173).
[20]   The humorous conclusion of the sentence has deliberately been omitted here.
[21]   In the second-last version the sentence reads as follows: "The heart, that used hardly to beat for Akaky Akakyevich, began to beat more strongly" (*Soch.*, II, 180).

becomes unfaithful to his first love, the static element disappears more and more. Thinking about the overcoat, he almost makes an error in copying. On the day on which the overcoat becomes his property, "the most glorious day in his whole life", for the first time he writes nothing at all in the evening.

He takes the following step when he begins in principle to discover the other world and with it the possibility of a sexual fulfilment. He who had never shown the slightest interest in any event in the street stops on the way to the soirée in front of a shop-window where a picture is hanging. The representation is that of a woman who is taking off her shoe, her *bashmak*, during which process she bares her well-shaped leg.

She is being stared at by a man out of the opening of a door. The reference to the erotic element was even clearer in an earlier version. There a second picture is mentioned, a sequel to the first; the same beautiful woman is represented in it, but she is now lying in bed naked.[22] Akaky Akakyevich smiles. Is it "because he had come up against something that was completely unknown to him, of which a certain consciousness is nevertheless preserved in everyone?" Gogol answers that one cannot know what a person is thinking. It is however not here a question of "thoughts". What is it but a rising up of desire, as a result of which Akaky Akakyevich almost breaks into a trot behind a lady who shoots past him and who shows such an extraordinary mobility in all her limbs? Once again, Gogol finds it necessary to point out twice that his hero does not himself realise from where that wave has come. The fact that there was indeed a definite intention in Gogol's mind appears from the passage which functions as a counterpart to the one just mentioned. After being robbed Akaky Akakyevich in fact sees a half-naked woman who is wearing merely one *bashmak*: his terribly old landlady who "from modesty holds her chemise pulled together over a bosom".[23] A sad contrast with what a few hours ago had been a vague enticement. If we become aware of this contrast, then we suddenly also surmise a hidden intention behind the seemingly arbitrarily chosen example of the teasings of the colleagues, who "told of his landlady, an old woman of seventy, that she struck him and asked when the wedding was to be."

It is, I think, undeniable that all these indications and references

[22] *Soch.*, II, 183.
[23] It is precisely the parenthetic sentence quoted which was added in the last version.

point to a process which is taking place in Akaky Akakyevich, the maturing and realisation of which are nevertheless prevented by the loss of the overcoat.

The growth of his personality also appears from quite different things. Before the robbery his increasing personal consciousness is expressed as an unmotivated anxiety; only afterwards does it properly appear how much has changed in him. The shy Akaky gaspingly shouts his reproaches to the night-watchman. His further reactions to the robbery are likewise completely normal. He does not allow himself to be fobbed off by the commissioner, "wants to show character once in his life", barks at clerks and even ventures to lie that he has come on departmental business. And when he is finally standing opposite the general, this person, the "important personality" is the one who has the most of a puppet about him. The acquired words and gestures of the powerful man are completely mechanical, but the unfortunate one who is shattered by them is a small, nervous man who, sweating from anxiety, defends his last human hope.

This development is not finished with his death. It is not difficult to see that the second part of the short story is, insofar as it concerns Akaky Akakyevich, a fantastic, but logical continuation of the first, in which he, if only in a feverish dream, had dared to express his anger while dying. Without anticipating our discussion of the composition, we must here devote some attention to that final section. Rozanov, had he done the same, would perhaps have been forced to another conclusion. As appears from the earliest rough drafts of this short story which have come down to us, Gogol originally had another title in mind, namely "Story of a chinovnik who stole overcoats", and under this name, Pogodin, who was better informed than anyone about the origin of the story, announced it as late as 1841 to the readers of *Moskvityanin*.[24] We can, I think, derive something with fairly reasonable certainty from this writing. It is of course possible to think of quite a different ending than that which the story now has. In other words, we can attempt to imagine a situation in which the hero would have committed an ordinary robbery. We then however land in great difficulties. After all, even if the main character in the first version does not yet have the name Akaky Akakyevich, he has so many typical features in common with him that we can scarcely imagine that such a man would steal anything, and least of all overcoats! He would never be able to wear his booty! The matter is however completely plausible if we assume

[24] *Soch.*, II, 620.

that the stealing of the overcoats, as it now takes place, was in Gogol's mind from the very start, and was even the real subject of the short story. If this is correct, then there immediately disappears the possibility of seeing in the fantastic conclusion an addition, for whatever purpose it may have been written. It must then on the contrary have a fundamental importance in the literal sense.

This becomes even more probable if we assume that the name Akaky Akakyevich was chosen not merely with regard to its silly sound. I have to thank Professor Becker for being able to throw further light on this name. He gave me the idea of looking up the name Akaky in a Russian calendar of saints. There appear to be eight saints worshipped under that name. Under the St. Akaky whose death is commemorated on 29th November, I found the following entry in the almanach compiled by Bukharev: [25]

St. Akaky lived in the sixth century. St. Akaky lived for nine years in the service of a certain evil *starets* and suffered all insults without complaint and performed scrupulously everything he was ordered to do. When he died, he answered to the question "Is he dead?" from the grave "I am not dead, for it is impossible for one who is a doer of obedience to die." The *starets* then repented his hardness and for the rest of his days led a life which was pleasing to God.

The similarities with the main figure in "The Overcoat" are so great that, in my opinion, there is no question of chance. It would scarcely be possible to find another name which expressed so strongly the character of its bearer and at the same time embraced the nucleus of his adventures.

If the fantastic element is however firmly established in the plan, and this can also be discovered upon careful reading without knowing the origin of the story, then this alters the aspect of our problem completely. The reductio ad absurdum is then deliberate, a reproduction of reality is naturally excluded and it is foolish to apply to Gogol the standards of a normal psychology.

It is at the same time easy to see where Rozanov is right and where he is wrong. He is right in his protest against the realistic view of the short story, right in his thesis that Gogol has violated life, but incorrect in considering that this assertion should imply an accusation. Rozanov did not after all go far enough. He remained at the then new and still valuable discovery of the non-realistic character of Gogol's later work, yet only in order to measure it thereafter by reality. If on the con-

[25] I. Bukharev, *Zhitiya vsekh svyatykh* (Moscow, 1892), p. 624.

trary we recognise the fantastic element in it as essential, we can also take the view that death seems to rule in this unreal world, but that life is victorious.

Analogous objections can be uttered against Bem's views. Their tendency, insofar as they concern Dostoyevsky, can be left out of consideration here, but Bem underestimated Gogol in certain respects. It is not correct that Akaky Akakyevich is a dead soul, not correct that his resurrection is really a humiliation, and not true that the "humane passage" is an abstract statement, serving to give the story afterwards an ethical-aesthetic tinge. It can however very easily be explained how Bem arrived at his opinion. Anyone who in our time takes the trouble to read Dostoyevsky's "Poor Folk" after "The Overcoat", will feel himself struck by the very wide gap which separates both works. Whereas, when reading, one begins to identify oneself with Makar Devushkin, one can perhaps still see in Akaky Akakyevich a "brother", but hardly oneself. There is much truth in Bem's remark that Gogol's world "makes us laugh or cry, but evokes no sympathy".

However, we should then ask what causes the tears, if it is not sympathy. The most obvious answer, in fact already given by Rozanov, is: reflection.[26] That would agree marvellously with Pushkin's well-known reaction upon the reading aloud of the beginning of "Dead Souls". He too sank into reflection before exclaiming: "How sad our Russia really is!"

However attractive this solution may seem, it is in my opinion not the true one. The fact that the reader's contact with Gogol's hero is much less direct than that with Dostoyevsky's once again has its cause in the fantastic character of Gogol's world and moreover in the way in which it is portrayed. If we view the nature of both somewhat more closely, then we at the same time find an answer to the other questions confronting us from Bem's study.

The contrast Gogol-Dostoyevsky has more than once been formulated in that the first evokes bodies, whereas the second evokes souls for us. Yet no-one who knows Gogol somewhat will doubt that he is a masterful psychologist, of a completely different type to Dostoyevsky however. The latter also continually moves in border areas, but there is one region in which he had dared less far in 1846 than his great predecessor, and that lies where normal life touches death. It need hardly be repeated here that triviality had become terrifying to Gogol,

[26] Rozanov presumes this reflection in Gogol himself.

that the faces of people had become death-masks, and that he reproduced their senseless movements with inexorable accuracy. Gogol
is however the artist who remained in this border area longer than
anyone else and who also professed life, the more vehemently the deeper
he had despaired, but who described reality in its aspect of death with
fanatical concentration.

This story of Akaky Akakyevich is such an example of border psychology. He stands infinitely far from us in his dead surroundings,
from every complete human being, from the most miserable titular
councillor; not because he too is dead, but because life has in him been
reduced to a smaller spark than in any normal person. The fact that
this spark is roused by a breath, weaker than ever passes through a
normal human soul, is completely acceptable and is no offence to
human dignity. It is also very understandable that Devushkin and
precisely he should feel differently. Dostoyevsky shows clearly that
Devushkin's attitude to literature is extremely naïve. He enjoys the
bumptious nonsense which his fellow-lodger Ratazyayev knocks together for the simple reason that he does not understand where the
man gets the words from. He also enjoys, it is true, Pushkin's "Station Master", but principally because the main figure is to him so
appealing. When he however thinks he recognises himself in Akaky
Akakyevich, he is insulted, and rightly so – from his point of view.
It is unbearable to him that one knows and describes his intimate life,
he no longer feels safe in his retired state. Above all, he feels himself
misjudged in a consciousness of his own value which Akaky Akakyevich misses and has to miss, but which Devushkin possesses. He is
continually in contact with the living world, his deprivations are sacrifices for a human being, he has already long since found himself.
Nobody can be less prepared to place himself on a level with Gogol's
hero than he who stands so close to him.

This difference between the heroes finds its complete expression in
the way in which their creators introduce them. Akaky Akakyevich is
first seen from the outside, sitting on his stool, with his myopic eyes,
his bald head and his haemorrhoidal complexion. We then hear how
he was baptised and got his name, afterwards how he is treated in the
department and then, finally, these few words are pressed out of him:
"Leave me alone, why do you pester me?" On the other hand, we see
directly into Devushkin's soul. From the very first line of the book he
reveals himself, even if he does not intend to, in long letter after long
letter, and only slowly do we see his figure rising up before us and it

bears a striking likeness to his prototype without being the complete expression of his inner nature. On the contrary.

Coupled with this is, of course, the presence of a narrator in "The Overcoat", in other words of a person who places himself, unnoticed or otherwise, between his hero and the reader, and the lack of such a figure in the novel, which consists of a correspondence between two persons. It is also not without significance to note that as a short story "The Overcoat" answers Jolles' definition, that the case is more important than the main person, this being precisely the opposite in the novel "Poor Folk". All this makes it even clearer that the distance which the short story in general requires between the reader and the subject is still increased by humour.

The small, defenceless, injured hero is at the same time very comical, even from his first grimace after birth. His monomania for writing is comical as is the eternal idea of the overcoat, the feverish dream on his deathbed. The tailor and the general are comical as are almost all the situations. The nameless and shapeless figure of the narrator who has chosen his position below the described objects and who as a result perceives all the small things magnified into the ridiculous,[27] appeals in this way to the "healthy" desire to laugh of the "normal" person. Yet, on a few occasions he moves and then not only is another light thrown on the situation and the hero, but also on everything that went before and follows. There arises in this changing light that uncertainty, that ambivalence of feelings which always accompanies humour.

It is understandable that at a time when social feeling was still new in literature, readers answered the above-indicated appeal to see Akaky Akakyevich as comical with less guile. Surprise at the humane passage and the tragic turn in the course of the short story must have been greater for them than for us. The one-sidedness of the classical view is, I think, to be explained in this way, also bearing in mind the character of Russian literature in the second half of the previous century.

Through this humour and the distance which is created between the reader and the hero, through the merciless stress which he lays on the comic element, Gogol appears to have taken a risk which is greater than Dostoyevsky's plea for pity for his Devushkin. He succeeded, his

---

[27] The remark is by Chizhevsky, see below p. 201. This technique is not however restricted to "The Overcoat" being already known to Gogol's readers from his first works. It can probably be traced back to Sterne whose influence was profound in Russia.

19th century readers came even further to meet him than he had asked. It is the merit of Rozanov and Bem to have pointed out this "too much" and their fault that they in their turn went too far.

If we have spoken above mainly about the content of "The Overcoat", we shall in the following summary of two important studies for the most part consider the form. We shall then investigate the extent to which it is possible to arrive at new views by an examination of form.

The first of these studies is that by B. Eichenbaum[28] resulting from the purely formalist occupation with literature as was in vogue in Russia in about 1920. Eichenbaum sees in "The Overcoat" a grotesque which is carried, neither by the material nor by the "sujet", if we wish to use the technical term, but by the tone of the narrator. This is dramatic rather than narrative. The narrator begins with puns, all sorts of plays on words (e.g. with the names) and seeks a comically effective sound system ("the mimic sound gesture"). Consider the beginning which suggests an improvisation and ends with the sentence which culminates in the comically elevated word "haemorrhoidal", followed by the quasi-powerless: "What can you do about it, it is the fault of the St. Petersburg climate". Eichenbaum also considers the "humane passage" as such a "sound gesture", which according to him has wrongly so far always been regarded as the idea of the work. Here the tone suddenly changes and passes over into the sentimentally melodramatic. Yet, just because of this, the short story becomes a grotesque. It is, according to Eichenbaum, simply unacceptable that this should be a personal utterance by Gogol. Each work of art is after all "formed", art and artificiality are clearly expressed in the melodramatic cadence of the sentences (notice the often repeated "and"). The cleverer the jokes were at the beginning, the more pathetic and more sentimentally stylised must the passage therefore be in which the comical play is abolished. It is no wonder that Gogol thereafter continues in the old tone. It moreover appears from the manuscripts that this passage was missing in the first version. The style is that of the grotesque: a world fantastically reduced in size, which is cut off from large reality, not with a didactic or satirical purpose, but merely to create room for a playing with reality in which all its elements can be arranged anew. It is here not at all a question of the worthlessness of

[28]   B. Eichenbaum, "Kak sdelana Shinel' Gogolya", *Poetika*, I (Petrograd, 1919), pp. 151–65.

Akaky Akakyevich, any more than of preaching humanity, but merely that Gogol could unite the irreconcilable, could make the small huge and the large infinitely small.

The death of Akaky Akakyevich is, according to Eichenbaum, related comically and is followed by another pathetic passage. The final section is the apotheosis of the grotesque and nothing more fantastic than the beginning.

These are the main points in Eichenbaum's argument which it is all too easy to criticise in one sense, namely the strange depreciation of the "humane passage". What on earth does the theory, true on the whole, that a work of art is "formed", prove in this case? Even if it were to follow logically from this that a writer never expresses himself directly where he forms and is an artist, even then we have the fullest right to ask whether this in fact never happens, possibly not in an artistic manner and with fatal consequences for the work? Everyone knows that this has happened thousands of times and will happen thousands of times, as long as there are ideas and feelings which lie closer to the heart of an author than the immanent conformity of his creation. The whole of "Tendenz"-literature provides proof of this. It is on the contrary on many occasions from the "lack of form" of a certain section of a work, i.e. from the way in which the tone or atmosphere of the whole breaks up, that we can gauge the value it had for the artist.[29]

What should be proved therefore is that the passage in question which is in fact out of tune, acquires its full meaning only if it is viewed as having been written for the sake of the contrast effect in a grotesque. Leaving out of consideration whether it is correct to seek the basic idea of the short story in this particular place, its "ideal" content is nevertheless too heavy to be argued away in such a simple way. The fact that we do not find this paragraph in the earliest version is of little value as an argument. This in itself still proves nothing about Gogol's insincerity or lack of seriousness. We know after all that he was usually in the habit of placing just such passages which set a preceding section in a new light, at the end of his works. He does this in fact from the first short story of the "Evenings", and the close of the story of the two Ivans is a classical example thereof. The only unusual thing in this case is consequently the placing of the reflection not at the end, but at the beginning.

[29] See my treatment of "Viy".

To me, this criticism strikes at the heart of Eichenbaum's argument. It is not possible to treat "The Overcoat" as a grotesque. This does not imply that his study does not contain much valuable material.

He discerned the fantastic character of the short story, and the way in which he characterises the role of the narrator also seems to me largely incontestable. Eichenbaum's main fault is that he places humoresque and grotesque on the same plane and in this way robs the story of all its content.

Another author who likewise arranged his investigation of "The Overcoat" on a formal basis is Chizhevsky,[30] whose conclusions agree in some respects with those of Eichenbaum, although for the most part he is a very long way from Eichenbaum as regards the main point, namely the fixing of the basic idea of the short story.

Chizhevsky begins his study by stating that Gogol in "The Overcoat" uses the word *dazhe* (even) surprisingly often. He then investigates what curious functions it fulfills. In his opinion it is, lexicologically speaking, in the first place an impoverishment, a means for approaching the spoken language. More important however, are the comic effects which Gogol achieves with it, which are based on "a kind of strange antithesis of what is significant and what is not".[31] After the word "even", we naturally expect a climax, which is then absent in Gogol. Sometimes the opposite of what one expects follows and we consequently have an alogism. In this way Gogol lays bare the inner emptiness of Akaky Akakyevich. For example,

Fire sometimes appeared in his eyes and *even* the most bold and audacious thought flashed through his mind: whether he should not after all get himself a fur collar of marten?

Not only Akaky Akakyevich, but his whole milieu are typified in this way, as Chizhevsky shows by means of many examples.

Gogol made his narrator approach the sphere of thought of the hero as closely as possible and tries, although complete identification is out of the question, to see the world with the eyes of the small man, again using the word "even" as a stylistic aid, for example, when

---

[30] D. Chizhevsky, "Zur Komposition von Gogol's 'Mantel'" in *Zeitschrift für slavische Philologie*, Vol. XIV (1937), pp. 63–94. The author published the same article, in a slightly modified form, in *Sovremennye Zapiski*, part LXVII (1938), pp. 172–95. I have quoted the German version thereof, since this enabled me to quote Chizhevsky's words literally.
[31] "eine Art eigentümlicher Antithetik des Bedeutenden und des Bedeutungslosen", *op. cit.*, p. 67.

he speaks about the misfortune "to which *even* privy, real, court and other councillors are exposed." He consequently sees the world from below and, as a result, what is small becomes large. In this way, Gogol forces the reader to change his point of view continually. For he becomes aware again and again of how insignificant those things are in reality which appear so important to Akaky Akakyevich.

"The Overcoat" occupies a very special place amongst the many Russian short stories about minor officials. In Chizhevsky's opinion the social importance was substituted surreptitiously by publicistic criticism. For as a protest against the social position of minor officials, the story has turned out rather surprisingly. "Is the person of Akaky Akakyevich convincing proof that the 'small man' is also our 'brother'?"[32] Gogol did not want to prove this at all. He intends according to Chizhevsky something quite different, namely

to develop a theme which is very essential to his view of the world, the problem of 'one's own position' of man, a problem which is much deeper and wider than that which later became so popular in Russian literature, namely of 'the superfluous person.'[33]

We may therefore also doubt whether Dostoyevsky's protest against "The Overcoat" really concerns Gogol. A defence of the "small man" was for Gogol superfluous, "since for his Christian consciousness (. . .) the equality of men before God is from the start an axiom!"[34] The subject of the short story is "the kindling of a human soul", in which the strange thing is that the object of love is merely an overcoat. Every person has his passions, the hero has nevertheless here set himself an ideal which lies far below everything that Gogol elsewhere portrays as an *object of human desire*. His passion is however "a peculiar variety of love", and he can therefore best be placed amongst other unfortunate lovers in Gogol's work – Petro from "St. John's Eve", Andry from "Taras Bulba", Piskarev from "Nevsky Prospect", Poprishchin from "The Diary of a Madman" and even Chichikov.

[32] "Ist die Person Akakij Akakievič denn ein überzeugender Beweis, dass auch der 'kleine Mann' unser 'Bruder' ist?"

[33] "ein für seine Weltanschauung sehr wesentliches Thema zu entwickeln, das Problem der 'eigenen Stelle' des Menschen, ein Problem, das viel tiefer und weiter ist als das später in der russischen Literatur so populär gewordene Thema des 'überflüssigen Menschen'," Chizhevsky however sees a relationship between Akaky Akakyevich and the type of the dandy (Chichikov, Khlestakov) and the greedy ones (Petro from "St. John's Eve", Chertkov from "The Portrait", also Chichikov and others). This relationship seems to me distant and vague.

[34] "denn für sein christliches Bewusstsein [. . .] ist die Gleichheit der Menschen vor Gott von vornherein ein Axiom!"

In Gogol's letters between 1840 and 1843 we find again and again the thought that a person can attach himself too much to the world. The world is dedicated to destruction and man is destroyed with it if he has no centre on which he can lean.[35] This "centrum securitatis" is God. If one has found peace in it, then one also knows one's place in the world and cannot attach one's existence so closely to it that one is destroyed with it. Now, several of Gogol's heroes do precisely that. Chertkov is destroyed by riches and fame, Piskarev and Poprishchin by love, Akaky Akakyevich by – nothing!

The world – the devil – catches people not only with great things, not only with a flaming love, not only with millions, with the piles of gold, which Chertkov sees in his dream, but also with "trifles" with everyday things, with miserable pennies, with the love of an overcoat.[36]

The material for "The Overcoat" is in a certain sense a reversal of the parable of the widow's mite. "Not only God, but also the devil can assess such a 'mite' correctly."[37] Now everything becomes clear to Chizhevsky: "Obviously Gogol wants to have the whole adventure with the overcoat understood as a 'temptation' of Akaky Akakyevich by the devil."[38] Finally, it is "quite clear" that Akaky Akakyevich is not intended as our brother, Gogol "could not himself have failed to appreciate that none of his readers would have wanted such a brother."[39]

To begin with this last point, we evidently have here a misunderstanding. From the stir which the – misunderstood or otherwise – "humane passage" has made, we should, on the contrary, conclude that at least Gogol's first readers were particularly keen on this brotherhood. There are also facts which make it seem likely that Gogol was really serious about this thought. In an earlier version the "idea of brotherhood" is expressed even more clearly. There it says about the young man who is repenting: ". . . something whispered into his ear:

---

[35] Chizhevsky quotes here a letter to Danilevsky of 20th June 1843, *P.*, II, 317.
[36] " Die Welt – der Teufel – fängt den Menschen nicht nur mit Groszem, nicht nur mit einer flammenden Liebe, nicht nur mit Millionen, mit den Haufen Goldes, die Čertkov im Traume sieht, sondern auch mit Kleinigkeiten', mit Alltäglichkeiten, mit elenden Groschen, mit der Liebe zu einem Mantel", Chizhevsky, *op. cit.*, p. 88.
[37] "Nicht nur Gott, sondern auch der Teufel kann ein solches 'Scherflein' richtig einschätzen." *Ibid.*, p. 88. Chizhevsky shows by means of a number of passages that the devil plays a part in "The Overcoat".
[38] "Offenbar will Gogol' das ganze Abenteuer mit dem Mantel als eine 'Versuchung' des Akakij Akakievič durch den Teufel aufgefasst wissen." *Ibid.*, p. 89.
[39] "ganz deutlich" . . . "hätte doch selbst nicht verkennen können, dass niemand von seinen Lesern solch einen Bruder hätte haben wollen." *Ibid.*

this is after all a human voice, this is after all an intelligible ... a kindred voice.' "[40] Human and kindred, this is also the way this voice sounds for the unprejudiced reader from the words of the final version. It is not possible to get away from this. Gogol wanted to place his hero, who stands at such a distance from us, in the context of humanity.

What should we however think of Chizhevsky's fundamental position? Is "The Overcoat" really a demonstration of the idea that the devil can also bring man into temptation and to ruin by the slightest means? This is, in my view, an example of the sort of interpretation which conjures forth from a text those ideas which the commentator himself has first hidden in it. It already falls with Chizhevsky's view of the "humane passage", but there is much more in the short story which is opposed to this strange interpretation. The story never lends support to the view that Akaky Akakyevich is destroyed by sinful desire, firstly because the hero does not lose himself through the overcoat but finds himself, as we have just shown. There is no question that his personality is impoverished, hollowed out by his passion, as is, for example, the case with Chertkov, any more than there is anywhere an attempt to represent his desire as misplaced or the means to satisfy it as wrong. Imagine that Akaky Akakyevich had been satisfied with his "place" and had not looked around for a new overcoat. He would then just as surely have perished as now. Who shall deny that Gogol was a Christian thinker? We are however terrified when we consider what would be obtained from "Dead Souls" with such a method of explanation.[41]

We must regret all the more the strange turn taken by Chizhevsky's thoughts since his study contains for the rest so much that is valuable. The way in which he analyses the use of the word *dazhe*, which was only indicated very briefly above, is original and convincing. The view about the story of the overcoat as a modification of the theme of unhappy love is also, in my opinion, completely acceptable. The theological development and combination of these ideas is however just as prejudiced as the social, formalistic or any other one.

---

[40] *Soch.*, II, 173.
[41] We find the same view stated more strongly in the work by Chizhevsky's pupil Dietrich Gerhardt, *Gogol und Dostoevskij in ihrem künstlerischen Verhältnis* (Leipzig, 1941), p. 69. "Der Sinn, den Akakij Akakijevičens Leben bekommen hat, ist Unsinn, ist ein verlierbarer Gegenstand. So verliert er den Gegenstand, den Sinn seines Lebens und den Verstand auf einmal. Seine Strafe wird uns gezeigt, seine Schuld müssen wir erraten." How true!

After these critical considerations, we can deepen our insight into Gogol's intentions through an attempt at a new analysis of the construction of this work.

If we try to form a picture of the structure of the short story, it is almost obvious to begin with a separation into two parts: Gogol himself preceded us in this and entitled the section after Bashmachkin's death as a "fantastic conclusion". If we leave this latter section, which was in my opinion Gogol's starting point, and restrict ourselves for the time being to the first, "realistic" section, then it is not difficult to make a bipartite division here also, with a separating line after the theft of the overcoat. There is then as an introduction to the first part the description of Akaky Akakyevich's birth and name-giving. This is all so obvious that we may ask ourselves whether there is any point in dwelling on it. Nevertheless, upon closer viewing, it appears that Gogol must have worked according to such a scheme and that all sorts of lines in the composition of these parts run parallel and that others link them.

Before we consider the relationship of the sections, it is however desirable to make a general observation about certain concepts which recur repeatedly in the first main section.

The first noun that Gogol uses is the word "department". He breaks off immediately, but only in order to take this word up again.

In the department ... but perhaps it is just as well not to say in which department. There is nothing more touchy and ill-tempered in the world than departments, regiments, government offices, and indeed any kind of official body.

There follows, as proof, a comic digression, after which Gogol resumes:

Consequently, to avoid an unpleasantness, we shall call the department in question a certain department, and so in a certain department there served a certain *chinovnik* ...

(a description of him follows), after which Gogol continues:

As for his *chin* (for with us rank is something that must be stated before anything else), he was what is known as a "perpetual titular councillor" ...

This translation has deliberately been kept as literal as possible, and because of their etymological link the words *chin* ("rank") and *chinovnik* ("civil servant") have not been translated. The word "department" is, as it were, the key-note of what is going to follow, and *chin* the dominant.

We can find throughout the whole short story that the department or rather the official hierarchy forms a firm and immutable lattice within which Akaky Akakyevich moves as a prisoner. He is of course not aware of that, his cage seeming to him to be nature, and he has there his fixed "natural" place, such an insignificant one that neither the door-keepers nor his chiefs find his presence of importance.

It is the overcoat which compels him to go outside this circle, at first anxiously, later elatedly. As soon as he does that, he comes into contact with another hierarchy: the police apparatus, which is just as immobile as the official one. It is a police watchman who brings him back from his first musings about the overcoat to the bounds of reality, i.e. of St. Petersburg, the city of officials; after the robbery a watchman again shows him the course of the police hierarchy, and finally it is the "important person" who gives him the final reprimand which is at the same time a rejection. He too refers to the hierarchy. There enter in between these the figures of the inspector and superintendent, such as in the world of officials there is continually reference to heads of departments, directors and councillors of all sorts of ranks. The illness of Bashmachkin is confirmed by a departmental doctor, his death by a departmental door-keeper, while after his resurrection he is first recognised by a departmental official.

This expresses all the more strongly that Akaky Akakyevich is living in a dead world, is moving in an immobile miniature universe. If he were rewarded for his love for his work, he would have become a Privy Councillor, but of course ... Fighting for his highest good, he tries to break through this network, he penetrates as far as the superintendent, as the "important person" against all hierarchy, and his boldest word, which also costs him his life, is "Secretaries are such unreliable people ..." The ghost then takes revenge on this whole world "without distinguishing rank or position".

But let us first view the unfortunate hero in the preceding stage and at the same time the composition of the part of the short story which is concerned more with the "natural" Akaky Akakyevich.

On unravelling the threads of the composition, it appears that Gogol always works with small means, which escape the eye upon rapid reading. These include the return of certain situations and the use of certain words which acquire the value of symbols.

One example thereof has already been mentioned in another context. The awakening of the erotic feelings of Bashmachkin is demonstrated in a *bashmak* (the picture in the shop-window prior to the theft). The first woman whom he sees after the theft is sparsely clad and has only one *bashmak*.[42] When we notice something of this kind for the first time, we think of chance but, on looking closely, the number of cases appears to be so great that chance must be considered out of the question. It cannot even be assumed that Gogol's play was always unconscious.

In connection with the overcoat Akaky Akakyevich has on two occasions to pay a painful visit, the first being to Petrovich, the last to the "important person".[43] These visits show striking points of similarity. They are moreover connected by a motif. Both Petrovich and the general are tyrants. Both apply themselves to disheartening Akaky Akakyevich.

Petrovich was very fond of strong *effects*, he liked suddenly to browbeat someone completely and then to view *out of the corner of his eye* what sort of face the browbeaten person would put on after these words.

When he has achieved his aim, he is "*satisfied* that he had *not thrown himself away* and had also upheld the art of the tailor."

That the "important person" is such a tiresome being is due to the fact that he never dares to begin a conversation with anybody without first asking himself whether "he is not in that way *throwing away* his importance." After his energetic address to Bashmachkin he is "*satisfied* that the *effect* he had produced exceeded all expectations and absolutely in raptures over the idea that a word of his could actually throw a man into a faint, glanced at his friend *out of the corner of his eye* . . ."[44]

Before Petrovich had expressed his verdict about the old overcoat, he had first grasped his snuff box

with a portrait of some general, though which particular general it was impossible to say, for the place where the face should have been had been poked in by a finger and then pasted over with a square bit of paper. Having treated himself to a pinch of snuff, Petrovich held the overcoat out in his hands against the light and gave it another thorough examination, and again shook his head; he then turned it with the lining upwards and again shook his head, again took off the lid with the general pasted over with paper, and, filling his nose with snuff, replaced the lid, put away the snuff-box and, at last, said, "No, sir. Impossible to mend it. There's nothing left of it."

---

[42] I do not dare to express myself in a psycho-analytical sense about the symbolic value which the shoe (perhaps as what is trampled upon?) could have had.
[43] There is, it is true, also mention of a further visit to the superintendent, but this is not reproduced in detail.
[44] The word was first added in the last version. Cf. *Soch.*, II, 110 and 189.

Then he comes out with the bold plan of a new overcoat.

At the word "new" a mist suddenly spread before Akaky's eyes and everything in the room began swaying giddily. The only thing he could still see clearly was the general's face pasted over with paper on the lid of Petrovich's snuff-box.

The visits, which are so curiously similar in some respects have a contrasting function in the short story. In both cases the hero seems crushed, but in the first it is the beginning of his new life, in the second the announcement of his death. And, strangest of all, through the symbol of the general without a face, the first passage forms a prelude to the second.[45] There is no longer a place in St. Petersburg for a living Akaky Akakyevich.

At the end of the first part, Petrovich and the general come together in Akaky Akakyevich's feverish dream which was in the penultimate version developed somewhat differently and more clearly than in the definitive one.

Now he dreamed of Petrovich and commissioned him to make an overcoat from a pistol, so that it [the overcoat, F.D.] could burst into flames during an attack, since thieves and rascals sat everywhere in his room; now it seemed to him that he was standing in front of the general and hearing the suitable scolding, at which he muttered: "Yes, excuse me, excuse me, Excellency!" And, finally, he even carried on, using pure coachman's terms or those with which one makes room in the street, something which had not happened to him in his whole life since the time of his birth. "I don't care that you are a general!" he then cried, "I shall take the overcoat from his father-in-law (?) ... I shall ... Platon Platonovich."[46]

If we compare this version with the last, then Gogol appears to have altered the text. Not only has he toned down, but also blurred. Petrovich and the general are no longer mentioned straight after one another, it is less clear that they have something to do with one another, the schematic element has disappeared.[47]

[45] The "important person" has become important through receiving the rank of General, he has acquired a "face". There is however no place for "living" people near him.
[46] *Soch.*, II, 190. The question mark and the ... are by Tikhonravov, the editor of the manuscripts. They are placed before words which are difficult or impossible to read.
[47] The addition of the expression "out of the corner of his eye" in the description of how the general enjoys his effect (see note 44) is not in contradiction with this. The passages in question are a long way from one another. Gogol's smoothing out of schematic lines in the composition can also be found at other places. There is

Very schematic and so striking that we can scarcely imagine unconscious intentions, is the indication of the contrast between the hero
and his great enemy, "the important person".

In the first version we read that Bashmachkin "hardly ever cast a
glance at himself and even shaved without a mirror".[48] The "important person" always thinks of his own attitude and even studies it in
front of the mirror when he has gained the rank of general.

Akaky Akakyevich does not count for anything in the world of
officials.

No particular respect was shown him in the department. Not only did the
caretakers not get up from their seats when he passed by, but they did not
even vouchsafe a glance at him, just as if a common fly had flown through
the waiting-room. His superiors treated him in a manner that could best be
described as frigidly despotic. Some assistant head clerk would just shove a
paper under his nose without even saying "Please copy it," or "Here's an
interesting, amusing little case!" or something in a similarly pleasant vein
as is the custom in all well-regulated official establishments.

It is, on the other hand, said of the "important person":

he introduced a rule that his subordinates should meet him on the stairs when
he arrived at his office; that no-one should be admitted to his office unless
he first petitioned for an interview and that everything should be done
according to the strictest order ...

The strictness which he maintained everywhere served no purpose,

for the dozen or so Civil Servants who composed the whole administrative
machinery of his office were held in a proper state of fear and trembling
anyhow. Seeing him coming from a distance they all stopped their work
immediately and, standing at attention, waited until the chief had walked
through the room.

We scarcely need to refer to the contrast in their characters. It is
however interesting to compare the way in which they liked to express
themselves. When Akaky Akakyevich is teased to breaking point, he
mutters softly: "Leave me alone"; the first of the three phrases which
the general has, is "How dare you?"

There would in itself not be much purpose in establishing all this
if this sharp contrasting effect were confined to the purely static
element – the characteristic of the persons. We could at the most see

---

an example on p. 211. The addition of a symbolic feature is of course doubly
interesting therefore.
[48]   *Soch.*, II, 612.

in it a reminiscence of the puppet theatre. But, as we noticed when considering the two visits, the dynamics of the short story are also determined to a large degree by it and even the basic intention of the short story appears clearly from it.

Before we finally analyse this, attention must be directed to a highly important parallel.

There is namely not one "humane passage", but two. This has of course been noticed for a long time, but strangely only the first is normally accorded careful attention. Eichenbaum in the above-mentioned article deals with the second in a few words. Chizhevsky does not even discuss it. We are interested precisely in this section because it is so clearly the counterpart of the famous words which are always quoted, i.e. because of its position as a parallel, also however because it appears from it how few grounds there are for the opinion that Gogol did not intend the first seriously.

And St. Petersburg carried on without Akaky, as though he had never lived there. A human being just disappeared and left no trace, a human being whom no one ever dreamed of protecting, who was not dear to anyone, whom no one thought of taking any interest in, who did not attract the attention even of a naturalist who never fails to stick a pin through an ordinary fly to examine it under the miscroscope; a man who bore meekly the sneers and insults of his fellow Civil Servants in the department and who went to his grave because of some silly accident, but who before the very end of his life did nevertheless catch a glimpse of a Bright Visitant in the shape of an overcoat, which for a brief moment brought a ray of sunshine into his drab, poverty-stricken life, and upon whose head afterwards disaster had most pitilessly fallen, as it falls upon the heads of the great ones of this earth!

Is it incorrect to see in this great city without this living being a city of the dead? Do we not clearly have here the dimensions[49] of this unimportant creature who only becomes large enough to attract attention under the microscope of fantasy? Is not real pity asked for his defencelessness and misfortune?

The fact that this long sentence has a less pathetic effect than the "humane passage" seems to be nothing but a subjective opinion, at least if we simply place the two paragraphs in question side by side. If we however bear in mind their position in the short story, then we are struck by a great difference. There is in the first passage reference to a tragic element for which the comical descriptions of the intro-

[49] I would point out that Gogol had already used the image of the fly for the description of Akaky Akakyevich in the waiting-room.

duction were not exactly a preparation – on the contrary. In the latter a tragic life is summarised. It is understandable that people have doubted the veracity of the first, while it is scarcely possible to contest that of the second. All contrasts with which humour had played are summed up here once again, but now without pleasantry.

As far as positioning is concerned, the second passage is precisely where we should expect it, namely at the end of the first part. If we bear in mind the scheme of the construction, then the first seems to be placed in such a way that the balance is complete, namely as far as possible near the beginning.

Thus we have found in the first part a triple play of contrasts and parallels – for the dynamic element in the two visits and the remarks about the *bashmak,* for the static element in the characteristics of the hero and his opponent, for the meaning in the humane passages. This finding now acquires greater interest because it can also be shown that the two heterogeneous parts, the "realistic" beginning and the fantastic ending are connected by a similar construction.

After all, the theft is precisely in the middle of the three pairs of related passages just mentioned. The final section which, so to speak, consists wholly of thefts of overcoats, also finds its climax in a robbery scene, namely that in which the "important person" is the victim.

Both Akaky Akakyevich and the general are robbed, coming from an evening party. The hero did not feel at home at his for he was visiting someone higher than himself, and nobody had really worried about him. The general, on the other hand, had had an excellent time. He had been able to talk to everyone, since no-one was below him in rank. Nevertheless, both had drunk two glasses of champagne to cheer themselves up.[50]

Both are interested in the female sex. The thief cries to Akaky Akakyevich: "That overcoat is mine", the general hears someone call out to him: "I need your overcoat". Akaky Akakyevich appears the following day at his office "very pale", the "important person" also sees him as deathly pale after his death. He however also returns home pale and his daughter notes the following day: "You are very pale, papa."

These details are, in my opinion, again too numerous to be chance, but their importance is intensified when we find that in the last part

[50] To be accurate: there were in an earlier version initially 3 to 4 goblets for the general, one goblet in a following one, in the last, two glasses.

all the persons against whom Akaky Akakyevich can have a grievance pass in review. The introduction and conclusion are formed by the ridiculous figure cut by the policemen. They also occur twice in the first part. Moreover there is an office official who recognises the body and sees how it threatens him with its fist, and then in the last version only the general.

Yet, in the second-last version there is also mention of an inspector and a superintendent with the degree of importance they had in the first part. Bashmachkin did not even go to an inspector! There is merely mentioned how there appeared from the house of an inspector the little pig that knocks down a faint-hearted servant. It is however a superintendent, a very worthy man who, when having a cup of tea with a merchant, tends to explain "that the phenomenon still in fact appears, although rarely", and then he is made to tell the anecdote with which the last version of the short story ends.[51] Gogol omitted this whole passage about the superintendent and thereby rendered the parallel in the plan indistinct. It is however clear that there was a plan.

But these facts gain even more importance if we make a final comparison between the overcoat of Akaky Akakyevich and that of the "important person". The title of the short story already ensures that we are here at the centre of things.

The poor hero has discovered a new world through his overcoat. He has found it trampled on the ground on the fateful evening, but he puts it on and now goes into the night with a new attitude. For a moment an erotic adventure even entices him. Then he loses everything with the overcoat, except himself. In order to recover his treasure, he dares the most unheard-of things, risks his life and dies.

How different things are for the general. After a fine evening party, he wraps himself "particularly nicely in his warm overcoat" and prepares himself calmly for an amorous pleasure. Gogol has a few things to say about this latter point. The "important person" was "not a young man, a worthy father of a family". He has two very promising sons and a sweet daughter who "every morning kisses his hand with the words 'bonjour papa' ". His wife is "still in the prime of life and by no means bad-looking". They likewise kiss hands.

But the "important person", although for the rest completely satisfied with the tendernesses which he found in his home and family, considered it only right to have a lady friend in another part of the town with whom he entertained friendly relations. This lady friend was not a bit younger or

51   *Soch.,* II, 193, 194.

better-looking than his wife, but there it is: such is the way of the world, and it is not our business to pass judgment on it.

In other words, this man has everything that Akaky Akakyevich lacks, but it does not mean anything to him, because he himself means nothing. After all, through this method of indication Gogol devalues not only the importance of the mistress, but also that of the general's family. In connection with the remark about the female friend, the statement that the general is a "good husband" and a "worthy father of a family" is only to be construed in one way. The same applies to those household "tendernesses" which consist of hand-kissing, but just as much to the mistress who is not more beautiful or younger than the wife, but with whom the general nevertheless considers it "only right" to maintain friendly relations. In other words, both the consummation of marriage and the "free" love of the general are merely conventions in a mechanical existence.

Now the general is robbed of his overcoat and thereby a piece of the mechanism is destroyed. The amorous adventure is immediately at an end, the bully has suddenly been changed into a weasel and also has lost for good his taste for appearing powerful. In a word, it is as if something of his "attitude" (just as recently acquired as that of Akaky Akakyevich) has been taken from him, as a result of which a small piece of a small person becomes visible again.[52]

Reality is consequently different from appearance in this fantastic conclusion: it is not a dead person who visits the living, but a living person who visits the dead. Akaky Akakyevich still lives in fact, for he has after all carried a "great idea" around with him.[53] I do not hesitate to take this ironic word of Gogol seriously for a moment.[54]

Thus we again see Gogol playing with his basic themes – life in death, death in life, and love which is both death and life. Death has grown enormously in importance since before, life is repressed to that one spark in that almost imbecile, stammering copyist with the ludicrous name and the microscopic soul. And the miracle takes place in this fantastic world: life triumphs. The overcoat has not only brought

[52] It should, merely for the sake of completeness, be mentioned that this robbery scene serves in the composition not only as a parallel to that from the first part, but also as a reversal of the situation in the general's reception-room.
[53] See p. 191 above.
[54] This chapter had already been fully set when I came across the study by L. Gantsikov, which I was unfortunately unable to take account of in the text. L. Gantsikov, "Dell' umiltà. (Commento a 'Il Mantello' di N. V. Gogol)" in *Ricerche Slavistiche* (Roma), Part III (1954), pp. 242–52.

about a transformation in Akaky Akakyevich. In the "important person", there falls away a layer of bark around his miserable humanity. Even into the poor minds of officials and policemen there gleams something of a threat, which can of course only be reflected in a ludicrous manner.

Thus the last problem with which this fantastic ending confronts us is also solved. Did Gogol really intend a fantastic play or merely want to objectify the speaking of the various consciences? No more than there can be any doubt that the admirer of Hoffmann, the writer of "The Nose" was "genuinely" indulging in fancies, can one deny the meaning in his fantasy. We must have only admiration for the sensitive way in which he has handled the two possibilities. If it were possible that tens of people began to suffer from the same hallucinations as a result of the same real events, then the whole miracle could be explained away. Gogol did not strive for this type of reasonableness.

Summarising, my conclusions are: in order to understand "The Overcoat", we must consider the ending as an integral part of the story. The threads which connect this part from the point of view of composition with the preceding part also give us the right to do so from the point of view of form. Seen historically, it is likely that Gogol had this ending in mind when planning the work.

The large first part is an example of the "Wendepunktnovelle", the overcoat brings about the turn, the theft of the overcoat the destruction of the hero. This theft is the centre of the construction, on both sides there are two parts which are kept in balance and at the same time linked by a number of parallels and contrasts.

The main symbol in the short story is of course the overcoat, a number of minor ones consolidate the composition. This is highly schematic in the plan. Through careful retouching Gogol has eliminated the scheme to such an extent that it is not striking. He nevertheless allows it at the same time to remain just perceptible, as a result of which the reader can become aware of the unreal, even puppet-like nature of situations and characters.

As regards meaning, "The Overcoat" is the story of an unhappy love, through which the hero discovers himself and comes to life. He is a borderline case of what is human, the departmental world around him is mechanical and dead. The ending is the revenge of the living on the dead.

The humane passages are the places where the tragic side of the humour is accentuated. They do not contain the full meaning of the short story, but form the confrontation of the fantastic and "sub"-human element with reality. The comic element is through these passages alone raised to humour. If they are looked at away from the whole, then they can only partially be understood.

Gogol's work develops not from fantasy to reality, but it shows the development of a fantasy which absorbs more and more reality and which, having awakened from the dream, continues and illuminates the world of day into its farthest corners. It is a fantasy which can juggle in such a way with the attributes of reality and which knows the rules of the game of reality so accurately that it can in the end hazard comparison with reality which it seems to cover completely, and which is its opposite. Gogol has never lost an opportunity of reminding his reader of the change. This is also in part the meaning of the fantastic ending. In earlier work, what had begun as a dream is confronted with reality, here reality has to account for itself to the dream.

The dreamer used to say at the end of each play: "I am awake, I am here", now the "realist" asks at the end of his bitter work: "What do you think of my fantasy?"

CONCLUSION

The conclusions that can be drawn from what has been said lead to a modified view of Gogol's person and work.

In the first place it has appeared that Gogol worked consciously, to a much greater extent than hitherto assumed, at his technique, and that he also shows an extraordinarily strong feeling for composition in his seemingly most capricious works. The division into chapters, the use of symbols and *Leitmotive*, the formal determination of a position opposite the reader are amongst other things proof of this.

It sometimes appeared possible, by following the, in most cases hidden, lines of composition, to bring difficult passages "into place" and consequently to render clearer the intention of a whole work ("The Overcoat").

It subsequently became clear that Gogol treats borrowed material arbitrarily ("St. John's Eve", "The Two Ivans"). He changes not only details, he transfers the material not only into his own sphere, but also changes its meaning.

As far as content is concerned, Gogol appears, more than had been noted, to express his own anxieties in his short stories. The discovery of this fact led to the writing of the first chapter. Gogol's personality is explained in it in a certain respect. We have investigated from what unconscious sort of feelings of guilt he suffered. He seems to have had remarkable links to both parents, as a result of which normal eroticism was out of the question for him, just as was normal social intercourse. He is strongly narcissistic. It follows from this that we can hardly expect a social tendency in this very personal prose of the short story.

Realism appears to be present in the short stories in the details only. They serve to strengthen the illusion of objectivity. Gogol begins to use this means more and more and, in that sense, he develops in fact to a realist. He nevertheless continues to move in a self-created world which only deceptively resembles the "normal" one.

The summary at the end of this study gives the results of the investigations of the individual stories, whereas it is possible here to survey the material once again and to make an occasional new remark by combining previous findings.

Gogol's youth appears in the "Evenings" from the content of certain short stories and repeatedly also from the language, not from the form, in which he is an immediate master. Even such an early work as "The Fair at Sorochintsy" is perfect and original as regards form, being a grotesque, consisting of a number of fantastic scenes, which are set in a few fragments of lyricism. It is a short story concerned with anxiety, but it remains completely in the sphere of the play: a mock-devil is marriage-broker in an amorous story, which no-one will take seriously. Seriousness exists only in the descriptions of nature and at the end where the writer mourns about his youth. It then appears that Gogol has done nothing but bring a beautiful phantasmagoria to life. Real life is not represented in the figures, only an airy dream which is unfortunately at an end. "St. John's Eve" forms a contrast with "The Fair", in which the penetration of a demoniac principle into the world is treated merely as an amusing subject for an operetta.

In "St. John's Eve" Gogol has created a twofold masterpiece. On the one hand, he has succeeded in processing a romantic short story by Tieck into a Ukrainian story which gives the impression of being completely genuine. He has, by putting the story into the mouth of Foma Grigoryevich, created just that distance from his readers through which the horrible element was subdued and humour was given a chance. On the other hand, he has certainly put the devil upon the stage as a ludicrous character, and has planned his story as a comic tale, but shuddering at the demoniac element is now no longer limited to the dramatis personae – the reader experiences it as well.

"A Terrible Revenge" is the heaviest and most terrible work dating from Gogol's youth. From the combination of saga and antilegend there arises a tale of mystery in which the whole world seems distorted by the demoniac element. This world has cosmic dimensions and is held together in the short story by two symbols, namely the Dnieper and the Carpathians. Movement is expressed in the river and petrifaction in the mountains. The latter wins. The action finds its end in the mountains and the story of the *bandurist* in the immobility of his listeners. Anxiety is once again the subject, now only being hidden by the form, for saga and antilegend suggest distance in a completely different way from that in which the narrator did in "St. John's Eve". Yet the "simple forms" carry a second possibility. They arouse the feeling of "repeatability". What takes place within their vague limits is never completely past. We gain the impression that this world still exists for Gogol and anyone who, be it unconsciously, has come under the oppression of cosmic revenge, must ask: what is being avenged? It is those lovers of realism who consider that there is one way only in which reality can appear, who find "A Terrible Revenge" a weak piece. Yet it is just as obvious that Andrey Bely, the symbolist, felt: here Gogol's reality lies right before me and almost open.

How we want to explain Gogol's anxiety is a secondary matter compared with the fact that we recognise it as fundamental. That is what Bely did. My explanation goes in a psycho-analytical direction. Something should be added here to my assumption given above, namely that the relationship of Katerina and her father forms the mirror image of that between Gogol and his mother. We have in the first chapter seen Gogol's world shrink to an anxiety which found its expression in his physical life. This expression was masochistic. Gogol punished himself, partly by denying himself food. If we go a step further with Freud, then we are consequently confronted with an oral masochism, inseparable from the sadism which is paired with it. If we assume that there was with Gogol a regression to this infantile stage, then "A Terrible Revenge" gives us the terrible objectification thereof. Gogol then expressed his most primitive horror by creating a world peopled by the dead who swallow a sinner in their revenge. Thus Gogol gave shape to his anxiety when, unconscious of his own deepest motives, he brought to life these awful figures. It may have become clear that, whatever we may think about all these hypotheses, an elementary force has acted in "A Terrible Revenge", as a result of which the story acquires its oppressive grandeur.

Breaking my order of treatment, I should now like to consider "Viy" for a moment. This short story forms the counterpart to "A Terrible Revenge". Once again, the world becomes petrified at the end, as does the hero, not now an "antichrist", but a free Cossack. The "realism" has increased. The wizard had the dimensions, but also preserved the vagueness, of a "legendary" figure. Homa Brut is tangible and human, he belongs to the day, this unworried eater and lover. He is however overtaken by the world of night and slowly driven to his destruction. Incest is completely invisible to the eye of the consciousness, but anxiety is visible all the more. Once again revenge takes place for the same guilt. If there is some truth in another hypothesis from our first chapter, then the judgment is all the more terrible because it is carried out by a loving father, who not only may not see, but also may not be looked upon, because he has been the object of unconscious sinful love. He is covered with earth. It is in fact the ending of "Viy" and not "Nights at a Villa", nor the letters to Pogodin, through which I have come to assume a homo-erotic component in Gogol's unconscious.

In "The Fair at Sorochintsy" there was a confrontation with reality, namely the close; in "St. John's Eve" it was constant, namely the narrator; in "A Terrible Revenge" it was merely indicated, namely the horror of *bandurist's* listeners (for "A Terrible Revenge" is "reality", and its terribleness continues to be expressed as horror up to the last line); in "Viy", we are assured at the end in peaceful Kiev that Homa would not have needed to die if he had not known what anxiety was.

Gogol's dream-world appears on two further occasions, in both cases tangibly. "Old-world Land-owners" had not much attention paid to its form in the above discussion. There are merely two dominating formal characteristics in this short story, namely the first word, "I", and the turning-point. They are both so heavily laden with content that the idyll is through them essentially destroyed. "I" – Gogol – "I" stand outside, "I" dream, this is said to us so clearly for the first time in Gogol's work. "My" dream-world is destroyed by death which broke in, as senselessly as that happens in a paradise. "I" know that, "I" too know the voice which Afanasy Ivanovich has heard. And from afar we see an ideal woman looming up in this "fatherland of the soul". Pulherya Ivanovna is indeed devalued sexually, she is not a mother but a grandmother character. Yet, at last there are quiet and charm around a woman. There is of course anxiety, it even forms the centre, but only for Gogol who sees his idyll disappear. The beauty of the dream dominates for the reader.

The idyll of "The two Ivans" is tarnished and yet radiant. The dynamics of the puppets of Gogol's model, Narezhny, are replaced by a static immobility which seems all life. The fat and the thin hero also shrivel up, as does everything in Gogol, and the sadness of the conclusion again forms the point at which reality is reached. The immediate cause of this stiffening is just as senseless as in "Old-world Land-owners", but it is comical. There is scarcely any question of anxiety, even though a world is also passing away here. The play remains the main thing, the humour is laughing, even if the end is melancholy.

"Shponka" and "The Overcoat" have more often been compared with one another, and at the end of these considerations I should like to do the same. The heroes are one another's complete counterpart, but Gogol likes to depict contrasts with related features. Thus, we can say that the humble Ivan Fedorovich Shponka shows similarities with the obedient Akaky Akakyevich Bashmachkin. We can certainly see in the material which is called "woman" an example of the coat which is woman. This similarity is however superficial. The short story of Shponka is, as mentioned above, an open play with anxiety, anxiety for the feminine which reveals itself grotesquely in a thousand figures to that almost human creature, that only knows: "I don't want to", "I am afraid", "I might be touched by life, but I cannot". For Shponka is a most pleasant, most friendly specimen of the *nebokoptiteli*, the useless thumb-twiddlers.

Akaky Akakyevich has begun at the point at which Shponka ended. He discovers the overcoat, himself, woman, and he holds on. Up till after his death he wants to grasp what has once aroused his life.

The realism in "Shponka" is a joke, in "The Overcoat", which is a thousand times more fantastic, it is serious. St. Petersburg, the world, is a reality, a dead reality, through which that one small figure wanders about as a ghost, having just before his death looked upon life. We have quoted Bem who spoke about Gogol's killing of what is alive. These words contain truth, almost the whole truth in fact, for in "The Overcoat" almost everything is dead. Is this story then the apotheosis of anxiety? No, I think I can in Gogol's last short story discern resistance to that force. Gogol's violent aggressiveness, his hate, is certainly active in "The Overcoat". Just as in "Dead Souls", the world has become a magnificent mechanical play of the dead. Yet here, the one living creature has awakened. Gogol has provided him with his own attributes – the ludicrous and the ideal. He is "haemorrhoidal", he has known his "place" (but differently from the way in which Chizhevsky meant), he has "served", he has been a "doer of obedience", as his saintly model. He is immortal.

If Gogol had been able to proceed along this path, if he had, starting from the humblest form of life, been able to create figures, struggling, defending themselves while dying against the dead world around them, he should not have needed to burn the second part of "Dead Souls".

SUMMARY *

The present study is concerned with an analysis of some of Gogol's short stories, mainly from the point of view of their composition. By this method the author hoped to arrive at a more satisfactory interpretation. In some cases, however, the composition defied complete analysis, some elements having apparently no logical or aesthetic relevance to the whole. Thus the question arose whether there could have been some inner, psychic necessity compelling Gogol to introduce "unformed" material. The results of this enquiry have been laid down in the introductory chapter, "Gogol and anxiety". Not being a psychologist, the author wishes to stress the preliminary character of this part of his investigations, which needs to be further amplified and confirmed.

GOGOL AND ANXIETY

Gogol's earliest memories indicate the presence of feelings of anxiety and aggression. Gogol's reaction to the death of his father shows that, mentally, the aggression becomes directed against himself. A sense of guilt towards his father is present. Gogol's letter of March 24, 1827, shows that he feels himself called to a great mission by his father, with whom he identifies himself. To answer the call is to expiate an unconscious guilt. Needless to say that the sense of guilt persists and that the expiation is never at an end. The feeling of having a great mission to accomplish at the same time reinforces the narcissism present from childhood.

---

* This English summary was published in the original Dutch edition and does not form part of the present translation. It has been reprinted here since it contains a few additional thoughts.

When Gogol flees from Petersburg in 1829, we see that he regards his first failure as a punishment sent by God. His infatuation at that time, although his letter on the subject makes an impression of being extravagant, may have been real enough. The beloved, who is "too exalted", appears to be a mother-image. We may assume that his flight was, in fact, an attempt to break away from his mother.

In this connection the fragment "Woman" is of importance. From it we may see that the *femme fatale* occurring repeatedly in Gogol's work, represents the mother-image. Gogol fails on every occasion to describe the figure with any degree of realistic conviction. In the fragment we further find definitions of woman and of love that are highly significant, provided one does not put too abstract an interpretation upon them. In masculine beauty Gogol recognises woman. This raises the question of a possible homo-erotic component in his love-feelings, for which further indications may be found in his relationship to Pogodin and to the young count Velgorskij (Nights in a Villa). Love is the "home of the soul"; in his union to a woman a man may regain his father, whom Gogol calls "eternal" and "God". We find a marked Oedipal relation to the mother and identification with the father-aggressor.

Towards Pushkin Gogol re-enacts the relationship to his father. On Pushkin's death there are once more indications of feelings of guilt.

Illness has, in Gogol's life, a multiple function:

1. Hypochondria permits the coexistence of anxiety and narcissism. Crises of anxiety occur in 1840, 1842 and 1845.
2. Illness is a form of self-dramatisation; self-pity allows Gogol to cling to his neurosis.
3. Illness justifies the failure of his "mission".
4. Illness is a means of self-punishment.

We see that, later in life, Gogol transfers the part played by the father-image to God, whom he tries to placate by magical means (Father Matvey may be regarded as an incarnation of the angry father). When Gogol dies, he is convinced that he is suffering from the "disease of his father"; in the story of the last days of his life attempts at penance and anxiety-defence are prominent. Both on psychological grounds and in view of the facts of the case it is hardly possible to give credence to the notion that Gogol destroyed the second part of "Dead Souls" by mistake.

EVENINGS

"Evenings in a Village near Dikanka" is the subject of the second chapter. The first part of the work has to be conceived as a whole. It consists of four tales, told alternately by two narrators, Foma Grigoryevich and the *panich* (who is Gogol himself).

The structure of "The Fair at Sorochintsy", which is dramatic within a lyrical frame, is to be understood from the character of the narrator, the *panich*. The central part is a grotesque interplay of contrasts: the devil and love, Cherevik's unhappy marriage and the courtship of his daughter, the scene of Cherevik's wife with the *pope's* son and the happy union of the lovers. In extended imagery the older and the younger generation are shown as overlapping; the young girl in love, looking in a mirror, sees her own love as a reversal of the affair between her stepmother and the *pope's* son. The central theme is not one of love, but of the demoniacal. Its symbol, the red *svitka*, is contrasted with the *Leitmotiv* of love, the white *svitka*.

True eroticism is to be found in the lyrical nature-description at the opening of the story, anxiety appears in the horror at the mechanical motions of the ending. In this passage we are confronted with reality, a device that recurs in all Gogol's stories. The beginning and the ending contrast again with the central part, a contrast that is romantic and aesthetic.

"St. John's Eve" is discussed in connection with its source Tieck's "Liebeszauber". Gogol changes his original in essentials. Tieck's story is part of "Phantasus" and appears as a frame-story, but the "narrator" is a reader and is Tieck himself. He allegorises one idea, how death may approach a man unexpectedly, as if by chance; he constructs a typical *Wendepunktnovelle*. His hero Emil is a dreamer, living in fear of insanity – music is its symbol. He is contrasted with his friend Roderich, who represents the comical element, but it is with Roderich's dagger that Emil murders his beloved. Tieck aims at presenting a notion of fate in a fairyland setting and so to demonstrate the misery of the world "wie von vielen muntern Farben gebrochen".

The difference between "Liebeszauber" and "St. John's Eve" is at once evident from the character of the narrator. Foma Grigoryevich pretends to tell one of his grandfather's stories, and introduces the devil as a comic personage – and eventually he leaves the stage in the same rôle. Tieck's ending is filled with terror, Gogol's has a subdued ironic laughter. In the telling, Foma relieves the tension of the tale, so

that Gogol's story is typical of the indirect epic method. The characterisation of the hero in the two stories is opposite: the gallant Cossack
Petro takes the place of the timid dreamer Emil. Gogol's motivation is
much more concrete than Tieck's. Gogol takes recourse to motifs from
popular literature: the devil's goods bringing disaster, the search for
hidden treasures, the properties of St. John's wort, the witch as the
baba-yaga. The poetry of "Liebeszauber" is individualistic in character,
that of "St. John's Eve" reminds us of Ukrainian folk songs. But literary borrowings of popular motifs are quite possible.

"The Fair" and "St. John's Eve" are opposites in tenor, composition and style, while the central themes (the devil in the service
of love, the devil's property carrying disaster) are similar. The contrast
is probably intentional. Both stories are essentially a play of fancy.
In the second, love may have approached very closely to the demoniacal, but the two have not coincided.

The second part of "Evenings" shows a looser construction. The
two stories that differ most from those in the first part have been
selected for discussion. "A Terrible Revenge" is a masterpiece of
composition. The story is divided into two unequal parts, the first
comprising chapters I–XV, the second chapter XVI. The first part
resembles a tale of mystery, the second a saga. The mystery comes to
a climax at the end of chapter XV. By tracing the structure of the story
it can be demonstrated that one by one elements from the revenge-
drama of chapter XVI make their appearance in the first fifteen chapters. Once we read the first part of the story with the knowledge we
have gained in the second, it becomes completely changed. Gogol's
mastery can be demonstrated even more clearly in the equilibrium of
the various chapters, as has been shown by an investigation of the
formal relation between the initial and final sections of the successive
chapters.

The action first rises to a climax in chapter IX. The Dnieper passage
in chapter X is of great importance. Up till that point the Dnieper is a
Leitmotiv, it now becomes the symbol of the Cossack world. In chapter
XII the Carpathians loom up, as the symbol of the other world, a
movement that has become petrified, as indeed the action itself ends
in petrifaction. Chapter XV concludes the drama of the wizard, and
completes the revenge. Chapter XVI contains the story of the *bandurist*, ending at this same point. The terror of the audience forms the conclusion of the tale as a whole. Formally the first fifteen chapters form
an interplay of contrast, tension and relief, the action being dominated

by two symbols, the Dnieper and the Carpathians. Each stands for a separate world, and in addition the two represent the two planes of the action. On the first plane a tragedy is enacted in the Cossack world, symbolised by the Dnieper; on the second plane we witness a cosmic tragedy, symbolised in the Carpathians, where it has its beginning and ending. The first part approaches to what Jolles calls the antilegend, a story of superhuman wickedness. The wizard is constantly presented in contrast to holiness. The sinner is as much chosen for his crimes as is the saint in the legend for his miracles. He is contrasted to Katerina, his daughter. She cannot understand him, since, bearing no guilt, she belongs to another world. Thus she sets him free when he makes his appeal by the holy apostle Paulus. His desire she rejects, even unconsciously.

On the first plane the wizard's crimes are motivated by incestuous lust – seen from the second plane this is how Ivan's revenge is fulfilled. On the first plane the wizard goes mad, on the second the whole cosmos turns against the sinner. "A Terrible Revenge" is a cosmic tale of fate. It has been interpreted by Bely as referring to Gogol's own estrangement from his "race", from the "collectivity" to which he belonged, from his *milieu*. Such an interpretation seems unconvincing. When Gogol wrote "A Terrible Revenge" he can hardly have been aware of being uprooted, and can certainly not have seen this as an inevitable fate.

On the unconscious level the problem has a different aspect. The first to make him familiar with the notion of revenge was his mother. The incestuous disposition father-daughter may be the reversed image of the Oedipal relation son-mother. Thus Katerina's innocence reflects the innocence of Gogol's mother, the wizard's fatal guilt the unconscious guilt of Gogol himself. The possibility of the sinful desire being satisfied is persistently rejected. The desire itself, however, is punishable. Thus Gogol is cast out from the collectivity of the human race; he stands alone and is destroyed.

We may add that aggression is the wizard's main characteristic; an inferiority-complex is clearly indicated: everything laughs, the horse included. Petro's crime re-enacts the murder of Cain and Abel (Bely); this may mean that to Gogol anxiety and guilt are qualities inherent in humanity.

For the gnawing at the dead bodies a parallel can be cited in the story of Ugolino in Dante's Inferno, cantos 32 and 33.

"Ivan Fyodorovich Shponka" is again a grotesque, achieved this time by realistic means. The technique is not that of story-telling, it is typically "written" work, and complete in spite of the fact that there does not seem to be a real ending. The grotesque character appears from the delineation of the personages, the feminine Ivan Fyodorovich as opposed to his masculine aunt and all the others, the schoolmaster, the colonel, Storchenko, Ivan Ivanovich. He acts like a marionette. The culminating point is his anxiety-dream about woman. Formally this summarises all we have been told in the preceding pages. In a way "Ivan Fyodorovich Shponka" is a parody of the *Wendepunktnovelle*: it is no trivial incident that forms the turning point, but a great event, love. Ivan Fyodorovich however, remains unchanged. A satiric intention is absent.

The story is of great importance in Gogol's development: as an idyll it is the transition to "Old-World Land-owners", its humour reminds one of "Dead Souls", while woman is introduced as the personification of anxiety. It is of psychological interest because this last element is dealt with fancifully; a warning to be cautious when applying the notion of "realism" to Gogol.

MIRGOROD

The tales have not been placed in a framework, the fiction of explicitly mentioned narrators has been abandoned. The tales all belong to Gogol's masterpieces.

"Old-World Land-owners" shows at once something new in form, it begins with the word "I" – Gogol appears in his own subjective character. The object of his love is bucolic life. This is contrasted with the "full", the "real" life, which is dominated by an evil demon. The tone is elegiac – the idyll belongs to the past. Whenever Gogol evokes the contrast with the "larger" life, he sides with the bucolic world. In this lies the meaning of the opposition habit-love.

In one point Gogol identifies himself with his hero: after describing how Afanasy Ivanovich was called by the dead Pulherya Ivanovna, Gogol himself tells us how he is always terrified by the death-call. This is again the point where we are confronted with Gogol's own reality – the passage is to be regarded as very important for an understanding of his intentions.

In "Old-World Land-owners" a childhood paradise comes back to life, which, however, cannot be fenced off against anxiety and death. Gogol retains distance by his humour (which however is missing in the central place, where Afanasy Ivanovich is called). As an example we may point to the way in which the old people give expression to their love, which is humorous, also in the higher sense: teasing his wife Afanasy Ivanovich plays already with the thought of death.

Belinsky's opinion, which shows an increasing understanding of this work, mirrors a conflict between his reflection and his feeling. He acknowledges in 1840 that "habit" is actually love. He could not know that Pulherya Ivanovna's place in Gogol's work would remain unique. She is the only woman who is only lovable and sweet and as such she belongs to his childhood paradise.

Belinsky's words have been cited out of context by many later critics (Khrapchenko, Stepanov, Yermilov). Chizhevsky blames Belinsky for the mistakes made by his followers.

Eichenbaum's opinion that Gogol's first words "I love" are also meant to be humorous, must be rejected – his reference to Gogol's letter to Dmitryev of 1832 is unconvincing. Gippius sees a conflict between individualistic, romantic rebellion and the resignation of sentimentalism. According to Gippius Gogol comes to the same conclusion as Aleko in Pushkin's "Gipsies". In "Gipsies" however the fatal development is caused by passion. Gogol's paradise on the contrary is passionless. The world in which the idyll is enacted, is "closed" and of the past.

In "Viy" the subject-matter of a fairy-tale is incorporated in the form of a "novelle". An examination of the style of the opening passage shows at once that it is not an imitation of a folk-tale. Gogol aims at an illusion of reality, he wants to prove the reality of the demoniacal. At the beginning of the action the demoniacal enters reality as a dream, but when the dream ends it merges again into reality (Kiev).

There is an interplay between two worlds, that of "night" and that of "day", the former pervades the latter and destroys it. In Homa's first night in the church we see a symbol of this: the beautiful girl changes to a dead body. Day resumes its rights: Homa becomes once more a lover and an eater. In the second night the second symbol is presented: half of Homa's hair turns grey (this is stated in an accurate realistic description). The day has lost a great part of its right, Homa has been caught (the circle he described in his attempt to escape). In the third night Homa is destroyed.

Remarkable for the composition are the *Leitmotive*: 1. the howling of the wolves, 2. the evil eye, the demoniacal look, 3. the icons (which are mentioned each night and in the third night fall face downwards to the ground).

A radical departure from the fairy-tales is formed by: 1. Homa's loneliness (the protective grandfather of the fairy-tales has been replaced by the old Cossack who accompanies Homa to his fate. The formula "the philosopher was alone" is repeated again and again). 2. The erotic voluptuousness (the vision of the *rusalka* – Homa's emotion is both terrifying and sweet – he feels for his heart – is it gone?).

There is sexuality of two kinds, the animal kind, belonging to the day-world, and the demoniacal. Homa knows the former as normal, the latter he experiences as lust and terror of death.

Demoniacal wickedness is incarnated in the old woman, who is also a young girl and a hideous dead body. In her beauty she has the features of Gogol's ideal and represents his mother (she rises from the dead: the unconscious cannot be killed).

The scene where "Viy" appears cannot be accounted for either genetically from the fairy-tales or aesthetically from the composition. The "Viy" is the symbol of Gogol's father. He revenges the incest. He is blind – (dead) and covered with earth, the implication being twofold: come from the grave, and earthly. The dreamer is afraid of being seen (i.e. of being punished) and of seeing (i.e. of loving). The dreamer loves the father-aggressor.

The final words of "The Two Ivans" *skuchno na etom svete,* "the world's a dreary place" have become classic. They form a farewell to Mirgorod. This is a world seen comically, and irrevocably gone. It is the comical character of a *vertep* rather than of the despicable aspects of reality.

There are two narrators: one is from Dikanka, the other is Gogol himself. The introduction seems to be given by the former. If one pays close attention to the style, however, one notices a constant change of present and preterite in the description, and also a deviation from the present-time attitude. In addition all the important persons concerned in the quarrel are mentioned in advance (Agafya Fedosyevna, "the late judge", the mayor, Anton Prokofyevich Golopuz). This introduction is an overture in which all the themes of the composition have been indicated in the proper order.

Gogol appears here in the disguise of Rudy Panko and again and again peeps round his mask. In the story we see him come to the fore in the quasi-elevated "literary" passages, and again in the last pages, when the rôles are reversed and Gogol only occasionally speaks in Panko's manner, as in "the world's a dreary place, gentlemen". This last word proves that the storytelling is still going on, it takes away from the sentence the absolute positiveness of a general statement, it is a subjective utterance.

A comparison with Narezhny's novel "The Two Ivans, or the Passion for going to Law" is very fruitful. Narezhny's book is a rather complicated novel of adventure with a didactic purpose. The quarrel is in full swing when the story begins, its origin is woven in as previous history, the main theme is the course of the quarrel which leads up to a catastrophe, after which a happy ending follows.

With Gogol we see first the friendship, then the cause of the quarrel which is the turning-point in the story. At this point there follows a series of accelerated and retarded movements that do not lead to catastrophe but almost to a reconciliation. Then the first change is repeated. When the lawsuit begins, the tale is broken off.

Narezhny's work is dynamic, Gogol's static, Gogol treats that phase in the quarrel which Narezhny hardly mentions; the reconciliation which is Narezhny's aim, is missing with Gogol. The optimist Narezhny addresses reality in moralising tones, the pessimist Gogol withdraws in aesthetic disgust.

About the "thematic filling-up" of the construction we can say this: with Narezhny the Ivans stand side by side, they are doubles just as their sons and daughters and those of their common enemy *pan* Khariton Zanoza.

The Ivans of Narezhny are intended as men, but neither their outward appearance nor their inner selves have become real. Gogol makes his two Ivans mortal enemies and yet they are each other's counterparts. He succeeded in giving each a "personality" consisting almost entirely of external features and no more inner life than those small peculiarities of character that make their quarrel possible.

Gogol's mastery is evident in the structure of his plot: the naïve story-teller revels in the complications between the two identical culminating points, while actually all this commotion is a standstill. A denouement is not possible. The final considerations are only an apparent conclusion ("zero ending"). One should beware of attaching too much importance to them.

THE OVERCOAT

After a detailed analysis of the form of this story, the author has come to the following conclusions: the fantastic ending is, in all probability, also genetically, the centre of the tale. An indication of this is the title the tale originally had: "An Official stealing Overcoats", and the name of Akaky (the Saint of that name worshipped on 29th November is the prototype of Akaky Akakyevich).

In composition there are connections between the ending and the first "realistic" part of the tale.

This first part is a *Wendepunktnovelle*. The overcoat brings about the turn, the theft of the overcoat causes the hero's death. The theft is the centre of the structure, and on either side are two parts, counter-balanced and at the same time connected by parallels and contrasts. The main symbol is of course the coat, a number of less important ones strengthen the composition, the frame of which is markedly schematic. By careful retouching, Gogol has so far blurred the scheme that it no longer obtrudes itself, but he left it still barely perceptible, so that the reader may be conscious of the unreal, even puppet-like nature of the situations and characters.

In meaning "The Overcoat" is a story of an unhappy love through which the hero discovers himself and comes to life. He is a borderline case of what we consider human; the departmental world around him is mechanical and dead.

The end is the revenge of a living man on these dead officials. The "humane passages" are those places where the tragic side of the humour is accentuated. They do not contain the *complete* meaning of the tale; here the fantastic and the "sub-human" are confronted with reality. It is these passages that raise the comical aspects to the rank of humour. In separation from the whole they can only be partly inter-preted.

Gogol's work does not develop from fantasy to reality, but the fantasy increasingly absorbs the reality, it conjures with the attributes of what is real in accordance with the rules of the game, so that in the end it can bear comparison with the reality. Yet the latter is its oppo-site. Gogol constantly reminds his readers of the change. In earlier work that which had started as a dream, was confronted with reality; here it is the reality that has to account for itself to the dream. From a psychological point of view "The Overcoat" is an, unfortunately, isolated attempt on Gogol's part to overcome his anxiety.

APPENDIX

NIGHTS AT A ROMAN VILLA

They were sweet and painful, those sleepless nights. He sat ill in an arm-chair. I was with him. Sleep did not dare to descend on my eyes. Silently and unwillingly, it seemed, it respected the sanctity of the night-watch. It was so sweet for me to sit with him and to look at him. We had already called each other "thee" and "thou" for two nights. How much closer he has come to me since! He was sitting there all the time just as gently, quietly and resigned. God, with what joy, with what happiness I should have taken his illness upon myself! And if my death could have given him back his health, how willingly I should have surrendered myself to it!

I had not been with him during this night. I had finally decided to spend it at home and to sleep. Oh, how mean and inferior that night was and my despicable sleep during it! I slept badly, although I had spent sleepless nights the whole week. Thoughts of him tormented me. I pictured him to myself, praying, pleading. I saw him with the eyes of my soul. I hastened on the following morning and went to him as a criminal. He was lying in bed and saw me. He smiled with that angelic laugh with which he usually smiles. He gave me his hand. I pressed it full of love. "Traitor!" he said to me, "you have betrayed me." "My angel," I said, "forgive me. I have my-self suffered your suffering. I was tortured last night. My rest was no rest, forgive me!" He was so good! He pressed my hand! How I was then completely rewarded for the suffering which that senselessly spent night had brought me! "My head is heavy," he said. I wafted coolness towards him with a branch of laurel. "Oh, how fresh and pleasant," he said. His words were then ... how shall I say it! ... What should I then not have given, what earthly goods, those despicable, mean, loathsome goods ... no, there is no point in talking about them! You, who will get into your hands these incoherent weak lines, the dull expression of my feeling – if that at least happens – you will understand me. Otherwise you will not get them into your hands. You will understand how repulsive that whole collection of treasures and homages is, that rattling alluring gesture of the wooden dolls which are called human beings. Oh, with what malicious pleasure I should then have trampled down and flattened everything which came to me through the powerful sceptre of the tsar from the North if I had known that I could have bought with them a smile which would have indicated a slight relief on his face!

"Why have you provided me with such a bad month of May?" he said to me, awakening in his chair, upon hearing the wind which rustled behind the windows and brought with it gusts of aroma from the blossoming wild jasmin and the white acacia and made them whirl up with the rose-leaves.

I came to him at 10 o'clock. I had left him three hours before in order to rest somewhat and to prepare something for him to provide him with some variety, so that my coming would cause him more pleasure. I came to him at ten o'clock. He had already been sitting for more than an hour alone. The visitors who had been with him had long since departed. The fatigue of the long waiting could be read from his face. He saw me. He just moved his hand. "My saviour!" he said to me. Those words still sound in my ears. "My angel! Has time seemed long to you?" – "Oh, terribly long!" he answered. I kissed him on the shoulder. He turned his cheek towards me. We kissed one another, he still held my hand.

EIGHTH NIGHT

He did not like lying down and hardly went to bed at all. He preferred the arm-chair and also a sitting position. That night the doctor ordered him to go and rest. He stood up reluctantly and, supporting himself on my shoulder, went to his bed. My dear boy! (*Dushenka moi!*) His tired look, his warm, coloured coat, the slow movement of his steps – I see it all again, it is all before my eyes. He whispered into my ear while he was leaning on my shoulder and cast a look at the bed: 'Now I am a lost man," – "You'll just stay in bed for half an hour," I said, "and then you'll go and sit in your chair again." I have looked at you, my dear, tender flower! All that time you slept or merely dozed in bed or in the chair, I followed your movements and gestures, tied to you by a mysterious force.

What a strange newness my life then had, and I at the same time felt it as a repetition of something that was far away and long ago! But I believe that it is difficult to give an idea of it. There returned to me a vanished, fresh fragment of my youthful years, that time in which the soul seeks friendship and fraternity amongst the young companions of one's own age and a genuine youthful friendship, full of dear, almost childish trifles and competing signs of intimate affection; the time in which it is sweet to look one another in the eyes, in which you are prepared to make all sacrifices which often serve no purpose. And all those sweet, young, fresh feelings, – inhabitants, alas! of a world which does not return, – all those feelings returned to me. God, why? I have looked at you, my dear, young flower. Was for that reason that fresh aroma of youth wafted towards me, so that I should thereafter suddenly and with one blow sink into that large, deathly chilliness of my feelings, so that I should suddenly be a whole ten years older, so that I should look upon the vanishing of my life with more despair and exasperation? In this way an extinguishing fire sends a last flame upwards, which flickeringly illuminates the sombre walls and then conceals itself for ever.

BIBLIOGRAPHY

This list does not include titles of works of reference and newspaper articles. Works in Western European languages on the history of literature or on literary technique are listed only if they are quoted in the text or in the notes.

Adams, V., "Gogol's Erstlingswerk 'Hans Küchelgarten' im Lichte seines Natur- und Welterlebnisses", *Zeitschr. f. slav. Philologie*, 1931, p. 323 ff.

Afanas'ev, A., *Russkie narodnye skazki*, pod red. A. E. Gruzinskogo, 3 vols. (M., 1897).

Ajzenštok, I., "Gercen – literaturnyj kritik", *Literaturnyj Kritik*, 1937, 5, p. 18 ff.

A. K. and Ju. F., "'Strašnaja Mest' Gogolja i povest' Tika 'P'etro Apone'", *Russkaja Starina*, 1902, 3, p. 641 ff.

Aksakov, S. T., *Istorija moego znakomstva s Gogolem* (M., 1890). Also in: *Sobr. soč. S. T. Aksakova*, pod red A. G. Gornfel'da, IV, (SPb., 1910), p. 345 ff.

——, "Neskol'ko slov o biografii Gogolja", *Ibid.*, IV, p. 153 ff.

——, "Pis'mo k druz'jam Gogolja", Ibid., IV, p. 449 ff.

A. L., "Ukrainofil'stvo Gogolja", *Kievskaja Starina*, 1902, 7/8, p. 115 ff.

Aleksandrovskij, G., "Gogol' i Belinskij", *P.G.D.*, otd. IV, p. 3 ff.

——, *Neskol'ko dannych iz psichologii Gogolevskogo tvorčestva* (Kiev, 1902).

Annenkov, P., *Literaturnye vospominanija* (L., 1928).

Annenskij, I., "Estetika 'Mertvych Duš' i ee nasled'e", *Apollon*, 1911, 8, p. 50 ff.

Arndt, J. L., "Autopsychodrama. Een bijdrage tot het neurosebegrip", *Genees- kundige Bladen*, 46th series, 9 (Haarlem, 1954).

——, *Zelfdramatisering* (Leyden, 1950).

Arnol'd, N., L. Kaplan, G. Fridlender, "Gogol' v neizdannych vospominanijach", *Literaturnoe Nasledstvo*, vol. 58 (1952), p. 773 ff.

Arsen'ev, K., "Značenie Gogolja dlja ego preemnikov", *Reči*, p. 21 ff.

Bartenev, P., "A. O. Smirnova o Gogole", *Russkij Archiv*, 1895, 4, p. 537 ff.

Baženov, N., *Bolezn' i smert' Gogola* (M., 1902).

Belinskij, V. G., *V. G. Belinskij o Gogole. Stat'i, recenzii, pis'ma*. Red., vstup. stat'ja i kommentarii S. Mašinskogo (M., 1949).

——, *Sobranie sočinenij v 3 tomach*. Pod obščej red. F. M. Golovenčenko (M., 1948).

——, *Sobranie sočinenij v 3 tomach*. Pod red. Ivanova-Razumnika (SPb., 1911).

——, *Polnoe sobr. soč. V. G. Belinskogo v 12 tomach*. Red. i prim. S. A. Vengerova (SPb., 1900).

Belozerskaja, N., "M. I. Gogol'", *Russkaja Starina*, 1887, 3, p. 690 ff.

Belyj, A., "Gogol'", *Vesy*, 1909, 4.

——, *Masterstvo Gogolja* (M.-L., 1934).

Bem, A., Review of D. Gerhardt, *Gogol' und Dostojevskij.* – In *Zeitschr. f. slav. Philologie*, 1942, p. 225 ff.
——, *Dostoevskij* (Prague, 1938).
——, "Il superamento di Gogol", *Cultura*, 1931, p. 157 ff.
——, *K voprosu o vlijanii Gogolja na Dostoevskogo* (Prague, 1928).
——, *O Dostoevskom*, 3 vols. (Prague, 1929, 1933, 1936).
——, "Pervye šagi Dostoevskogo", *Slavia*, 1-2, 1933, p. 134 ff.
Berliner, G., "Černyševskij i Gogol' ", *M.I.*, 2, p. 472 ff.
Blok, A., "Ditja Gogolja", *Reč'*, 20 March 1909; also in *Sočinenija v odnom tome* (M.-L., 1946), p. 531 ff.
Bobrov, E., "Dva voprosa iz tvorčestva N. V. Gogolja", *Izv. otd. russk. jaz. i slov. Imp. Akad. Nauk*, 1911, p. 63 ff.
Bocjanovskij, V., "Odin iz veščnych simvolov u Gogolja", *Sbornik otd. russk. jaz. i slov. Akad. Nauk S.S.S.R.*, 1928, 3, p. 103 ff.
Bogaevskaja, K. and Ja. Černjak, "Pis'mo Belinskogo k Gogolju", *Literaturnoe Nasledstvo*, vol. 56 (1950), p. 513 ff.
Bolte, Joh. and G. Polivka, *Anmerkungen zu den Kinder- und Hausmärchen der Brüder Grimm*, 5 vols. (Leipzig 1913–32).
Borozdin, A., "Razvitie vzgljadov N. V. Gogolja na tvorčestvo", *Reči*, p. 31 ff.
Boutonier, Juliette, *L'angoisse* (Paris, 1949).
Brik, O., "Formal'nyj metod", *Lef*, 1923, 1, p. 213 ff.
Briksman, M., "K voprosu ob otnošenii Gogolja k 'neistovoj poetike' ", *Izv. Azerbajdžanskogo gos. Univ. im. V. I. Lenina*, 1927, 8-10, supplement, p. 81 ff.
Brjusov, V., "Ispepelennyj", *Gogolevskie dni v Moskve* (M., 1909), p. 157 ff. Reprinted in *Vesy, 1909*; also appeared separately (M., 1909).
Brodiansky, Nina, "Gogol' and his Characters". *The Slavonic Review*, 1952, p. 36 ff.
Brynner, Cyril, "Gogol's 'The Overcoat' in World Literature", *The Slavonic Review*, 1954, p. 499 ff.
Bucharev, I., *Žitija vsech svjatych* (M., 1892).
Budde, E., "Značenie Gogolja v istorii russkogo literaturnogo jazyka", *Žurnal Min. Nar. Prosv.*, 1902, 7.
Bykov, N., "K biografii N. V. Gogolja", *Russkaja Starina*, 1888, 1, p. 767 ff.
Cejtlin, A., "Marksisty i 'formal'nyj metod' ", *Lef*, 1923, 3.
Chalanskij, M., "N. V. Gogol' kak romantik i poet russkoj dejstvitel'nosti", *Ch. S.*, p. 171 ff.
Charciev, V., "Puškinskie principy v tvorčestve Gogolja", *Ch. S.*, p. 163 ff.
Chrapčenko, M., *N. V. Gogol'* (M., 1936).
Čagovec, V., "Semejnaja chronika Gogolej", *P.G.D.*, otd. III, p. 3 ff.
Černyševskij, N. G., *Estetika i literaturnaja kritika* (M.-L., 1951).
——, *Očerki Gogolevskogo perioda russkoj literatury*, 2nd ed. (SPb., 1893).
Čiževskij, D., see also: Čyževs'kyj and Tschizewskij.
——, "Neizvestnyj Gogol' " *Novyj Žurnal*, 1951, p. 126 ff.
——, "O 'Šineli' Gogolja, *Sovremennye Zapiski*, 1938, p. 172 ff.
Čudakov, G., Otnošenija tvorčestva Gogolja k zapadno-evropejskim literaturam (Kiev, 1908). Also in *Univ. Izvestija*, Kiev, 1907, 7, 1908, 3, 8, 10.
——, "Otraženie motivov narodnoj slovesnosti v proizvedenijach N. V. Gogolja", *Univ. Izvestija*, Kiev, 1906, 12, p. 1 ff.
Čyževs'kyj, D., *Hegel bei den Slaven* (Reichenberg, 1934).
Danilevskij, G., *Sobranie sočinenij*, XIV (SPb., 1902).
Danilov, V., "O. M. Somov, sotrudnik Del'viga i Puškina", *Russkij Filol. Vestnik*, 1908, 3, p. 190 ff.; 4, p. 316 ff.

——, "Vlijanie bytovoj i literaturnoj sredy na 'Večera na chutore bliz Dikan'ki' ", *S.N.*, 99 ff.

Dauenhauer, A., "Gogol's 'Schreckliche Rache' und 'Pietro von Abano' von L. Tieck", *Zeitschr. f. slav. Philologie*, 1936, p. 315 ff.

Denisov, V., "Sociologičeskij analiz dvuch redakcij 'Propavšej gramoty' Gogolja", *Literatura i Marksizm*, 1930, 2, p. 110 ff.

Deržavin, N., "Fantastika v 'Strašnoj mesti' Gogolja", *Naukovi Zap. Nauk.-doslidčoï katedry ist. Ukr. kul't.*, 1927, p. 329 ff.

Desnickij, V., *Na literaturnye temy*, 2 vols. (M.-L., 1933, 1936).

——, "O realizme Gogolja", *Literaturnyj Sovremennik*, 1935, 4, p. 195 ff. Also in *Na literaturnye temy*, II, p. 367 ff. and *M.I.*, 2, p. 61 ff.

——, "Zadači izučenija žizni i tvorčestva Gogolja", *Na literaturnye temy*, II (L., 1936), p. 295 ff., reprinted in *M.I.*, 1, p. 1 ff.

——, "Žizn' i tvorčestvo N. V. Gogolja", *Na literaturnye temy*, I, p. 173 ff.

Dobrovol'skij, L., V. Lavrov, "Bibliografičeskij ukazatel' sočinenij Gogolja i literatury o nem na russkom jazyke za 1916–1934 gg", *M.I.*, 1, p. 377 ff.

——, "Gogol' v ukrainskoj literature (USSR) 1917–1934", *M.I.*, 1, p. 474 ff.

Durylin, S., " 'Delo' ob imuščestve Gogolja", *M.I.*, 1, p. 359 ff.

——, "Gogol' i Aksakovy", *Zven'ja*, 3-4 (1934), p. 325 ff.

——, *Iz semejnoj chroniki Gogolja* (M., 1928).

Efimenko, A., "Ukrainskij element v tvorčestve Gogolja", *Južnaja Rus'*, 1905. Originally in *Vestnik Evropy*, 1902, 7, p. 238 ff.

Eichenbaum, B., "Gogol' i delo literatury", *Moj Vremennik* (L., 1929), p. 89 ff.

——, "Illjuzija skazki", *Skvoz' literaturu* (L., 1924), p. 152 ff.

——, "Kak sdelana 'Šinel'' Gogolja", *Poetika*, 1 (P., 1919), p. 151 ff.

——, "Tolstoj i Paul de Kock", *Zapadnyj Sbornik*, 1937, 1, p. 291 ff.

El'sberg, A., *Nasledie Gogolja i Ščedrina i sovetskaja satira* (M., 1954).

Erlich, Victor, *Russian Formalism* (The Hague, 1955).

Ermakov, I., *Očerki po analizu tvorčestva N. V. Gogolja* (M.-L., 1924).

Ermilov, V., *Gogol'* (M., 1952).

F(ranko), I., "Vij, Šoludivyj Bunjaka i Juda Iskariotskij", *Ukraina*, 1907, 1, p. 50 ff.

Freud, S., *Abriss der Psychoanalyse* (Frankfurt a.M., 1953).

——, *Gesammelte Schriften*, 12 vols. (Leipzig-Vienna-Zürich, 1925–34).

Früchte, G., "Dostojevskij und Gogol", *Das literarische Echo*, 1918, p. 145 ff.

G., V., "Dvorjanskoe delo Gogolja", *Literaturnyj Vestnik*, 1902, 1, p. 131 ff.

Galagan, G., "Malorusskij vertep", *Kievskaja Starina*, 1882, 10, p. 1 ff.

Gancikov, L., "Dell' umiltà (Commento a *Il Mantello* di N.V. Gogol')", *Ricerche Slavistiche*, 3, Rome 1954, p. 242 ff.

Georgievskij, G., "Gogol' v ego novych pis'mach", *Russkaja Starina*, 1903, 3, p. 451 ff.

——, *Gogolevskie teksty* (SPb., 1910).

Gerbel', N., "N. Ja. Prokopovič i otnošenija ego k Gogolju", *Sovremennik*, 1858, 2, p. 266 ff.

Gercen, A., see: Herzen.

Gerhardt, D., *Gogol' und Dostojevskij in ihrem künstlerischen Verhältnis* (Leipzig, 1941).

Gersevanov, N., *Gogol' pred sudom obličitel'noj literatury* (Odessa, 1861).

Geršenzon, M., "Gogol' ", *Istoričeskie Zapiski*, 1923, p. 163 ff.

Gesemann, G., "Der Träumer und der Andere", in *Dostojevskij-Studien*, ges. und herausgeg. von D. Čyževs'kyj (Reichenberg, 1931).

——, "Grundlagen einer Charakterologie Gogols", *Jahrbuch der Charakterologie*, 1924, p. 51 ff.

Gippius, V., see also: Hippius.
——, *Gogol'* (L., 1924).
——, *N. V. Gogol' v pis'mach i vospominanijach* (M., 1931).
——, "Literaturnoe obščenie Gogolja s Puškinym", *Učenye zapiski Permskogo Gos. Univ., otd. obšč. nauk*, vyp. 2, 1931, p. 60 ff.
——, "Literaturnye vzgljady Gogolja", *Literaturnaja učeba*, 1936, 11, p. 52 ff.
——, " 'Večera na chutore bliz Dikan'ki' Gogolja", *Trudy otd. novoj russk. lit. Akad. Nauk. S.S.S.R.*, 1948, 1, p. 9 ff.
Gogol', N. V., *Polnoe sobranie sočinenij*, 14 vols. Edition of Akademija Nauk S.S.S.R. (M., 1937–52) (I had access to vols. II, VIII, IX, XI, XII, XIII only).
——, *Pis'ma N. V. Gogolja*. Redakcija V. I. Šenroka, 4 vols. (SPb, no date) (1902).
——, *Sočinenija N. V. Gogolja*, 10th ed. (M., 1889–96), Vols. I–V edited by N. Tichonravov, vols. VI and VII by V.I. Šenrok.
——, *N. V. Gogol'. Materialy i issledovanija*, pod red. V. Gippiusa, 2 vols. (M.-L., 1936).
——, *Gogol'. Reči posvjaščennye ego pamjati* (SPb., 1902).
——, *Gogol'. Stat'i i materialy.* (L., 1954).
——, *N. V. Gogol' v russkoj kritike*. Published by A. K. Kotov and M. Ja. Poljakov (M., 1953).
——, *Gogol' v vospominanijach sovremennikov.* Pod red. S. Mašinskogo (M., 1952).
——, *Opisanie rukopisej i izobraziteľnych materialov Puškinskogo doma*, I, *N. V. Gogol'* (M.-L., 1951).
Gogol', O. V., *Iz semejnoj chroniki Gogolej* (Kiev, 1909).
Gogol', V. A., "Prostak", *Osnova*, 1862.
Gorlin, M., "Hoffmann en Russie", *Revue de littérature comparée*, 1935, 1, p. 60 ff.
——, *N. V. Gogol and E. Th. A. Hoffmann* (Leipzig, 1933).
Grigor'ev, A., "F. Dostoevskij i škola sentimental'nogo naturalizma", *M.I.*, 1, p. 249 ff.
——, "N. V. Gogol' i ego perepiska s druz'jami", *Sobr. soč. A. Grigor'eva*, pod red. V. F. Savodnika, part 8 (M., 1916), p. 6 ff.
——, "Russkaja literatura v seredine XIX veka", in the same edition, part 9 (M., 1916), p. 18 ff.
Haertel, Emmy, "Gogol als Maler", *Jahrbuch für Kultur und Geschichte der Slaven*, 1929, 2, p. 145 ff.
Herzen, A., "Du développement des idées révolutionnaires en Russie", *Polnoe sobr. soč.*, pod red. M. K. Lemke (P., 1917–20), VI, p. 269 ff.
——, "Über den Roman aus dem Volksleben in Russland", in the same edition, IX, (references to Gogol', p. 87 ff.).
——, "Une nouvelle phase de la littérature russe", in the same edition, XVII, p. 191 ff.
Hippius, V., "Die Gogol-Forschung 1914–1924", *Zeitschr. f. slav. Philologie*, 1925, p. 530 ff.
Hoch, Paul H. and Joseph Zubin, *Anxiety* (New York, 1950).
Hofmann, M. and R., *Gogol, sa vie, son œuvre* (Paris, 1946).
Ivanov, G., "Narodnye rasskazy o ved'mach i upyrjach", *Sbornik Char'k. ist.-filol. Obščestva*, 1891, 3.
Ivanov-Razumnik, "Belinskij i Gogol'", *Sočinenija* (P., 1916), V, p. 246 ff.
Janet, P., *De l'angoisse à l'extase* (Paris, 1938).
Jilek, H., "Das Weltbild N. V. Gogols", *Zeitschr. f. deutsche Geisteswissenschaft*, 1938, p. 162 ff.
Jolles, A., *Bezieling en Vorm* (Haarlem, 1923).
——, *Einfache Formen* (Halle/Saale, 1929).

——, „Het Sprookje". *Hand. v. d. Maatsch. der Ned. Letterkunde te Leiden 1923–1924* (Leyden, 1924), p. 18 ff.

Jung, C. G., *Psychologie und Religion* (Zürich-Leipzig, 1940).

Kadlubovskij, A., *Gogol' v ego otnošenijach k starinnoj malorusskoj literature* (Address) (Nežin, 1911).

Kallaš, V., N. V. *Gogol' v vospominanijach sovremennikov i perepiske* (M., 1924).

——, "Melkie zametki o Gogole", *Literaturnyj Vestnik*, 1902, 1, p. 3 ff.

——, "Zametki o Gogole", *Istoričeskij Vestnik*, 1902, p. 679 ff.

——, "Zametki o Gogole", *Golos minuvšego*, 1939, 9, p. 234 ff.

——, *Žukovsko-Gogolevskaja jubilejnaja literatura* (M., 1902).

Kamanin, I., "Naučnye i literaturnye proizvedenija N. V. Gogolja po istorii Malorossii", *P.G.D.*, otd. II, p. 75 ff.

Kantor, R., "Pis'mo N. V. Gogolja k V. G. Belinskomu", *Krasnyj Archiv*, 1923, p. 309 ff.

Karskij, E., "Značenie Gogolja v istorii russkogo literaturnogo jazyka", *Russkij Filol. Vestnik*, 1909, 1–2, p. 205 ff.

Katranov, V., *Gogol' i ego ukrainskie povesti* (Voronež, 1910).

Kaun, A., "Poe and Gogol", *The Slavonic Review*, 1937, p. 387 ff.

Kaus, O., *Der Fall Gogol* (Münich, 1912).

Kierkegaard, S., *Le concept de l'angoisse*, traduit du danois par Knud Ferlov et Jean J. Gateau (Paris, 1935).

Kirpičnikov, A., *Opyt chronologičeskoj kanvy k biografii N. V. Gogolja* (M., 1902).

——, "Somnenija i protivorečija v biografii Gogolja", *Izv. otd. russk. jaz. i slov. Imp. Akad. Nauk*, 1900, 5, p. 591 ff.

Koenig, H., *Literarische Bilder aus Russland* (Stuttgart-Tübingen, 1834).

Korobka, N., "Detstvo i junost' Gogolja", *Žurnal Min. Narodn. Prosv.*, 1902, p. 239 ff.

——, "Kuliš o malorossijskich povestjach Gogolja", *Literaturnyj Vestnik*, 1902, 1, p. 73 ff.

Korolenko, V., "Tragedija velikogo jumorista", *Russkoe bogatstvo*, 1909, 4, 5, reprinted in *Gogol' v russkoj kritike*, p. 536 ff.

Korš, E., "O komizme Gogolja", *Gogolevskie dni v Moskve* (M., 1909), p. 190 ff.

Kotljarevs'kyj, Ivan, "Moskal'-čarivnyk" in *Tvory* (= *Biblioteka ukraïns'koho slova*, 9) (Berlin, 1922), II, p. 57 ff.

Kotljarevskij, N., *Gogol' (1829–1842)*, 4th ed. (P., 1915).

Krijgers Janzen, E., *De justificatie*. Utrecht thesis (Amsterdam, 1940).

Kuliš, P., "Gogol' kak avtor povestej iz ukrainskoj žizni", *Osnova*, 1861, 4, p. 67 ff.

——, *Zapiski o žizni N. V. Gogolja*, 2 vols. (SPb., 1856).

Künzli, A., *Die Angst als abendländische Krankheit* (Zürich, 1948).

Lanskij, L. and S. Mašinskij, "Neizdannye pis'ma k Gogolju", *Literaturnoe Nasledstvo*, vol. 58 (1952), p. 797 ff.

Lanskij, L. and I. Sergievskij, "Gogol' v neizdannoj perepiske sovremennikov", *Literaturnoe Nasledstvo*, vol. 58 (1952), p. 533 ff.

Lavrin, Janko, *Gogol* (London, 1925).

——, *Nikolai Gogol. A Centenary Survey* (London, 1951).

Lazurskij, V., "Velikij melancholik", *S.N.*, p. 37 ff.

Lebedev, A., *Poet-Christijanin. N. V. Gogol' v russkoj literature i iskusstve (1829–1908)*, 2 vols. (Saratov, 1909–11).

Léger, L., *Nicolas Gogol* (Paris, 1913).

Lipovskij, A., "K voprosu ob izučenii Gogolevskogo stilja", *Literaturnyj Vestnik*, 1902, 1, p. 44 ff.

Literaturnoe Nasledstvo, vol. 58 (*Puškin, Lermontov, Gogol'*) (M., 1952).

Ljubič Romanovič, V., "Gogol' v nežinskom licee", *Istoričeskij Vestnik*, 1902, 2, p. 548 ff.

Loks, M., "Problema stilja v chudožestvennoj proze", *Problemy Poetiki*, sbornik statej pod red. V. Brjusova (M.-L., 1925).

Loosli-Usteri, M., "De l'anxiété enfantine", *Schweizerische Zeitschrift für Psychologie*, 1943. Supplement 3.

Luk'janovskij, B., *K voprosu o "perelome" v biografii Gogolja* (Warschau, 1912).

Majkov, V., *N. V. Gogol' i S. T. Aksakov* (SPb., 1892).

Makedonov, A., "Gogol' i 'obnovlennyj feodalizm'", *Literaturnyj Kritik*, 1936, 11, p. 181 ff. (Criticism of Chrapčenko).

Maksimovič, M., "Oborona ukrainskich povestej Gogolja", First appeared in *Den'*, 1861, no. 3, 5, 7, 9, 13. Reprint in *Literaturnyj Vestnik*, 1902, 1, p. 104 ff.

Malinin, V., "Gogol' kak epičeskij pisatel'", *P.G.D.*, p. 227 ff.

Mandel'stam, I., *O charaktere Gogolevskogo stilja* (SPb.-Helsingfors, 1902).

Mašinskij, S., *Gogol'* (M., 1951).

——, "Gogol' i 'Delo o vol'nodumstve'", *Literaturnoe Nasledstvo*, no. 58 (1952), p. 495 ff.

——, *Gogol' i revoljucionnye demokraty* (M., 1953).

Merežkovskij, D., *Gogol'. Tvorčestvo, žizn' i religija* (SPb., 1909).

Michajlov, K., "Vnov' najdennye rukopisi Gogolja", *Istoričeskij Vestnik*, 1902, 2, p. 596 ff.

Miloradovič, V., "Etnografičeskij element v povesti Gogolja 'Zakoldovannoe Mesto'", *Kievskaja Starina*, 1897, 8, p. 55 ff.

Močul'skij, K., *Duchovnyj put' Gogolja* (Paris, 1934).

Močul'skij, V., "Čto zaveščal Gogol' sozdannoj im natural'noj škole", *S.N.*, p. 13 ff.

Mordovčenko, N., "Gogol' i žurnalistika 1835–1836 gg.", *M.I.*, 2, p. 106 ff.

Nabokov, V., *Nikolai Gogol* (Norfolk, Conn. 1944).

Narežnyj, V., *Izbrannye romany*, edited by V. Pereverzev (M.-L., 1933) (Contains "Aristion ili perevospitanie", "Bursak" and "Dva Ivana ili strast' k tjažbam").

Nazarevskij, A., "Gogol' i iskusstvo", *P.G.V.*, otd. II, p. 49 ff.

——, "Iz archiva Golovni", *M.I.*, 1, p. 313 ff.

Nekrasova, E., "Gogol' pered sudom inostrannoj literatury", *Russkaja Starina*, 1887, p. 553 ff.

Nevirova, K., "Motyvy ukrains'koï demonologiï v 'Večerach' ta 'Myrhorodi' Hoholja", in *Zap. Ukr. Nauk. Tov. v Kyïvi*, 1909, p. 27 ff.

Nikitenko, A., *Zapiski i Dnevnik*, pod red. M. K. Lemke, 2 vols. (SPb., 1904–05).

Odier, Ch., *L'angoisse et la pensée magique* (Neuchâtel-Paris, 1948).

Odoevskij, F., "Dve zametki o Gogole", *M.I.*, 1, p. 223 ff.

Oerlemans, A. C., *Development of Freud's Conception of Anxiety*. Amsterdam thesis (Amsterdam, 1949).

Oksman, Ju., "'Krovavyj bandurist'. Novye stranicy N. V. Gogolja", *Niva*, 1917, 1, p. 2 ff.

——, "Puškin, 'Pis'mo k izdatelju'", *Atenej*, 1924, 1, p. 6 ff. and p. 15 ff.

Osipov, N., *Žizn' i Smert'* (Prague 1935).

Ovsjaniko-Kulikovskij, D., *Gogol'*, 2nd ed. (SPb., 1907).

——, *Gogol' v ego proizvedenijach* (M., 1909).

Pabst, Walter, "Die Theorie der Novelle in Deutschland (1920–1940)", *Romanistisches Jahrbuch*, 1949, 2, p. 81 ff.

——, *Novellentheorie und Novellendichtung. Zur Geschichte ihrer Antinomie in den romanischen Literaturen* (Hamburg, 1953).

Pamjati Gogolja. Naučno-literaturnyj sbornik, izdannyj Istoričeskim obščestvom Nestora Letopisca pod red. N. P. Daškeviča (Kiev, 1902).

Pamjati N. V. Gogolja. Sbornik rečej i statej, izd. Imp. Univ. Sv. Vladimira (Kiev, 1911).

Panaev, I., *Literaturnye vospominanija* (L., 1950).

Peretc, V., "Gogol' i malorusskaja literaturnaja tradicija", *Reči*, p. 47 ff.

——, "Kukol'nyj teatr na Rusi", *Ežegodnik Imp. Teatrov 1894–95* (SPb., 1896), p. 85 ff.

——, *Novye dannye dlja istorii starinnoj ukrainskoj liriki* (SPb., 1907).

——, *Novyj trud po istorii ukrainskogo teatra* (SPb., 1911).

Pereverzev, V., "Narodnyj jazyk u Gogolja", *Literaturnyj Kritik*, 1934, 9, p. 80 ff.

——, *Tvorčestvo Gogolja*, 3rd ed. (Ivanovo-Voznesensk, 1928).

Petrov, N., "Južno-russkij narodnyj element v rannich proizvedenijach N. V. Gogolja", *P.G.D.*, p. 52 ff.

——, *Očerki iz istorii ukrainskoj literatury XVII i XVIII vekov* (Kiev, 1911).

——, *Očerki istorii ukrainskoj literatury XIX stoletija* (Kiev, 1884).

——, "Starinnyj južno-russkij teatr i v častnosti vertep", *Kievskaja Starina*, 1882, 12, p. 438 ff.

Petrov, V., "Peterburž'ki povisti M. Hoholja", in M. Hohol', *Tvory*, redakcija P. Fylypovyča (Char'kiv-Kyïv, 1932), IV.

Petuchov, E., "Gogol' i Žukovskij", *Ch. S.*, p. 1 ff. Also in *Pamjati N. V. Gogolja i V. A. Žukovskogo* (Jur'ev, 1903), p. 1 ff.

Pfister, O., *Das Christentum und die Angst* (Zürich, 1944).

Piaget, J., *La représentation du monde chez l'enfant*, 2nd ed. (Paris, 1938).

Piksanov, N., *Dva veka russkoj literatury* (M.-P., 1923).

——, "Ukrainskie povesti Gogolja", in *O klassikach* (M., 1933), p. 43 ff.

Plokker, J. H., S. Dresden, K. Baschwitz, and W. Banning, *Angst en Crisis der Moraal* (The Hague, 1949).

Pokrovskij, V., *N. V. Gogol', ego žizn' i sočinenija*, 3rd ed. (M., 1910).

Polonskij, V., *Soznanie i tvorčestvo* (M., 1934).

Pospelov, G., *Tvorčestvo N. V. Gogolja* (M., 1953).

Puškin, A. S., *Dnevnik Puškina (1833–1835)*, Pod red. [. . .] B. L. Modzalevskogo (M.-P., 1923).

——, *Sočinenija A. S. Puškina*, izd. Imp. Ak. Nauk, *Perepiska*, pod red. i s primeč. V. I. Saitova, 3 vols. (SPb., 1906–11).

Pypin, A., "Die Bedeutung Gogols für die heutige internationale Stellung der russischen Literatur", *Archiv für slav. Philologie*, 1903, p. 290 ff.

——, "Značenie Gogolja v sozdanii sovremennogo meždunarodnogo položenija russkoj literatury", *Reči*, p. 1 ff.

Reve, K. van het, *Goed en Schoon in de Sovjetcritiek* (Amsterdam, 1954).

Rochedieu, E., *Angoisse et religion* (Genève, 1952).

Rodzevič, S., "K istorii russkogo romantizma", *Russkij Filol. Vestnik*, 1917, 1–2, p. 194.

Rost, P., "Gogol", *Auslandstudien*, 2, 1926, p. 177 ff.

Rozanov, N., *Gogol' kak vernyj syn cerkvi* (M., 1902).

Rozanov, V., "Kak proizošel tip Akakija Akakieviča", in *Legenda o velikom inkvizitore*, 3rd ed. (SPb., 1906), p. 266 ff.

——, "Puškin i Gogol'" in *Legenda o velikom inkvizitore*, 3rd ed. (SPb., 1906), p. 253 ff.

Rozov, V., "Tradicionnye tipy malorusskogo teatra XVII–XVIII vv. i junošeskie povesti N. V. Gogolja", *P.G.V.*, otd. 2, p. 99 ff.

Rümke, H. C., *Inleiding tot de karakterkunde*, 3rd ed. (Haarlem, 1951).

——, *Psychiatrie*, I (Amsterdam, 1954).

Rybakova, N., "Kak rabotal Gogol'", *Literaturnaja Učeba*, 1931, 7, p. 53 ff.
Sainte-Beuve, A., "Nouvelles russes par Nicolas Gogol", *Revue des Deux-Mondes*, 1845, 12, p. 883 ff.
——, see: N. Lerner, "Sainte-Beuve o Gogole" (translation of a letter from S.-B. to Prince A. Golicyn), *Zvezda*, 1903, 1, p. 219 ff.
Sakulin, P., *Teorija literaturnych stilej* (M., 1927).
——, "Tvorčeskie muki Gogolja", in *Gogolevskie dni v Moskve* (M., 1909), p. 216 ff.
Sbornik izdannyj Imp. Novorossijskim Universitetom po slučaju stoletija so dnja roždenija N. V. Gogolja (Odessa, 1909).
Schloezer, Boris de, *Gogol* (Paris, 1932).
Schultz, F., *Klassik und Romantik der Deutschen* (Stuttgart, 1935).
Setschkareff, V., *N. V. Gogol. Leben und Schaffen* (Berlin, 1953).
Slonimskij, L., *Technika komičeskogo u Gogolja* (P., 1923).
Smirnova-Rosset, A. O., *Zapiski, Dnevnik, Vospominanija, Pis'ma* (M., 1929).
——, *Avtobiografija* (M., 1931).
Sobolevskij, A., "Gogol' v istorii russkoj etnografii", *Mirnyj Trud*, 1909, p. 176 ff.
Sokolov, B., "Gogol' – etnograf", *Etnogr. obozrenie*, 1909, 2–3, p. 58 ff.
Sollogub, V., *Vospominanija* (SPb., 1887).
Stekel, Wilh., *Nervöse Angstzustände und ihre Behandlung*, 4th ed. (Berlin-Vienna 1924).
Stender-Pedersen, A., "Gogol und die deutsche Romantik", *Euphorion*, 1923, p. 628 ff.
——, "Johann Heinrich Voss und der junge Gogol", *Edda*, 1929, p. 98 ff.
——, "Der Ursprung des Gogolschen Teufels", *Göteborgs Högskolas Årsskrift*, 1926, p. 72 ff.
Stilman, Leon, "'Gogol's Overcoat' – Thematic Pattern and Origins", *The American Slavic and East European Review*, 1952, p. 138 ff.
Straszer, Ch., *Mirgorod-Seldwyla* (Zürich, 1936).
Sumcov, N., "Gogol' i Žukovskij", *Ch. S.*, p. 5 ff.
——, "Paralleli k povesti Gogolja 'Vij'", *Kievskaja Starina*, 1892, 3, p. 472 ff.
Šambinago, S., *Trilogija romantizma (N. V. Gogol')* (M., 1911).
Šarovol'skij, I., "Gogol' sredi velikich jumoristov novogo vremeni", *P.G.V.*, otd. 1, p. 16 ff.
——, "Junošeskaja idillija Gogolja", *P.G.D.*, otd. 2, p. 13 ff.
Ščeglov, I., *Podvižnik slova* (SPb., 1909).
Ščegolev, P., "Iz školnych let N. V. Gogolja", *Istoričeskij Vestnik*, 1902, 2, p 509 ff.
——, "K biografii N. V. Gogolja", *Literaturnyj Vestnik*, 1902, 1, p. 48 ff.
——, "K biografii P. A. Kuliša", *Istoričeskij Vestnik*, 1902, 3, p. 242 ff.
——, "Otec Gogolja", *Istoričeskij Vestnik*, 1902, 2, p. 655 ff.
Šeluchin, S., "Gogol' i malorusskoe obščestvo", *S.N.*, p. 59 ff.
Šenrok, V., "Gogol' i Jazykov", *Vestnik Evropy*, 11, p. 134 ff. and 12, p. 597 ff.
——, *Materialy dlja biografii Gogolja*, 4 vols. (M., 1892–97).
——, A. O. Smirnova i N. V. Gogol'", *Russkaja Starina*, 1888, 2, p. 31 ff., p. 597 ff.
——, *Učeničeskie gody Gogolja* (M., 1887).
Šklovskij, V., *O teorii prozy* (M., 1929).
Tarasenkov, A., *Poslednie dni žizni N. V. Gogolja* (SPb., 1857).
Terebinskij, V., "O bolezni N. V. Gogolja", *Russkij vrač v Čechoslovakii*, 1939, 1–2, p. 5 ff.; p. 61 ff.
Tichonravov, N., "Puškin i Gogol'", *Sočinenija*, III², p. 182 ff.
Tomaševskij, B., *Teorija literatury*, 6th ed. (M., 1931).

Trachimovskij, N., "Marija Ivanovna Gogol' ", *Russkaja Starina*, 1888, 7, p. 24 ff.
Trilling, Lionel, *The Liberal Imagination* (New York, 1954).
Tschizewskij, D., Review of M. Gorlin, *N. V. Gogol und E. Th. A. Hoffmann*. — In *Deutsche Lit. Zeitung*, 31 March 1935, p. 555 ff.
Tynjanov, Ju., "Dostoevskij i Gogol' ", *Archaisty i novatory* (L., 1929), p. 412 ff.
Tyrnéva, R., *Gogol' écrivain et moraliste* (Aix, 1901).
Vengerov, S., *Pisatel'-graždanin, Gogol'* (SPb., 1913).
Veresaev, V., *Gogol' v žizni* (M.-L., 1933).
——, *Kak rabotal Gogol'* (M., 1934).
Verwey, A., *Proza*, 10 vols. (Amsterdam, 1921–23).
Veselovskij, A., *Etjudy i charakteristiki*, 2nd ed. (M., 1903).
——, *Zapadnoe vlijanie v novoj russkoj literature*, 4th ed. (M., 1910).
Vilinskij, S., "Gogol' i russkaja literatura", *S.N.*, p. 48 ff.
Vinogradov, I., *Bor'ba za stil'* (L., 1914).
Vinogradov, V., *Etjudy o stile Gogolja* (L., 1926).
——, *Gogol' i natural'naja škola* (L., 1923).
——, *Evoljucija russkogo naturalizma. Gogol' i Dostoevskij* (L., 1929).
——, "Jazyk Gogolja", *M.I.*, 2, p. 286 ff.
——, "Jazyk Gogolja i ego značenie v istorii russkogo jazyka", *Mat. i issled. po ist. russk. lit. jaz. Akad. Nauk S.S.S.R.*, M. 1953, 3, p. 4 ff.
Vinokur, G., "Poetika, lingvistika, sociologija", *Lef*, 1923, 3, p. 104 ff.
Vladimirov, P., "Iz učeničeskich let Gogolja", *Univ. izvestija*, Kiev, 1890, 5.
——, "Očerk razvitija tvorčestva Gogolja", *Univ. izvestija*, Kiev, 1891, 2.
Vogüé, E. M. de, *Le roman russe*, 20th ed. (Paris, 1927).
Wälzel, O., *Das dichterische Kunstwerk* (Leipzig, 1926).
——, *Gehalt und Gestalt im Kunstwerk des Dichters* (Berlin, 1923).
Wijk, N. van, "N. W. Gogol", *Onze Eeuw*, 1911, 1, p. 404 ff.
——, *Hoofdmomenten der Russiese Letterkunde* (Zeist, 1919).
Zabolockij, P., *Gogol' i slavjanstvo* (Nežin, 1911).
——, "N. V. Gogol' v russkoj literature. Bibliografičeskij obzor", in *Gogolevskij sbornik*, pod red. M. Speranskogo (Kiev, 1902), p. 13 ff.
Zajcev, B., "Žizn' s Gogolem", *Sovremennye Zapiski*, 59 (1935), p. 272 ff.
Zamotin, I., "Tri romantičeskich motiva v proizvedenijach Gogolja", *Zapiski obščestva istorii, filologii i prava pri Imp. Varš. Univ.*, 1902, 2, p. 28 ff.
——, *Romantizm dvadcatych godov XIX stoletija v russkoj literature*, II, *Romantičeskij idealizm* (SPb., 1907).
Zavitnevič, V., *Religiozno-nravstvennoe sostojanie N. V. Gogolja v poslednie gody ego žizni* (Kiev, 1902). (Also in XVI of the *Čtenija v Istor. obšč. Nest.-Letop.*).
Zeldenrust, E. L. K., *Over het wezen der hysterie*. Utrecht thesis (Utrecht, 1954).
Zelinskij, V., *Russkaja kritičeskaja literatura o proizvedenijach N. V. Gogolja*, 3 vols., 3rd ed. (M., 1903).
Zen'kovskij, V., "Die aesthetische Utopie Gogol's", *Zeitschr. f. slav. Philologie*, 1936, p. 1 ff.
——, "Gogol' als Denker", *Zeitschr. f. slav. Philologie*, 1932, p. 104 ff.
——, *Russkie mysliteli i Evropa* (Paris, no date).
Zinke, Paul, *Paul Heyses Novellentechnik* (Karlsruhe, no date).
Zonin, A., "Tragedija Gogolja", *Na literaturnom postu*, 1927, 5–6, p. 25 ff.
Zundelovič, Ja., "Poetika groteska", in *Problemy poetiki*, 1925, p. 63 ff.
Žirmunskij, V., *Byron i Puškin* (L., 1924).
——, "Formprobleme in der russischen Literaturwissenschaft", *Zeitschr. f. slav. Philologie*, 1925, p. 117 ff.
——, *Voprosy teorii literatury* (L., 1928).

INDEX OF PERSONS *

* The numbers printed in italics refer to the notes.

SLAVISTIC PRINTINGS AND REPRINTINGS

Edited by Cornelis H. van Schooneveld

Some titles:

MOUTON & CO · PUBLISHERS · THE HAGUE

In this book the composition of eight of Gogol's short stories is analysed. This work succeeds more than any other in eludicating the finer points of Gogol's technique: the division into chapters, their effective opening and closing motifs, the surprise transitions, the contrasts and parallels, the leit-motifs, the use of symbols, the rôle of the narrator, etc. In handling these questions, the author frequently arrives at new interpretations, which he contrasts with existing views. For instance, after making a penetrating analysis of the double-narrative style in "The Two Ivans" with its different forms of irony and the apparently indiscriminate use of past and present tenses, he throws new light on the function and significance of the end of this story. In the same way, by unravelling the structure of "The Overcoat", he brings us nearer to the solution of a controversial problem: the disputed function of the "fantastic" ending of this story. At the same time, his investigation of this point leads him to make a fresh assessment of the genre of this short story, an assessment which runs counter to characterisations of "The Overcoat" as a grotesque or realistic-cum-tragic tale with an underlying humane significance.

No less important is Driessen's penetrating insight into the actual extent of Gogol's borrowing from other literary works and folk-tales. He shows how slight these influences often are or how individual their treatment is in the light of the completely different structure and thematic development of Gogol's product, as is seen in "A Terrible Revenge", which is alleged to have been influenced by Tieck and Hoffmann, or in "The Two Ivans", which is supposed to show the influence of Narezhny's work, although